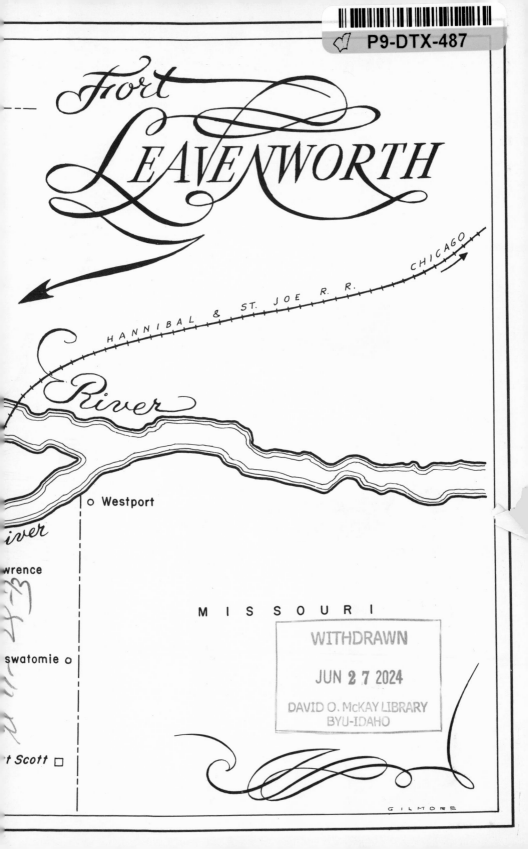

SENTINEL OF THE PLAINS:
FORT LEAVENWORTH
AND THE AMERICAN WEST

SENTINEL OF THE PLAINS:

OTHER BOOKS BY GEORGE WALTON

The Wasted Generation
Let's End the Draft Mess
Twelve Events That Changed Our World
Tarnished Shield
The Private War of Captain Madam

COAUTHOR OF:
The Devil's Brigade
Faint the Trumpet Sounds
The Champagne Campaign
Rome Fell Today

Fort Leavenworth and the American West

≫→←≪

GEORGE WALTON

PRENTICE-HALL, INC.
Englewood Cliffs, N.J.

Library of Congress Cataloging in Publication Data
Walton, George H
    Sentinel of the plains.
    Bibliography: p.
    1. Fort Leavenworth, Kan. 2. The West–History.
I. Title
UA26.L4W34   978.1'38   79–99756
ISBN 0–13–806729–5

For my sons
FRANK and JOSEPH

THE AMERICAN FORTS SERIES
Consulting Editor: Richard Dillon
Author of BURNT-OUT FIRES

GUNS AT THE FORKS
(Forts Duquesne and Pitt)
by Walter O'Meara

LOUISBOURG: KEY TO A CONTINENT
by Fairfax Downey

SUTTER'S FORT: GATEWAY TO THE GOLD FIELDS
by Oscar Lewis

THREE FLAGS AT THE STRAITS: THE FORTS OF MACKINAC
by Walter Havighurst

FORT LARAMIE AND THE SIOUX INDIANS
by Remi Nadeau

FORTS OF THE UPPER MISSOURI
by Robert G. Athearn

THUNDERGATE: THE FORTS OF NIAGARA
by Robert West Howard

VINCENNES: PORTAL TO THE WEST
by August Derleth

★ ★ ★

SENTINEL OF THE PLAINS: FORT LEAVENWORTH
AND THE AMERICAN WEST
by George Walton

ACKNOWLEDGMENTS

Two people, Helen S. Walton and Sara D. Jackson, are perhaps more responsible for this book in its final form than the author. Both spent long, tedious hours of research in the National Archives and have my deep appreciation.

The assistance of Mildred C. Cox, who for a long time was only a phone call away, will always leave me in her debt. Colonel O. W. Martin, Jr., Editor-in-Chief of the *Military Review* and President of the Council on Abandoned Military Posts—U.S.A., Inc., Colonel Milton B. Halsey, an authoritative Fort Leavenworth historian, Colonel Forrest Blackburn, USAR, of the staff of the Kansas State Historical Society, and Sara D. Jackson of the National Archives read the manuscript and made suggestions. Charles E. Hoffhaus, Esquire, of Kansas City, Missouri, a distinguished student of the pre-Anglo Saxon West, contributed information that would otherwise have been impossible to obtain.

I am also grateful for the help given to me by Egon Weiss, Librarian of the United States Military Academy at West Point; George J. Stanfield, Librarian of the National War College; Katherine E. Howell and Mary Francis Kilburn of the Wilmington, North Carolina, Public Library; Camille Hannon, Reference Librarian of the Library of the National Archives; Edna Besore of the staff of the Library of the Command and General Staff College at Fort Leavenworth; William Sartain of the Library of Congress, Robert Pennington of the Bureau of Indian Affairs, Department of the Interior; The Honorable Arthur J. Stanley, Jr., Senior United States District Court Judge for Kansas; Josephine Motylewski and Mary M. Johnson, both of the staff of the National Archives; and Martha Bayliss of Winchester, Virginia.

My sincere thanks goes also to Patricia Hall who typed the manuscript. Her long, hard hours and attention to detail went far and beyond the call of duty.

I am also again indebted to Louis and Dolores McGuinness for their hospitality, help, and encouragement. Part of the book was written in their home in McLean, Virginia.

To these and the many others who contributed to the venture go my heartfelt thanks. In no sense, however, do they share any responsibility for my thoughts or conclusions nor blame for any errors or inadequacies; rather they are entitled to full credit for any light this book may shed on the history of Fort Leavenworth.

CONTENTS

≫≫→←≪≪

	INTRODUCTION	*xi*
One	THE ROAD TO SANTA FÉ	*1*
Two	CANTONMENT LEAVENWORTH	*7*
Three	NEIGHBORING INDIANS	*19*
Four	THE EXPEDITIONS	*27*
Five	FORT LEAVENWORTH	*41*
Six	THE OREGON TRAIL	*63*
Seven	THE MEXICAN WAR	*69*
Eight	THE MORMON WAR	*79*
Nine	LIFE ON THE POST	*87*
Ten	BLEEDING KANSAS	*105*
Eleven	THE CIVIL WAR	*119*
Twelve	THE BUFFALO SOLDIERS	*139*
Thirteen	THE POST AFTER THE CIVIL WAR	*147*
Fourteen	THE SCHOOLS	*161*
	CHAPTER NOTES	*179*
	APPENDICES	*189*
	BIBLIOGRAPHY	*193*
	INDEX	*203*

INTRODUCTION

The story of Forth Leavenworth is the story of the making of a nation. The fort was founded (in 1827) to protect the Sante Fé Trail, the first route from the East to any of the vast lands acquired by the Louisiana Purchase. It later became the strategically situated bastion for the forces that guarded the Oregon Trail, leading to California and the Pacific Northwest. There is hardly a hero and hardly a villain in the settling of the West—from the Texas war for independence through the Civil War—who did not touch base, at one time or another, at this frontier post.

The name of the fort, which is the name of its first commandant, may evoke the image of prison to most people who hear it: the army's first disciplinary barracks were established near the fort in 1875, and a federal prison was built in the city of Leavenworth in 1942. But to a historian, the name evokes a colorful pageant, both tragic and heroic, in which march betrayed Indian chiefs, wise and foolish army officers, venal fur trappers, humane missionaries, improvident emigrants, exploitive steamboat and ferry operators, fanatical pro- and antiabolitionists, and cynical politicians. Leavenworth was the first capital of its state, and the base of the federal forces that futilely attempted to establish order in the days of "Bleeding Kansas," the prelude to the Civil War.

To a military man, Leavenworth means "the generals' school." The fort became an army educational base before the close of the nineteenth century, and that has been its chief function thus far in the twentieth century. As a postgraduate school for high-ranking army officers, it numbers among its alumni such World War II luminaries as Marshall, Eisenhower, Bradley, Ridgway, Mark Clark, and Maxwell Taylor.

If they succeed in their purpose, the following pages will carry the reader gently from an intimate view of a soldier's life on a rugged frontier post, surrounded by hostile Indians, through the days of conflict with his fellow white citizens—Mormons, outlaws, prosecessionists—to the quiet times today when denizens of the fort use their weapons only as laboratory specimens.

"God and the soldier we adore
In time of trouble, not before
When the danger is over
And all things are righted
God is forgotten
And the soldier, slighted."
> Graffito on a Sentinel Box,
> Gibraltar, about 1870.

CHAPTER ONE

>>>→<<<

THE ROAD TO SANTA FÉ

When the nineteenth century dawned, the United States knew little of the vast vacuum that stretched west from the Mississippi River to the Pacific Ocean. But the consummation of the Louisiana Purchase in 1803 aroused in President Thomas Jefferson and his countrymen a great curiosity as to what had been bought for the then huge sum of fifteen million dollars.

The need for exploration became apparent immediately, and it was obvious that army officers were, both by training and experience, ideally suited for such a task. As Jefferson advised Congress, such officers "might explore even to the western ocean; have conferences with Indian nations on the subject of commercial intercourse . . . agree on convenient deposits for an interchange of articles, and return with the information acquired, in the course of two summers." Jefferson added, with an eye toward the watchdogs of the treasury in Congress, "Their pay would be going on, whether here or there."

On May 14, 1804, a party numbering forty men set out by boat from St. Louis for the West. Their leader, a blond Virginian and former secretary to Jefferson, was considered quite a dandy in Washington. The appointment of Captain Meriwether Lewis to head the expedition was said to have been a gesture to those who revered Washington. Fielding Lewis, the captain's uncle, had married the general's sister.

Studious and precise in preparation for his command, Lewis spent the summer of 1803 in Philadelphia, principally studying botany, geography, and celestial navigation under the eminent

1

scientists Doctors Benjamin Rush, Casper Wister, and Benjamin Smith Barton, all of the University of Pennsylvania.[1] In August, Robert Patterson, the cryptologist-mathematician, gave him further instruction in celestial observation and in the determination of longitudes and latitudes.

Lieutenant William Clark, younger brother of the explorer George Rogers Clark, was the personal choice of Lewis as his second-in-command. Another Virginian, though raised in Kentucky, he was the more experienced of the two officers. Also with the expedition was George Drouillard as scout, interpreter, and chief hunter. Having a French father and a Shawnee mother, he was skilled in the Indian sign language and was a crack shot and a canny trader. Chief navigator Pierre Cruzatte spoke Omaha and was acquainted with the rapids and shoals of the temperamental Missouri River.

Before setting out, Lewis had been instructed by Jefferson to chart the Missouri and Columbia rivers as a practical water route across the continent. He was also to observe the Indian inhabitants, make notes on the weather, fix geographical positions, and map the country over which his party passed. Careful records were to be kept of the topography, soil, and on the fur-bearing animals.

Traveling up the river in three keelboats, the men occasionally passed canoes and bullboats[2] loaded with furs bound for St. Louis. They encamped near the present site of Kansas City and then, traveling north, passed the high cliffs where Fort Leavenworth was to be built twenty-three years later. On July 4, 1804, near what is now the city of Atchison, the party held the first celebration of Independence Day to be held in what is now Kansas.

The information brought back by Lewis and Clark disclosing the great commercial potential of the West was of great value to the nation, but it could fill only a narrow gap and was merely a beginning point. As William H. Goetzmann noted,

> Despite the fact that Lewis and Clark had made known such essentials as the width of the Continent, the existence of numerous ranges of high mountains, the location and description of the major rivers of the Northwest and the rich resources of the whole region, what was eventually to become the American West was still largely a geographical mystery in the immediate years after their return. Not until 1814 with the

publication of their report [edited by Nicholas Biddle and Paul Allen], was there even a satisfactory cartographic representation of the whole region south and west of the Missouri River. Instead, for a long time the West remained an immense unknown, whose limits were gradually being defined by the explorers sent out into it by the government and fur trading companies along its margin.[3]

The Lewis and Clark Expedition had nevertheless focused the attention of the people of the United States on the lands included in the Louisiana Purchase and had thus hastened the events that would lead to the establishment of Fort Leavenworth.

In 1806, another army officer, Lieutenant Zebulon Montgomery Pike, who had previously attempted to explore the sources of the Mississippi, was directed by General James Wilkinson to locate the headwaters of the Red River. Wilkinson was a double agent. Besides being the ranking general of the United States Army, he had long been in the pay of the Spanish crown.[4] Driven by a lust for wealth and power, the general had dreams of carving out an empire for himself in the Southwest, and was much more interested in Santa Fé than in the source of the Red River. It is likely that the general had given Pike secret instructions to scout New Mexico. It is beyond doubt that he deliberately betrayed Pike by warning his Spanish friends that the lieutenant would eventually head toward Santa Fé. A large Spanish force under the command of Lieutenant Don Facundo Malgaras was dispatched to intercept Pike.

On July 15, 1806, two months before the return of Lewis and Clark, Pike set forth from Bellefontaine on the Missouri River. In Missouri, he visited the Osage Indians and then struck out northwest across the plains to the Pawnee villages, where he was able to persuade the tribe to stop flying the Spanish flag. Pike then headed across country to the Arkansas River in central Kansas. He spent most of November and December exploring the Rockies en route. Next, in a bitter mid-winter march south, he and his men suffered such extreme hardships that he was forced to leave five who had developed gangrene. Pike eventually reached the Rio Grande River where he was intercepted by an alerted Spanish force under the command of Lieutenant Ignacio Saltelo. His men were taken as prisoners to Santa Fé.

General Wilkinson had selected not only an able officer, but also a good reporter. During the time Pike was confined by the Spanish, he made careful observations not only of the province of New Mexico, but of the country of Mexico as far south as Chihuahua, where he was taken before the Governor, General Don Nimesio Salcedo, for questioning. Upon his return to the United States in July, 1807, Pike wrote an account of his journey which was published in 1810. In the book, a best seller, Pike emphasized the great possibilities for profitable trade with New Mexico.

The lieutenant had not been the first to suggest the commercial possibilities of the Southwest. As early as 1714, a Frenchman, Captain Etienne Veniard Sieur de Bourgmont, Commandant of the Missouri, Chevalier of the Royal and Military Order of St. Louis, and the first European definitely known to have been in the area where Fort Leavenworth now stands, by diplomatic negotiations with the Kansa and with the Padouca at their village near the present site of Ellsworth, Kansas, was successful in opening a route from the Missouri River to Santa Fé. Bourgmont wrote in his journal of the general area west of the Missouri River:

> This is the finest country and the most beautiful land in the world; the prairies are like the seas, and filled with wild animals; especially oxen, cattle, hind, and stag in such quantities to surpass the imagination.

In 1739, Pierre and Paul Mallet, together with eight or nine companions, journeyed up the Missouri River past the future site of Fort Leavenworth to the Platte River, and thence overland across what is now Nebraska, northwest Kansas, Colorado and New Mexico, to Santa Fé. The success of the Mallet expedition resulted in a number of other caravans setting out for the Southwest, but most of them foundered on the rock of official Spanish opposition. This hindrance to northern commerce with Santa Fé ended with Mexico's successful revolution, and its subsequent independence, in 1821.

Pike was the first to propound the myth of the Great American Desert. His conclusion that the plains resembled the deserts of Siberia was, in the years that followed, adopted by such eminent Americans as Major Stephen H. Long, Washington Irving, George Catlin and William Babcock Hazen.

Wilkinson's machinations came to nothing, but they did inadvertently result in the eventual establishment of Fort Leavenworth.

If Pike was the father of the Santa Fé Trail, Senator Thomas Hart Benton of Missouri was the godfather. On January 25, 1826, after a Christmas visit to the aging Jefferson at Monticello, Benton made a major speech in the Senate calling for such a road, and for the protection of its travelers by the United States Army. Benton painted a romantic picture "of men and horses crossing the desert plains like the great caravans of Asia."[5] The speech was applauded throughout the nation.

Senator Benton's efforts were successful; Congress was persuaded to provide a survey of the trail. It was to extend from Franklin, Missouri, to the "Great Bend of the Arkansas," and be marked by mounds of earth. From the Arkansas River it was to go on to Taos and, finally, to Santa Fé.

Within a few years, long lines of pack mules, closed black carriages (in which the traders rode and slept), covered wagons, and droves of cattle were winding over the more than seven hundred miles of dusty tracks to Santa Fé—and returning with considerable profit for their owners.

The question of protection for these traders remained. The caravans, especially the smaller ones, were tempting targets for marauding Indians. As their attacks increased, demands for action by the government became more and more insistent, and once again Senator Benton stepped forward. He introduced a resolution in Congress calling for an inquiry as to the wisdom of establishing a military post near where the trail crossed the Arkansas River. At the time, however, such a cantonment would have been impossible to supply, and several counterproposals were made to the Senate by Major General Jacob Brown, then commanding the army. It was finally agreed that the best location for the proposed fort would be a site on the Missouri River near the eastern terminus of the Santa Fé Trail. The War Department accordingly directed Colonel Henry Leavenworth to establish such a post.

CHAPTER TWO

>»>>-<-«««

CANTONMENT LEAVENWORTH

The few Indians and fewer whites who lived near the banks of the Missouri River, west of St. Louis, in mid-April, 1827, might have witnessed a scene that caused them considerable wonderment. Over a hundred swearing, sweating men were pulling three heavily loaded keelboats up the river. Similar crafts, conveying fur traders, had been along before, but these men appeared to be different; in spite of their nondescript clothing, they had a vaguely military look. Even more amazing must have been the sight of a number of white women and children seated on the decks among the boxes and barrels. Any spectator might have concluded that something of great and far-reaching importance was in the making. And he would have been right: the troops that were traveling west were about to establish a frontier post that would eventually become a gateway for white men to the land that had been the domain of the Plains Indians for centuries.

The soldiers who were propelling the keelboats had no conception of the role they were playing in the history of the western expansion of their country. They were obeying the orders of Colonel Henry Leavenworth, who had received instructions from the War Department that he would, with four companies of the 3rd Infantry Regiment, ascend the Missouri River from St. Louis, ". . . and when he reached a point on its left bank near the mouth of the Little Platte River, and within a range of twenty miles above or below its confluence, . . . he will select such position as in his judgment is best calculated for the site of a permanent Cantonment. The spot being chosen, he will then construct with the troops of his

7

command comfortable though temporary quarters sufficient for the accommodation of four companies. This movement will be made as early as the convenience of the service will permit."[1] Directing his second-in-command, Captain William G. Belknap, to follow him with the four companies of infantry, Colonel Leavenworth left immediately for the Little Platte.

The river on which Belknap and his detachment embarked is as crooked as the path made by a snake. It is never constant, but continually changes its channel, eating the banks along its sides, and is probably the most contrary body of water known to man. Someone has said, "Of all the variable things in the world the most uncertain are the actions of a jury, the state of a woman's mind, and the condition of the Missouri River." Stanley Vestal describes the Missouri as being "about equally unsuited to every kind of river craft: too swift for oars, too deep for poles, too shallow for keels, and without permanent banks for a towpath."[2] The trees that it sucks down from its sides are a constant hazard to its navigation, as are the rocks and eddies.

The keelboats in which the troops traveled were about seventy-five feet long and twenty feet wide, and had a light draft of thirty inches. A cabin used for cargo storage, and holding from ten to twenty tons, extended four or five feet above the keel. There were multiple methods of propulsion: the cordelle, or rope, thirty feet long, by which anywhere from twenty to thirty men on the bank pulled the craft; poles, for the more shallow parts of the river; oars, which were used when it became necessary to cross the river; and sails, set when there was a favorable breeze.[3] The trip up the river on these primitive craft, while interesting for a few days, must have become terribly tedious for the officers and their dependents. The lack of privacy and any conveniences was particularly unpleasant for the officers' wives, one of whom was pregnant.[4]

The men on the boats were typical of the soldiers then on the frontier. Unmilitary in appearance, they were subject, nevertheless, to hard, brutal discipline. Life for them meant poor food, deadly monotony, none of the comforts of civilization, and an ever-present danger of death from disease or hostile action. The hours were long, the work grueling, and the compensation a mere pittance; but the army still found it possible to enlist, and often retain, good men. There were among them hard cases, men whose pasts were better forgotten and who might desert at the first opportunity; but there were also the eager, the adventurous, and those with a pride in their profession.

Belknap and his detachment left St. Louis on April 17, 1827. Samuel Peter Haintzelman of the 3rd Infantry wrote in his diary that it took 30 days to reach the Little Platte, and that they arrived at the site of the future Cantonment Leavenworth on Friday, 18th of May, 1827.

The garrison found the climate a continuing ordeal that first year. During summer they experienced days of searing heat when the wild winds and dust tornadoes whipped and browned any clothes hung on a line. Frightening thunderstorms, accompanied by deluges of rain that did not penetrate the soil but ran off in torrential streams, swept across the land. Often they were pelting hailstorms, stripping the foliage from bushes and trees, and covering the ground with a sea of melting ice. The winter that followed was equally extreme. There were blizzards with howling winds in which a man could be lost and might freeze to death only a few feet from his door. It was not a climate for the timid.

Cantonment Leavenworth was not the first post to be established by the United States Army along the Missouri River. About forty miles below the present site of Kansas City, near where the town of Sibley now stands, Fort Clark (later to be called Fort Osage) was founded in 1808, but by 1826 it had been abandoned. In 1818, preliminary to the expedition that would establish Fort Atkinson at Council Bluffs, Iowa, Captain Wyly Martin left Bellefontaine on August 30, going northward up the Missouri with ten keelboats, 347 men, ten officers, and large quantities of supplies. In late October, he landed his force at Isle de Vache, or Cow Island, about ten miles north of where Fort Leavenworth would later be located. Martin set his men to building a temporary post which he modestly designated as Camp Martin. The captain and his men spent the winter on the island. In September, 1819, Colonel Henry Atkinson and the 6th Infantry arrived. Cantonment Martin was abandoned, and the combined force moved up the river.

Henry Leavenworth had an impressive military record when

he was selected to establish the cantonment that was to bear his name. Tall and dark-haired, with a narrow face, a sharp nose, and a small mouth, the future general was then forty-four years old. He was born in New Haven, Connecticut, in 1783, the son of Jesse and Catherine Frisbie Leavenworth. His mother, proud of her bluntness, had a reputation as a shrew. When British soldiers sacked the Leavenworth house in her husband's absence during the Revolutionary War, she is said to have given the redcoats a tongue-lashing that was never forgotten by anyone within hearing distance.

Jesse Leavenworth returned during the war, and in 1780 secured a franchise from the legislature to operate a ferry at New Haven. His wife's scoldings finally became too much for the veteran, and he left for Vermont with three-year-old Henry and a woman who had been an intimate of the family. On October 27, 1786, he finally settled in Danville. There Jesse built a mill, married the woman who had accompanied him, and later served three terms in the Vermont legislature.

Henry, who had an analytical and inquisitive mind, decided to become an attorney. His father was able to arrange for him to read law in the office of a former war comrade, General Erastus Root, in Delhi, New York, and the young man was admitted to the bar there in 1804.

Before the war, Jesse had been a member of the Connecticut Governor's Foot Guard captained by his neighbor, Benedict Arnold, and in the Revolutionary Army, he had risen to the rank of colonel. When the War of 1812 began, Henry, against the pleadings and advice of his legal preceptor, forsook a lucrative law practice to follow his father's tradition, and was commissioned a captain in the 25th Infantry. Affable, responsible, and quick-witted, he rose rapidly. On August 15, 1813, he was named a major in the 9th Infantry, which was attached to General Winfield Scott's brigade, and he commanded the regiment in the invasion of Canada from the Niagara frontier.

Breveted[5] a lieutenant colonel, then colonel, for gallantry at Chippewa on July 6, and at Niagara on July 25, 1814, Henry also won special mention for his action at Lundy's Lane. He was transferred to the 2nd Infantry on May 17, 1815, and was granted a leave of absence later that year to serve a term in the New York state legislature, to which he had been elected. He found politics not to his liking, declined to run for reelection, and returned to active duty with the army.

In 1816, Leavenworth was named Indian agent for the Northwest Territory with headquarters at Prairie du Chien, a trading post on the Wisconsin near its confluence with the Mississippi. Two years later he became a lieutenant colonel of the 5th Regiment stationed at Detroit. He led his command to the falls at St. Anthony, where, on the banks of the Mississippi, he established the cantonment later to become Fort Snelling, at that time the most northerly outpost of the frontier.

The general's personal life in his early years was not a smooth one. His first marriage to Elizabeth Eunice Morrison ended in divorce. His second wife, eighteen-year-old Electa Knapp, whom he married in 1810, died the following year. In 1813, he had married Harriett Lovejoy, who accompanied him to many of his western stations. While he was at Prairie du Chien, his wife and daughter, traveling by way of New Orleans and St. Louis, joined him. Leavenworth sent fourteen Indians with a palanquin to St. Louis to escort them the remaining seven hundred miles through the unbroken wilderness. Four of the Indians carried the palanquin, five marched in front, and five formed a rear guard. At night, two stood as watchmen, and they were "all polite and obliging." Harriett Leavenworth and her daughter are believed to have been the first white women to have traveled through this area, a trip that took thirty-four days.

On October 21, 1821, before the permanent buildings at Snelling had been completed, Colonel Leavenworth was reassigned to the 6th Infantry and given command of Fort Atkinson[6] on the banks of the Missouri River in what is now Nebraska. From there, in the summer of 1823, he led an expedition seven hundred miles up the Missouri against the Arikara who, for years, had been harassing the fur traders. In early June, they had attacked the ninety-man fur brigade of William H. Ashley, killing fifteen men and wounding nine. Realizing that unless prompt action was taken trade along the upper river would be decimated, Leavenworth immediately, without waiting for orders, organized a force and headed north.

In addition to over two hundred officers and men, the colonel had with him fifty fur trappers, led by Joshua Pilcher, and hundreds of Sioux warriors anxious to join in the attack upon their ancient foes, the Arikara. Moving up river with five keelboats carrying two six-pounders and the supplies, Leavenworth's expedition was plagued by difficulties from the very start. The Missouri was at its meanest. Tons of supplies were lost, and seven men were drowned when one of the boats was wrecked; a second boat ran aground and could not be budged.

On the morning of August 9, the palisades of the Arikara village were sighted. The Sioux auxiliaries, who were several miles in advance of the troops, immediately attacked and had been engaged for an hour before Leavenworth and his men reached the village. The colonel was finding it difficult to form a line that would allow his men to fire on the enemy without killing the Sioux, when the Arikara withdrew behind the palisades leaving fifteen of their dead.

Impressed by the stockade, Leavenworth decided to await the arrival of his cannon on the keelboats. The Sioux, feeling they had not been supported, multilated the dead and withdrew to the nearby hills to observe the outcome of the fight.

In the first full-scale engagement between the United States Army and the Plains Indians, Leavenworth the next morning attacked the Arikara by lobbing shells into the village. Opposing some eight hundred warriors, he realized the weakness of his small, undisciplined, and motley force and was quick to accept the hostiles' suggestion for a parley.

The fur traders were furious; they had wanted the entire tribe annihilated and the Plains Indians taught a bitter lesson. Pilcher told Leavenworth, "You came to restore peace and tranquility to the country. You came, to use your own language, 'to open and make good this great road,' instead of which, you have, by the imbecility of your conduct and operations . . . left impassable barriers."[7]

Conversely, Colonel Leavenworth was stoutly defended by the military and commended by his departmental commander, the Secretary of War, and President James Monroe. In the East, however, there was criticism of the expedition. Ashley's brigade, it was said, had been illegally on Indian lands, and the army should not have been used against those who were defending their rights.

Colonel Leavenworth, who had been breveted to brigadier general on July 25, 1824, formally received his eagles on December 16, 1825, and was given command of the 3rd Infantry, then stationed at Green Bay, Wisconsin. The following year he was sent to Jefferson Barracks, St. Louis, Missouri, to establish an infantry school. Although its existence was brief, the school had a profound influence on the standards of duty and discipline of the army in its formative years. As General George B. Davis, judge advocate general of the army, later wrote in the *U.S. Cavalry Journal:*

> He [Leavenworth] was one of the first, as he was certainly the most active and intelligent of the small number of regimental commanders upon whom devolved the duty of adopting European methods of drill, discipline and administration to the peculiar needs of our own military service. How well this task was performed was seen a little more than ten years later in the splendid behavior of the Regular regiments in the War with Mexico.

It was while at Jefferson Barracks that Leavenworth received his orders for the establishment of a post near the confluence of the Missouri and the Little Platte rivers. How he reached his destination is not known, although it was probably by horseback. Upon his arrival, he made a reconnaissance of the area and decided to disobey orders. He selected as the site for the new cantonment a location on the west side of the river rather than on the left bank, as he had been directed. A less imaginative officer would have followed instructions literally, even though the right bank provided a more desirable site for the new post. In his report to the War Department, Colonel Leavenworth wrote:

> A short examination of the country convinced me that there was no good site for military purposes on the left bank up the Missouri within the distance of this place mentioned in the General Orders on that subject. I accordingly proceeded up the river eighteen or twenty miles and found a good site for a cantonment on the right bank of the Missouri, about the distance from this place. The site is 150 feet above the surface of the river and had an altitude of 896 feet.

In addition to the advantage of being on the same side of

the Missouri as the road to Santa Fe, this position (the one I
have selected) possesses the very material one of having a
dry, rolling country, on the south and southeast of it. This
will greatly contribute to the healthiness of the position. In
addition to all this, I can safely say that there is no other
place that will answer the purpose required within the prescribed distance of the Little Platte.[8]

Fortunately for the colonel, the desk-borne officers in the War
Department, who knew little of the West, were convinced, and
on September 19, 1827, gave approval of the site selected as
"deemed to be judicious," and the post was officially designated
as Cantonment Leavenworth.[9]

The Colonel had not waited for official sanction from Washington,
but had put the troops to work immediately. The temporary tents
were soon replaced by log-and-bark huts, and work was begun
on the permanent buildings of the cantonment. By the following
June, a year after his arrival, Leavenworth was able to report to
the quartermaster general that quarters for the enlisted men consisting of four one-story frame-and-brick buildings, fifty-two by thirty-
six feet with basement kitchens, and a hospital of the same construction sixty-four by thirty-six feet had been completed. He also
reported that part of the timber for the officers' quarters was available.[10]

There were occasional visitors to the cantonment even before
the log huts had been completed. Captain Daniel Ketchum of
the 6th Infantry, with a battalion of troops bound for Jefferson
Barracks, stopped to leave property and supplies from the deac-
tivated Fort Atkinson. Major John Dougherty, newly appointed
Indian agent for the upper Missouri, was with Ketchum.

In 1808, when he was seventeen, Dougherty had left his home
in Kentucky for St. Louis to join a western expedition of the Missouri
Fur Company. The lad had few employable skills, but like most
Kentucky youths, he had been an avid hunter. It was in this capacity
that his name was entered on the roles of the party. Eager to
be of use and thirsting for adventure, Dougherty was not only
able to keep the party well supplied with meat, but gained a considerable reputation for physical prowess. During a hunt that followed
a heavy snow and a hard freeze, Dougherty's companion hunter,

a Sioux, boasted that he killed only with a knife. About twelve miles from camp, they sighted a large herd of elk. The young men, who were on foot, pursued the herd into a box canyon and plunged their knives into the shoulders of twenty-five of the cornered animals. To add to the sport of the chase, Dougherty and his companion agreed to race each other back to the camp to get the pack mules needed to carry the meat. Dougherty arrived half an hour before the Sioux and had made all preparations for retrieving the kill when the Indian got there. It was said that the Sioux's chagrin was so great that he died a few months later, but not without first bestowing the name "Iron Legs" on Dougherty.

During the several years he traveled throughout the Pacific Northwest, Dougherty learned not only to speak French fluently, but how to converse in seven Indian dialects. This knowledge earned him an appointment as interpreter for Major Benjamin O'Fallon, the Indian agent for the upper Missouri tribes.

At Colonel Leavenworth's suggestion, Dougherty decided to make the Kansas cantonment his permanent headquarters. On September 25, 1827, he returned there with his wife, the former Mary Hertzog of St. Louis; their son was the second white male child born in Kansas. (Anne Clark Belknap, wife of the senior captain, was one of the few other women on the post.)

On October 31, 1827, the post complement had included four companies of the 3rd Infantry; sixteen officers and 164 enlisted men. Early in 1828, they were joined by the remainder of the 3rd Infantry. Small steamboats had appeared on the river for the first time, and the troops took advantage of this new means of transportation. A number of recruits embarked from St. Louis for Leavenworth on April 23, on the steamer *Illinois* that had been advertised the previous month as a "new and substantial craft."

In the same year, the troops of the cantonment were detailed to open a road to the town of Barry, a few miles from Liberty, Missouri. The road, twenty-feet wide, was cut from the Missouri River to Bee Creek, across which a ford was constructed. Citizens from Clay County did some work on the eastern end. In 1828, a license was granted to one Robert Todd to operate a ferry across the Missouri and Little Platte rivers. Before the year was out, Todd had sold his franchise to Zadock Martin who, with his six sons and six slaves, operated the ferry. There were loud protests from the customers who accused Martin of charging exorbitant prices for the passage.

The wisdom of the post commander in building a hospital became apparent the summer of 1828; the statement in his earlier report to the War Department that the site selected was healthful, had proved less than prophetic. Assistant surgeon Thomas S. Bryant, then at the cantonment, must have spent a busy time during June and July when 163 cases of malaria occurred, eleven of them fatal.[11] Among the fatalities was the six-year-old son of Lieutenant Samuel W. Hunt. According to Elvid Hunt, of "174 enlisted men, seventy-seven were sick and sixty-five were occupied with duties connected with taking care of them, which left only thirty-two for duty." The spring of 1829 brought no improvement in the health of the troops. The situation became so acute that on May 16, 1829, the entire garrison, with the exception of a small detachment, was ordered to Jefferson Barracks, and Colonel George Croghan, after an inspection tour, recommended that the post "be abandoned as too sickly."[12] The troops left Fort Leavenworth on May 21 aboard the steamer *Liberator;* they arrived in St. Louis ten days later.

The order had been greeted with enthusiasm by the officers, the enlisted men, and their dependents. It was a return to civilization; for the women, it meant resumed shopping and social life, and for the bachelors, the resumed pleasures of the companionship of the opposite sex. For one company, however, this respite was short-lived. Reports reached St. Louis of an outbreak of hostile Iowa on the Chariton River in Randolph County, Missouri. Colonel Leavenworth immediately ordered a detachment of one company of the 3rd and five companies of the 6th Regiment, under the command of Lieutenant Colonel Daniel Baker, to return to Cantonment Leavenworth. The colonel was not far behind the detachment. As recorded by the Secretary of War in his report for 1829, Colonel Leavenworth . . .

> caused to be assembled, through the instrumentality of the Indian agents, the tribes represented to have been engaged in the affair on the Chariton. The General [Leavenworth] stated to them that it was his object to ascertain, if possible, whether the Indian or the white people were the aggressors that the guilty might be punished. He, therefore, demanded of them

that they deliver into his hands all those who were concerned in the affair, and until this could be done, he detained as hostages some of the principal chiefs then present. The Indians accordingly delivered up nineteen of the Ioways who were the party engaged with whites on the Chariton. Measures were also taken to ascertain the names of the white men engaged in that conflict, and the whole of them have been presented to the proper authorities to be dealt with according to law.

After the successful and bloodless dealings with the Iowa, Leavenworth was given command of the entire southwestern frontier, with instructions to negotiate peace between the warring Indian tribes. Accordingly, he set out with four hundred troops from Fort Gibson[13] on June 15, 1834. The expedition was ill-fated from the start. The march was a hard one, and fever continually plagued the troops. Leavenworth was one of those who fell ill.

The Colonel's illness was not malaria, however, but the result of an injury he had suffered when, as he was chasing a buffalo calf near the mouth of the False Washita, his horse stepped into a gopher hole. George Catlin, the renowned painter of Indians, who had accompanied the expedition, was with him at the time of the accident and wrote of his concern:

> From that hour to the present, I think I have seen a decided change in the General's face; he has looked pale and feeble, and has been continually troubled with a violent cough. I have rode by the side of him from day to day, and he several times told me that he was fearful he was badly hurt. He looks very feeble now, and I very much fear the result of the fever that has set in upon him.

During his illness, Leavenworth told the artist, "I have killed myself in running down that devilish calf; and it was a very lucky thing, Catlin, that you painted the portrait of me before we started for it is all that my dear wife will ever see of me."

Doctor Melinas Conklin Leavenworth, the colonel's nephew, a graduate of the Yale Medical School and an army surgeon with the expedition, devoted his entire attention to the injured man. Despite his efforts, the colonel died in a hospital wagon near Cross Timbers, Indian territory, on July 21, 1834. The order promoting

him to Brigadier General arrived just four days after his death.
Mrs. Leavenworth and her daughter had been at Fort Jesup during
the Colonel's absence. With Leavenworth's friend, Major Belknap, the widow accompanied the body from Cross Timbers to
Delhi for burial. As the cortége passed through New York City,
escorted by the volunteer corps, crowds of mourners lined the
streets. In 1902, his body was disinterred and reburied at Fort
Leavenworth where thousands attended the ceremony.

(Jesse Henry Leavenworth, the general's son by his first wife,
graduated from West Point in 1830. He served in the Black Hawk
War and during the Civil War as a colonel on the western frontier.
Later, as an Indian agent, he was a severe critic of the army for
what he termed its provocative treatment of the Indians.)

CHAPTER THREE

➤➤➤—➤—◄—◄◄◄

NEIGHBORING INDIANS

Fort Leavenworth was soon to find itself in the midst of the great western Indian migration. The rich farmland east of the Mississippi River had been preempted. Avaricious whites who coveted the Indian reservations in the East, argued that it was impossible for the two races to live next to one another in peace. Had these Eastern Indians, they asked, not fought with the British in the War of 1812, and were they not an ever-present threat? And even sincere friends of the Indians agreed that the eastern tribes would fare better separated from the whites.

In 1825, Secretary of War James C. Calhoun proposed that the eastern tribes be moved to the western plains. It was not an original idea on Calhoun's part, but it was a popular one. Congress delayed action, however, until five years later, when during the administration of Andrew Jackson, it passed the Indian Removal Act. This was followed in 1834 by the Indian Trade and Intercourse Act, which defined as Indian territory all lands west of the Mississippi not parts of Louisiana, Alabama, or Missouri.

Treaties with the eastern tribes were rapidly concluded. Although they knew the white man rarely kept his agreements, surrounded and outnumbered as they were, the Indians had no alternative but to make their marks on the proffered documents. In contrast to their western brethren, they knew the power of the United States Government.

On their face, the treaties were fair, if not generous. The tribes were guaranteed protection on their western journeys, and they were to hold their lands in perpetuity, "as long as the green grass

19

grows and the water flows." They were promised local self-government and representation in Congress. Few of these commitments were to be kept, but under the treaties, army troops escorted over eighty thousand Indians to their western lands. The marches were hard, and the suffering severe, with many Indian women and children dying before reaching their new homes. The route followed by the Redmen would long be remembered as the "trail of tears."

With the arrival of the eastern tribes in the Leavenworth area, the personnel at the post were busily engaged in looking after the welfare of the displaced Indians, maintaining peace among them, and at the same time protecting the interests of the government. It was not an easy task, but it was ably performed by the small garrison.

The Kaw Indians, who lived north of the Kansas River, and the Osage, who lived toward the south, had agreed in 1825 to give up their lands and settle on reservations, in return for supplies of farm implements and stock. The Pawnee and the Oto tribes were also induced to transfer all of their lands between the Platte and the Kansas rivers to the United States. Consequently, a vast area of the plains was opened for the eastern tribes. The area immediately adjacent to Fort Leavenworth, containing over two million acres, was allotted to the Delaware, the Kickapoo, the Shawnee, and the Sac-Fox.

The Delaware, or Lenni-Lenape, Indians had originally occupied New Jersey, western Long Island, parts of New York west of the Hudson River, and eastern Pennsylvania and Delaware. Their name Lenni-Lenape means "original" or "true men." Although they had signed the famous treaty with William Penn under the oak at Kensington, they had later become bitter antagonists of the white man. Gradually they had been crowded west by the ever-spreading influx of colonists, and in 1742, the tribe had finally settled along the Susquehanna River in Pennsylvania. By 1770, after a brief stay in Ohio, they had migrated to the section of Indiana between the Ohio and the White rivers.

Though the tribe originally was ten thousand strong, war and disease had reduced it to three thousand by the time its members were gathered up and moved to Kansas. On their reservation neighboring Fort Leavenworth, the Delaware built small log cabins and did some farming. In the Seminole War they furnished the army with over one hundred scouts, and officers generally agreed that for this purpose, they were the most reliable of all Indians.[1]

The Delaware tribe had learned a hard lesson, and in Kansas they avoided hostile acts against the whites. Their warlike spirit did survive, but they expended their energies in fighting other Indian tribes. Francis Parkman, Jr., spoke of this after visiting their reservation in 1841:

> The tribe, the Delaware, once the peaceful allies of William Penn, are now the most adventurous and dreaded warriors upon the prairie. They make war upon remote tribes . . . and they push their new quarrels with true Indian rancor, sending out their little war parties as far as the Rocky Mountains, and into the Mexican territories. Their neighbors and former confederates, the Shawnees, who are tolerable farmers, are in a prosperous condition; but the Delawares dwindle every year, from the number of men lost in their warlike expeditions.[2]

The Kickapoo were a proud people. They were first discovered by Europeans in the late seventeenth century. They lived between the Fox and Wisconsin rivers in what is now Columbia County, Wisconsin; by 1800, the bulk of them were in central Illinois and numbered about two thousand. Between 1809 and 1819, various groups ceded their lands to the government and were removed first to Missouri and then to Kansas, where they were located to the north, immediately adjoining Fort Leavenworth. In the French and Indian wars, they were allies of the French and fought the English colonists. In the War of 1812 and the Black Hawk War, they opposed the United States.

The roots of the Shawnee were deep in the alluvial soil of the lands bordering the Cumberland River in southern Kentucky and northern Tennessee, where the white men first discovered them. Other branches of the tribe were later found near the Savannah River and in parts of South Carolina. Also victims of the western drive by the Anglo-Americans, they were scattered over Ohio and Indiana. They were almost constantly at war with the English colonists and later the Americans. Their hatred of the whites constituted the most serious opposition to the settlement of the Ohio valley. Under their great leader, Tecumseh, they attempted alliances with other Indian tribes to oppose and harass the western push of the paleface. At the mouth of the Tippecanoe River in Indiana, a large body of them was decisively defeated in 1811 by the troops of General William Henry Harrison. During the War of 1812, while fighting with the English, Tecumseh was killed in the Battle of the Thames.

The earliest known Sac had lived in the area of Saginaw Bay, Michigan, from which they had been driven by the Ottawa. In 1804, they were in northwestern Illinois and Wisconsin, but after the Black Hawk War, they sought refuge in Iowa with the Fox, and two years later both these tribes were removed to lands in eastern Kansas near Fort Leavenworth. Between 1857 and 1859, without the consent of the Fox, the Sac agreed to take up land in severalty and cede the remainder of their Kansas territory to the government. The Fox, in a pique, re-migrated to Iowa and in 1867, the Sac were again removed by the United States Government to Oklahoma.[3]

The first of the Shawnee to be taken to Kansas were those who migrated to Missouri in 1825. Six years later, that part of the tribe that had remained in Ohio joined their western kinfolk in Kansas. Because of their division into a multitude of separate tribes, it is impossible to determine their numbers, but there were probably less than one thousand in 1840 on the reservation immediately south of Fort Leavenworth.

In the fall of 1830, a party to survey the lands alloted to the eastern Indians reached Fort Leavenworth. The group was headed by the Reverend Isaac McCoy, a Baptist missionary who had long been a friend of the chiefs of the Delaware.

Born in Uniontown, Pennsylvania, in 1784, Isaac McCoy had been raised on the Kentucky frontier and was self-educated. By his nineteenth birthday, he had become a Baptist minister and in that same year married Christiana Polk, who dedicated her life to his work. In 1817, McCoy began his first work with the Indians and, as the first Baptist missionary to the Redmen, he ranks with Father Pierre Jean de Smet among the great clergymen of the West. In 1823, he reached the conclusion that the Indians were corrupted by their proximity to the whites and proposed their removal beyond the Mississippi. Thereafter he labored toward this goal, and spent much of his time in Washington where he was influential in working for the passage of the Indian Removal Act of 1830. Right or wrong in his pleadings for Indian migration, there could be no doubt of his sincerity, and this was recognized by his friends among the eastern tribes.

Others who accompanied McCoy were his sons, Rice McCoy and John Calvin McCoy; John Quick, the 2nd chief of (Missouri) Delawares whose council had recently elected him their representative and the expedition's chairman; Congreve Jackson; and Albert Dickens. Joining the party from time to time was Shane, a half-Shawnee Indian who acted as interpreter for his tribe; and James Connors who acted in a similar capacity for the Delaware. Jo Jim or Joseph James, a half-caste Kansa was hired by McCoy as interpreter after the party left Fort Leavenworth.

McCoy's party surveyed the lands neighboring the post for the Delaware, Shawnee, Wyandot, Potawatomie, and Kickapoo tribes. Before leaving Washington, the surveyors had not been given instructions for the omission of the Cantonment Leavenworth reservation from the Indian lands. Realizing that this must have been an unintentional oversight, McCoy, meeting with Major William Davenport, the post commander, and John Quick, finally reached an agreement as to the limits of the post and its separation from the Indians' province.

In this same year, an Indian peace council was held at Leavenworth. Called by Major John Dougherty, the Indian agent, the council included delegates from the Oto, Omaha, Iowa, Sac, Delaware, Shawnee, and Kickapoo. This initial council was a huge success and set the tone of many future meetings.

At Isaac McCoy's suggestion, representatives of the Pawnee, who lived in southern Nebraska, were summoned to the fort. They arrived on September 22, 1830. To those on the post who were unfamiliar with the appearance of the Plains Indians, the tall, erect, almost nude savages, wearing only a loincloth with a buffalo skin thrown over the shoulder, were an awesome sight. The chiefs were told that McCoy intended to survey a portion of their lands, and that to avoid complications, he wished to do so during their fall hunting season, while the warriors were away from the villages. The Pawnee gave their consent, and McCoy, escorted by a detachment of fifteen troopers from the post, later conducted his survey without incident.

The settlement of the Delaware on the land they had been

assigned was not without difficulties. The Pawnee and their allies, the Oto, in spite of their previous treaty, continued to hunt on the land between the Platte and the Kansas rivers. Friction inevitably developed, with the Pawnee being the aggressors. Parties of the Delaware were ambushed and their villages attacked. It finally became impossible for them to hunt safely north of the Kansas, and they retaliated. Led by Chief Sou-wah-nocke, they sacked and burned a large Pawnee village in 1833. It was now open war between the two tribes, and the government had to intervene. Accordingly, Henry Ellsworth was named United States Commissioner to settle, once and for all, the title to the disputed lands, induce the Pawnee to move north of the Platte, and conclude peace treaties between the contending tribes.

Following the arrival of Ellsworth, Major Dougherty sent messages to the Delaware and the Pawnee to come to the fort and meet in council. As they arrived, great care was taken to see that they were not encamped too close together.

Before the council convened, a problem arose that today would seem trifling, but which for a time threatened to disrupt the conference. The Delaware claimed to be the oldest of all the tribes and firmly believed all other Indians were descended from them. They accordingly insisted that the Pawnee address them as great-grandfather, which the latter adamantly refused to do. Fortunately, Major Dougherty, by the judicious use of a little flattery, was able to convince the chiefs of the Pawnee that the matter was not important and that, for the sake of peace, they should address the Delaware by the title.

Several days were spent in powwow, with all the delegates demanding to be heard. After interminable hours of oratory on the part of each representative, the commission asked the conferees to get down to business. The terms of a treaty were finally agreed upon. It embodied all the items that the government had specified and, the next morning, it was signed by the Indian chiefs. The Pawnee-Delaware War was over.

In the years that followed, aside from difficulties from time to time with the Pawnee, the post had little trouble with its red neighbors. Major Dougherty and Isaac McCoy had laid a firm foundation of mutual respect between the two races in the Leavenworth area.

The Great White Father in Washington did not keep his promises for very long. Within fifteen years after the treaties of 1830 had been signed, agitation began for removal of the Kansas Indians still further west. Within weeks after the Kansas-Nebraska Act of 1854 opening those territories to white settlers, new treaties were forced on the Indians.

CHAPTER FOUR

>»»→<—«««

THE EXPEDITIONS

While Fort Leavenworth has played a significant part in the history of the United States and of the army over the years, its military role has been a passive one. Its garrisons have never heard a shot fired in anger, or the war whoops of Indians, or the twang of their bows. As Colonel George Croghan reported after an inspection visit on August 26, 1836, "There is about as much propriety in calling this post Fort Leavenworth as there would be in calling an Armed schooner a . . . battleship, for it is not only not a Fort but it is even devoid of the regularity of a common barracks. Of defenses it has none."[1]

Established primarily to guard the Santa Fé trail, it soon became the gateway to the West, the starting point for the conquest of vast new territories. When that role ended and it found itself in the backwash of the Indian Wars, it took its place as the keystone of the army's educational system.

Through its gates passed not only the major early western exploratory missions but the troops that were sent to punish or pacify the Indian tribes of the plains. Many of these expeditions were commanded by officers permanently stationed at the fort.

The first of the many forces that were to leave Fort Leavenworth for the West was one commanded by Captain Bennett Riley, for whom Fort Riley was later named. Escorting a caravan of traders bound for Santa Fé, the 6th Infantry left the post on June 5, 1829. After a hard five-day march, during which they averaged only seven miles a day, they reached the Great Plains.

Their first contact with hostile forces occurred on July 23 when two of their mail couriers were ambushed by a party of fifteen Indians who succeeded in making off with the mail and their horses. Both men, Corporal Arter and Private Nation, were wounded. Nation got a spear through his chest and eventually died. The attack occurred some fifteen miles from the main party, and for thirteen days the wounded Arter, living on snakes and frogs, wandered about on foot before he found Captain Riley.

Riley continued his escort of the wagon train to Choteau's Island, on the Mexican border. There, the regiment went into camp while the traders continued south. They had not gone far when they were attacked by some five hundred Iowa and Comanche. A rider was sent back to Riley for help, and the captain immediately went to the aid of the embattled caravan. Approaching the hostiles, Riley opened fire at long range with grape and round shot from a six-inch cannon. After eight of their number had been killed, the Indians withdrew. Thereafter, Riley remained with the wagon train until it reached Sand Creek, then he returned to his camp on the border.

It had been agreed that the command would wait for the return of the traders until October 10, but by that date no caravan had been sighted. Supplies were low, the men were ragged, some were without shoes, and cold weather was setting in, so the next day Riley determined to return to Fort Leavenworth. He had not gone far when the column was overtaken by galloping horsemen from a detachment of the Mexican Army under the command of Colonel José Antonio who were escorting the delayed wagon train north.

Riley decided to delay his march to Leavenworth, and the two military forces remained together for three days. Philip St George Cooke, a young lieutenant and a West Point graduate of 1827, wrote a colorful description of the meeting with the Mexicans:

> I distinctly remember the feast we gave them. Seated cross-legged around a green blanket in the bottom of the tent, we partook of bread, buffalo meat, and as an extraordinary rarity, of some salt pork, but to crown all were large onions for which we were endebted to our arriving guests. A tin cup of whiskey which like the pork was for an unusual occasion was followed by another of water. The next day we had time to look around us and to admire the strangest collection of

animals and men that perhaps ever met on the frontier of the United States. There were a few Creoles, polished gentlemen magnificently clothed in Spanish costumes; a large number of grave Spaniards exiled from Mexico and on their way to the United States with much property in stocks and gold. There was a company of Mexican regulars as they are called, in uniform, mere apologies for soldiers or even men. Several tribes of Indians or Mexicans much more formidable as warriors, were grouped around their horses, with spears planted in the ground. Frenchmen were there of course, and our hundred and eighty hearty veterans in rags, but well armed and equipped for any service. Four or five languages were spoken. To complete the picture must be mentioned the two thousand horses, mules and Jacks which kept up an incessant braying.[2]

At a dinner given by the Mexican colonel the next day, the Americans were much impressed by the variety of wines served by their host. Resuming the return march on October 14, the troops arrived back at Fort Leavenworth November 8.

Early in 1834, Colonel Henry Dodge arrived with four companies of dragoons and took command of Fort Leavenworth. A shaggy-haired, unconventional, but kindly man, the colonel unfortunately had political ambitions and wanted the men to like him. He accordingly left all matters of discipline to his second-in-command, Lieutenant Colonel Stephen Watts Kearny. Dodge came to be considered by the officers as too soft, while the enlisted men thought Kearny too harsh.

The following year, the colonel was told by Major Dougherty that on a recent visit to the Pawnee and Otoe tribes to pay government annuities, he had talked with several chiefs of the Arikara. They had told him that their people had been driven from their lands on the Missouri by their enemy, the Sioux, and that they wanted to remain for the winter on the Platte River with the Pawnee. The agent had replied that they could stay there until he had word to the contrary from the Indian Bureau. On January 18, 1835, Colonel Dodge advised the War Department of his conversation with Dougherty, pointing out that the Arikara were a treacherous people who had never made peace with the government, and that "their wants may place them in a situation that will force them to make a peace with the United States that will be lasting." The colonel suggested, "A considerable show of force might well overawe this tribe and other hostiles."

The War Department agreed. On May 29, 1835, Dodge set out together with three companies of dragoons and Indian Agent Dougherty, with J. C. Gantt as the expedition's guide. Gantt, an Indian trader, had seen army service as a volunteer from 1816 to 1829 and had established the first trading post in Arikara country near the present site of Pueblo, Colorado. Dodge and his dragoons went as far as the Rockies by following the Platte River on a course that would later be called the Oregon Trail. The return march was by the Arkansas River and the Santa Fé Trail.

The colonel brought back a vast fund of information about the area traversed, and the expedition's show of force had a salutary effect on the Indian tribes. The departmental commander and the Secretary of War were gratified with the results of Dodge's efforts, the former recommending that the colonel be given a sword, the other officers a brace of pistols, and each of the noncommissioned officers an extra month's pay.

Local citizens in Clay County, Missouri, however, were most unhappy. They felt that in the absence of such a large force of troops from Fort Leavenworth they had not been protected from possible Indian attacks. A petition was dispatched by the Missourians to the Secretary of War, protesting that "there was no earthly use to the government resulting from the Dragoons' journeying to the distant Rocky Mountains."[3]

Information reached the War Department in 1839 that there was trouble in the Cherokee nation and that the Cherokee had killed their chiefs who had cautioned moderation in their dealings with the whites. Colonel Stephen Watts Kearny was ordered to quell the disturbance, and he left Leavenworth in June, 1839, with the largest military force ever assembled to that time by the United States. As the quartermaster at the fort did not have sufficient funds to equip the expedition, the colonel, who was from a wealthy New Jersey family, advanced the necessary funds. He was later reimbursed.

Traffic steadily increased through Fort Leavenworth, and the caravans grew longer and more frequent down the Santa Fé Trail.

In the spring of 1843, Captain Philip St George Cooke led an escort of a New Mexico-bound wagon train and made the usual camp at the Mexican border. From the agitated commander of some nearby Mexican troops he learned that one Jacob Snively purporting to be a captain in the United States Army had been confiscating property on both sides of the border. Catching up with Snively, who produced what appeared to be a regular army commission, Cooke concluded that the credentials were forgeries, put Snively and his entire band of a hundred men under arrest. Cooke's actions were later vindicated by a court of inquiry.

In May, 1845, Colonel Kearny led another expedition westward to cow the Indians and thus give protection to the trains along the Oregon Trail. Kearny, who died three years later, was ill with digestive troubles that would probably be diagnosed today as an ulcer, but he readily accepted the assignment. Actually, nearly all of the officers and men who survived the various western expeditions never fully recovered from the fevers or malaria they contracted. This time the affluent colonel may have been short of immediate funds, for the force was a small one, consisting of only five companies of dragoons. They carried with them two mountain howitzers from which exploding shells could be fired, as well as military rockets which when seen at night were most impressive. The three hundred officers and men were equipped with carbines and pistols.

Kearny followed the Dodge trail west, traveling an average of twenty-one miles a day. On June 11, he camped on the North Platte River below Scott's Bluff, where he could see a large village of Brûlé Sioux on the opposite side. Sending his guide, Thomas Fitzpatrick, to the Indian encampment, he invited a group of the warriors to visit the soldiers. Some fifty of them accepted, and after a speech by Kearny telling them of the white man's peaceful intentions, they were given a demonstration. After the deafening exploding shells of the howitzers, the rapidity and accurate firing of the breech-loading carbines, and the awesome "rockets' red glare," the Brûlé Sioux, visibly shaken, quickly agreed to meet in council at Fort Laramie two days later.

On the 16th, Kearny faced an assemblage of fifteen hundred Brûlé, Aglala, and Arapaho. Telling them that the caravans along the Oregon Trail were not to be interfered with, he had his troops give another demonstration of the white man's firepower, followed by a more peaceful bit of persuasion: gifts of cloth, beads, looking glasses, knives, and tobacco for the visiting delegates. The following day, Kearny headed west, arriving at South Pass on June 30. Returning eastward, he came upon a village of two hundred Cheyenne at Chugwater. The same routine of speeches, firepower displays, and gifts was repeated, and the Cheyenne were equally impressed. Nadeau related an amusing incident of the Chugwater Council:

> During the parley the rest of the command were standing idly in the camp, taking in the scene. One officer, with the unusual features of a red beard and thick spectacles was bending over the shoulder of a young squaw to view her handiwork, when she suddenly turned and saw him. Shriek followed shriek, and whenever the poor officer turned other Cheyenne maidens joined the chorus, some of them running, hiding, and laughing. At length it was understood that they believed glasses enabled the wearer to see through clothing and that their redbearded guest was violating their modesty.[4]

From the Chugwater, Kearny and his command headed southward, stopping at Bent's Fort[5] on the Arkansas, where the traders entertained the officers at a sumptuous dinner. They returned to Fort Leavenworth on August 24, after having covered more than two thousand miles in less than a hundred days without the loss of a single man. Kearny had not only impressed the Indians, but he had gained valuable knowledge of the terrain. In his report, Kearny recommended that a similar patrol be sent out yearly rather than establishing a string of forts for the protection of the Oregon Trail.

The first wagon train from Fort Leavenworth to reach the newly purchased Fort Laramie, arrived on July 28, 1849. With the escort party was Lieutenant Colonel Aeneas Mackay, sent to make an inspection, and Captain Langdon C. Easton with a detachment of dragoons. Although it went "exactly in the right direction" there had been some question as to whether the Great Platte Road was the best route from Fort Leavenworth to Fort Laramie. On August 1, before his return to Kansas, Colonel Mackay ordered Captain

Easton to take a detachment of ten dragoons and return to Fort Leavenworth by way of the Republican Fork and the Kansas Rivers and to make an examination of the country he passed through with a view to establishing a more direct route for the emigrants to Oregon and the gold fields of California. Mackay died a few months after dispatching Easton eastward.

Exploring the West was an undertaking that even the most experienced army officers were hardly prepared for. Easton, a frank, outgoing, and even-tempered Missourian, was a West Point graduate of the class of 1838. He had served in the Seminole War from 1838-1842, had been stationed at Fort Towson in Indian Territory, and had been on quartermaster duty at Fort Leavenworth for the last two years, but was without previous exploring experience. Easton's second-in-command, Nathan George Evans, a spanking new lieutenant from the West Point class of 1848, was equally inexperienced.

Besides the ten dragoons, Easton had in his party his guide, Joseph Huneau, a Dr. George B. Parks of Boston who was anxious to see as much of the country as possible, the thirteen-year-old son of Colonel Mackay who had been sent along "for the improvement of his mind and body," ten teamsters and two servants. There were five mule teams with the detail. Unfortunately, the troops were riding the same horses they had ridden to Laramie, and after only three days of rest and grazing, they were in poor condition.

After traveling nine miles on the first day, Easton discovered at Cherry Creek that the cartridges he had been issued at Laramie were of faulty manufacture; they had too much oil on the cloth patching. Delaying his march until the following day, he sent a trooper back to Laramie for a new supply.

On August 4, at Horse Creek—a sizable tributary of the North Platte—Easton came upon a large Sioux village. The Indians did their best to convince the party that they were friendly, even helping to move a wagon mired in the creek. Discovering that a cholera epidemic was raging in the village and "had carried off a large number of the tribe," Easton moved three miles beyond and camped on Bear Creek.

There, one Trooper Covey killed a rattlesnake with his saber, but foolishly picked up the head and was bitten on the thumb. There was no ammonia in the medical supplies, so Easton applied gunpowder after cutting the thumb, and the powder was then exploded with a coal of fire. Covey was seriously ill for twelve hours, constantly retching, and his arm became quite swollen, "after which time he became better" and was back on duty in ten days. Later, one of Dr. Park's servants was bitten on the leg. The same treatment was equally effective.

Easton reached Pole Creek on the 6th and followed its meandering course for about ten miles past the present site of Pine Bluffs, Wyoming, from where he struck out to the southeast. There he saw a herd of buffalo, and Huneau killed a young bull. This, along with an antelope, was the first fresh meat the troops had had since leaving Laramie.

On Mackay's march from Kearny to Laramie, the troops had been stalked by a band of Cheyenne. The same band appeared at Rush Creek and, as they had stolen supplies from the previous expedition, Easton allowed only two of the Indians in the camp at a time. The frustrated Indians tried to rush the sentinels, but when Lieutenant Evans ordered the troopers to take a menacing posture, the Cheyenne left.

Easton and his group crossed the south fork of the Platte on August 10. After traveling southeast for four days, they finally reached what they thought was the Republican River, but which was actually the Arikaree. The weary and thirsty men had gone four days without seeing a stream of water or timber, and a cheer went up as they reached a knoll that overlooked a pleasant valley and a stream shaded by cottonwoods. Their roars of joy turned to laughter when an Irish teamster bellowed out, "By Jesus, we're in sight of land again."

Easton reached the north fork of the true Republican on the 16th, and there the party encountered a buffalo herd so large that it was within sight or hearing for a full week. There was an ample supply of meat as they followed the river valley in a generally easterly direction.

On the 26th, Huneau and a dragoon, returning from butchering a buffalo, were met by a small party of Pawnee, who were on a stealing forage against the Cheyenne. Huneau dismounted and offered the Indians some of the meat. In appreciation, one of the

Pawnee put his arms around the guide; this affectionate embrace cost Huneau his bowie knife. At the same time another Indian helped himself to more meat, while a less successful brave was stopped from removing a bridle. These Indians proved to be masters of theft—despite the fact that Easton posted extra guards, Lieutenant Evans's favorite pony was missing the next morning.

It was not until a month later that the party reached the Oregon Trail. By the time they had stopped at the village of Uniontown and at the farm of a Potawatomie Indian to get supplies, the horses and mules were exhausted, and the men weary. The trek to Leavenworth finally ended on September 18.

Easton's group had covered a distance of fourteen hundred miles in a month and a half. They brought back considerable information on the soil, grazing land, and the sources of water and timber in the area covered; but Easton had certainly not enhanced his reputation as an explorer. He later admitted that he had made two principal errors: first in unduly lengthening the journey; and second in advising that the Republican River route offered no advantage over the great Platte road.

In mid-May, 1849, Lieutenant Colonel William Wing Loring, commanding the regiment of mounted riflemen, left Fort Leavenworth for the Columbia River in Oregon to map and investigate the land in that general area. Accompanying Loring were George Gibbs, a Harvard naturalist, and William H. Tappin, a botanist who spent most of his time sketching the landscape.

Loring, a Floridian, had lost an arm at Chapultepec. (Following the Civil War, during which he became a major general in the Confederate Army, he entered the service of the khedive of Egypt as a divisional commander. Participating in the Abyssinian Campaign of 1875, he was made a pasha, thereafter returning to the United States.)

The trail itself now bore little resemblance to the one followed by their exploratory predecessors. The thousands of emigrants who had since passed that way had been, in the modern term, litterbugs. Furniture, utensils, and even tools had been discarded. Mounds of stones and crosses were mute testimony to the rigors of the voyage. And, in early versions of "Kilroy was here," Independence Rock bore thousands of carved signatures of those who had passed. Philip St George Cooke described the sandstone outcropping as

"a natural Monument, with all the names of all the fools that pass
this way." To add to the confusion, the trail was jam-packed with
Forty-Niners on their way to the gold fields of California.

In Oregon, the wholesale desertion by his troops became Loring's
principal problem. Pay of as high as thirty dollars a day in the
gold fields was attractive to men who, as privates, were receiving
only eight dollars a month. On one occasion, a group of a hundred
men deserted in a body.

Loring's report, like Easton's, was a disappointment. The information he brought back to Fort Leavenworth was helpful but hardly
scientific. The army had continued to disregard what it had long
known—that those they sent out on exploratory missions should
have had training over and above that necessary to command troops.
Prior to Loring's trek, the army had formally organized, as a separate
branch, a corps of topographical engineers,[6] to be commanded by a
colonel. Its officers, popularly called topogs, were almost all West
Point graduates. Their education, however, did not end when they
left the academy; they traveled abroad, studied European ideas,
kept in contact with the leading American and European scientists,
and exchanged papers among themselves. The army was thus better
prepared for the extensive explorations that were to follow in the
West. Colonel John J. Abert, commander of the topogs, was a
frequent visitor at Fort Leavenworth.

It had been originally planned that Captain Howard Stansbury
and his assistant, Lieutenant John W. Gunnison—both topogs
—with eighteen men, horses, and mules, would accompany Loring's expedition as far as Fort Hall, Idaho. Unfortunately, they
were late in arriving at Fort Leavenworth, and Loring had already
left. Stansbury, accordingly, formed his own expedition and headed
for Laramie from the fort on May 31, 1849.

Stansbury had been directed to make a reconnaissance along
the Platte River route and across the Wasatch Mountains to Salt
Lake City. He was to map the Salt Lake, report on the Mormon
inhabitants of the area, and thereafter march to Fort Hall, returning
by way of Santa Fé.

From Laramie, the group went on to Fort Bridger[7] where
the famous scout Jim Bridger joined them. From Bridger, Stansbury
sent Gunnison on to Fort Hall with the wagons. Stansbury and
Bridger attempted to find a suitable route for a railroad by way

of Ogden's Creek through the Wasatch Mountains. Their conclusion was that the course was not satisfactory for the purpose.

Stansbury's reception in Utah was not cordial. A rumor had preceded him that his survey of the area was but a prelude to the dispossession of the Mormons by the government. After a conference, however, Stansbury not only convinced Brigham Young to the contrary, but secured the services of the famous Mormon scout, Albert Carrington.

At the Salt Lake, Stansbury explored the western shore and mapped the entire area. He spent the winter in Salt Lake City, the center of the Mormon empire, and his report on the people was objective and friendly.

In the spring, disregarding his instructions, he traveled south to the old Spanish trail and spent his time still trying to find a suitable railroad route through the Rockies and the Wasatch Mountains. But the exploration was brought to a speedy halt when Stansbury was thrown from a horse and suffered a severe injury. Nevertheless, the Union Pacific ultimately followed much of the route he mapped. Stansbury's report, *Explorations of the Valley of the Great Salt Lake of the Utah*, was published in 1853.

With the exception of the armies that set forth for Santa Fé and California during the Mexican War, there were no large expeditions out of Fort Leavenworth until the year 1857, when one commanded by Colonel Edwin Vose Sumner left the fort.

In the autumn of 1856, a well-outfitted, Utah-bound emigrant train, including many women and children, traveled west toward Utah along the Kansas River to Fort Riley, where it took the road to Fort Kearny. Some two hundred miles from the latter post, at the crossing of the Republican River, it went into camp on "a broad open bottom"[8] where there was good grazing for the oxen. No Indians had been sighted, and the members of the caravan relaxed.

Fires were lighted for the noonday meal, the cattle were turned loose, and most of the group were either cooking, mending harness, or dozing in the sun, when without warning a large band of Indians attacked the camp. The men barely had time to get their weapons before the battle was over with a hundred emigrants killed. The few survivors made their way to Fort Kearny and told their story.

When word of the massacre reached Washington, Secretary of

War Jefferson Davis immediately directed Colonel Sumner, commanding Fort Leavenworth, to take the field as early as possible in 1857, seek out the Indians who had committed the atrocity, and "inflict a punishment they will long remember."

Sumner, a white-bearded old cavalryman with a large powerful frame, was called "Bull of the Woods" by his enlisted men and has been described as "the greatest martinet in the service." Captain Richard F. Ewell, later to become a Confederate lieutenant general, wrote of Sumner in 1847, "Old Sumner has had one good effect on us, he has taught us to pray who never prayed before, for we all put up daily petitions to get rid of him." Nevertheless, Sumner was one of the most capable officers of the old army.

On May 20, 1857, Sumner set out with two companies of dragoons for Fort Kearny where he increased his force by two additional companies. He had previously sent Major John Sedgwick ahead with four companies of the 1st Cavalry. These forces were to meet on July 4 at Fort St. Vrain, a trading post on the South Platte River about twenty miles north of the present city of Denver.

The colonel proceeded along the north fork of the Platte River to Fort Laramie where he left one detachment of his dragoons. Leaving Laramie on June 27 with two companies of cavalry, three of infantry, and two pieces of artillery, he made contact with Major Sedgwick at Fort St. Vrain two days later than planned.

Leaving behind all encumbrances and taking only half rations for twenty days, the five-hundred-man column left immediately for the site of the massacre. Although several months had passed since the killing of the emigrants the previous autumn, the trail they had left could still be followed. The Indian encampment had been only forty miles south of their murderous attack, and on the 29th, the scouts reported that the hostiles were not far ahead. Sumner found them on a broad, open plain between Solomon's Fork and a low bluff. Estimates of the Indian strength have varied from two hundred to 1500 warriors, the truth probably being nearer the first.

When his force came within sight of the enemy, Sumner continued to advance at a slow cavalry walk. Riding ahead of the center of his force, he proceeded at the same pace until, within a few hundred yards of the hostiles, he directed the trumpeter to sound "trot." The Indians, who had expected a different tactic from the "long knives," began restlessly stirring about. Less than three hundred feet from the enemy, the colonel signaled drawn sabers and ordered the charge. This was too much for the hostiles, and they began to withdraw. Breaking through the Indian center, the troopers pursued the fleeing enemy several miles from the encounter until their horses became jaded. Sumner's casualties had been one officer and eight enlisted men wounded. The officer was Lieutenant J. E. B. Stuart of later Confederate fame. One of the wounded men caught an arrow in his abdomen. Breaking off the feathered end, he extracted the rest of the arrow himself and eventually recovered completely. That night, Sumner encamped on the battlefield.

Sending the wounded, his artillery, and the wagons back to St. Vrain, Sumner continued in pursuit of the enemy. On the 31st, he found the Indian village, but the hostiles had fled. After burning 150 lodges and their contents, he resumed the chase, but the Indians dispersed into small bands and disappeared. After reaching the Arkansas River, the command went on to Fort Atkinson, near the present site of Dodge City, where Sumner rested his worn troops for a few days.

Stopping at Fort Bent on the return journey, Colonel Sumner was enraged when he learned that before the battle, the Indian agent at the fort had distributed presents, including arms and ammunition, to the Cheyenne. Some of the bullets that had wounded his men had unquestionably been gifts from the very government that had ordered the attack.

The return march became virtually an endurance contest. Few of the horses were able to carry their riders, and the men suffered from lack of salt. Luckily, a supply train reached them at Walnut Creek, and the force was back at Fort Leavenworth by September 13.

The Sumner expedition accomplished its purpose: the Indians had been taught a lesson. However, unlike Custer's later Washita Massacre, this attack had harmed not a single Indian woman or child.

After 1857, the expeditions left from the newer western forts, west of Leavenworth. While most of their supplies still came by way of Fort Leavenworth, the exploratory phase of that fort's history had come to an end.

CHAPTER FIVE

※→←※

FORT LEAVENWORTH

The last outpost situated in the wilderness, "nearly twenty miles outside the United States," as the Reverend Samuel Parker wrote in 1833, Fort Leavenworth nevertheless enjoyed a steady stream of visitors, some of worldwide reputation.

The first of these distinguished visitors was Prince Paul of Württemberg, who in 1830, accompanied by two servants and a secretary, visited at the quarters of an old friend, Captain Bennett Riley.

In the spring of 1832, a Baron Braunsberg stopped at the post. He was actually Maximillian, Prince of Wied-Neuwied, traveling incognito. Accompanying him was a Swiss artist, Karl Bodmer, and a servant, Dreidoppel. The Prince—a slim, toothless, and shopworn looking man in his fifties—spoke with a strong Prussian accent. As a major general in the Napoleonic Wars, he rode at the head of his division when the allies entered Paris. He had wanted to be a botanist, not a soldier, and after leaving the military, he had spent two years studying the flora and fauna of Brazil. His book on his findings put him in the top rank of European scientists, and his visit to the fort was preliminary to making a similar study in the American West. Truly impressed by the arrival of such a distinguished visitor at the lonely frontier post, the officers and ladies outdid themselves in entertaining the visiting royalty; the Prince, despite his shrunken cheeks, was even seen to smile.

When he returned the following year, his reception was evidently not so cordial. In acid words, the Prince, known as the epitome of arrogance and a master of invective, was later to describe his

41

reception at Fort Leavenworth. When he and his party arrived at the boat landing, a sentinel informed them that they "must immediately appear before the commanding officer, and compelled us in an imperious manner, to keep close and march before him. We arrived like prisoners at the home of the commander, where Captain Riley received us with tolerable politeness, and supplied me with provisions, meat, bread, etc., which I required, taking care however, to be well paid for them."[1] The noted scientist was more kindly disposed toward the post surgeon, Dr. Benjamen F. Fellowes, whom he had previously known and who he said received him "with much cordiality and gave me a great deal of information respecting this interesting country."[2]

The former lawyer and self-taught portrait painter George Catlin of Philadelphia, arrived at the Fort on the steamer *Yellowstone* in the same year. Thirty-six years old at the time, he was starting the eight-year period that he would devote to depicting the Indians of the Plains as well as those of Arkansas and Florida. The 497 portraits of Indians and paintings of their lives and culture that are now in the collection of the Smithsonian Institution have placed him among the foremost of American artists. "Catlin was the first painter of the West who had any effect,"[3] Bernard De Voto has written. "So far as the Plains Indians are concerned—American ethnology may be said to begin with him."

Catlin's stay at Fort Leavenworth was evidently more pleasant than Maximillian's. "In this delightful Cantonment," he wrote, "the presence of officers' wives and daughters create a very pleasant little community who are almost continually together in social enjoyment of the peculiar amusements and pleasures of this wild country . . . riding on horseback or in carriages . . . picking strawberries and wild plums, deer hunting, grouse shooting, horse racing and other amusements."[4]

John Treat Irving, Jr., author and nephew of Washington Irving, was at Fort Leavenworth in 1833. In his "Indian Sketches," he told of his first impression:

> It was mid-day when we first caught sight of Fort Leavenworth but it was near sunset when we arrived there. About a dozen white-washed cottage-looking houses composed the barracks and abodes of the officers. They were so arranged as to form the three sides of a hollow square; the fourth is open and

looks out over a wide prairie. It is a rural-looking spot—a speck of civilization in the heart of a wilderness. There is nothing here to tell of war; and but for the sentinels upon their posts, the lounging forms of the soldiers or the occasional drum as the signal for the performance of some military duty, we would not have known that we were in the heart of a military station.

Four years later in London, Irving published *A Tale of the Indian Country*. The locale of the novel was Wolf Hill, which is actually Fort Leavenworth. The story—involving hunters, Indians, and mounted rangers—is an improbable tale of adventure, but the book was avidly read on the post.

In early July, 1835, Lieutenant George H. Crosman of the 6th Infantry was host to the popular British author, the Hon. Charles Augustus Murray. Murray was accompanied by a Scottish servant and a German youth named Vernunft. While at the fort, Murray attended the Independence Day celebration where a twenty-four-gun salute was followed by a sumptuous repast during which a series of champagne toasts were exchanged. Before the dinner ended, Indian Agent Dougherty arrived from the Platte country with a hundred and fifty Pawnee chiefs and warriors, a dozen of whom were invited to join in the festivities. The rest withdrew a short distance from the dinner party and roasted huge pieces of a freshly killed ox on rough sticks. On July 7, Murray and his companions left with the Pawnee for the upper Republican River, and then returned in September to visit Crosman for almost a week. Murray evidently was most impressed with the cuisine at Fort Leavenworth—he later wrote in his "Travels in North America":

> The Fort is supplied with beef and other meats chiefly by a farmer who lives in the bottoms immediately opposite. Among other articles for the supply of the table, one of the most abundant to be met with here is catfish. I found it somewhat coarse but not impalatable eating. These fish are caught of a most enormous size and in great quantities by the settlers, one of whom told me that he caught four in one morning about fifty pounds each.

A number of clergymen visited Fort Leavenworth in its early

years. The first, and certainly the most interesting of them, was
Father Pierre Jean de Smet, who made one of the first of his
many visits in 1831[5], following an inspection tour of the nearby
Indian tribes. A native of Belgium, the short but well-proportioned
young priest with his aquiline face, long blond hair, black cassock,
and large crucifix, cut an exotic figure among the soldiers and
frontiersmen. John Upton Terrell was later to say that the priest
was "for more than thirty years . . . the most influential man
in the Western Wilderness."[6] An adviser to four Presidents
—Pierce, Buchanan, Lincoln, and Johnson—Father de Smet was
able to gain not only the friendship but the complete confidence
of the Plains Indians.

In the summer of 1833, a Methodist minister, the Reverend
Jerome C. Berryman, arrived at the fort. He had been appointed
by the general conference of his church to establish a mission
among the Kickapoo Indians whose 152,000-acre reservation
adjoined Leavenworth on the north. He consulted with Agent
Dougherty and several of the Kickapoo chiefs as to the best location
for his headquarters. It was finally agreed that it should be about
five miles north of the outer limits of the post. How long Berryman
remained at Fort Leavenworth is not known but, during his eight
years with the tribe, he is said to have visited the fort frequently
to conduct Sunday services.

Writing to the Methodist General Conference, Berryman
reported:

> It did not take me long to have some log cabin buildings
> erected for my family, and a schoolhouse of the same sort
> in which to open a school and by midwinter I had about ninety
> children in attendance. Here for eight consecutive years, with
> my faithful wife and other helpers, I labored in teaching the
> young and old.[7]

In the spring of 1834, the Presbyterian church of Ithaca, New
York, raised a fund to support a mission among the Pawnee, and
the Reverends Samuel Allis, John Dunbar, and Samuel Parker
were named missionaries for the project. They had planned to
accompany a group of traders from St. Louis, but they were delayed
and did not arrive until six weeks after the traders had left. With

no other group headed in their direction, Parker left for Mackinaw where he was told that an agent for the Hudson's Bay Company might be of assistance. Allis and Dunbar journeyed on to Liberty, Missouri, and eventually reached Fort Leavenworth. The two clergymen remained there for several months, during which time Allis contracted and recovered from the fever that had plagued the garrison. Parker, who had failed to reach the Pawnee by the northern route, later joined them. All three conducted services at the post, sometimes several on the same Sunday.

In his journal of *An Exploring Tour Beyond the Rocky Mountains*, which Parker published in 1838, he was to write of western Missouri near Fort Leavenworth:

> Liberty, and the country around, is inhabited by people of considerable enterprise, and when it shall be brought under Christian influence, there will be but a few places more inviting.

He found considerable humor in local speech:

> It is amusing to observe the provincialisms which are common in this part of the country. If a person intends to commence a journey some time in the month of May: he says, "I am going in all the month of May." For a large assembly of people, they say "a smart sprinkle of people." The word "balance," comes into almost every transaction—will you not have a dessert for the balance of your dinner?"—"to make out the balance of his night's rest, he slept until eight in the morning." If your baggage is to be carried, it will be asked, "shall I tote your *plunder?*" This use of the word plunder, is said to have originated in the early predatory habits of the borderers. They also speak of a "mighty pleasant day," "a mighty beautiful flower," "mighty weak."

Father Charles Felix Van Quickenborne, S.J., the master of the Jesuit novices in the United States, who planned a mission among the Kickapoo, was frequently at the post in 1835. Another Belgian, the tall, artistocratic priest was a cultured man of the world. With Bishop Louis de Bourg, he had founded St. Louis Academy, which later became St. Louis University, the first institution of higher learning west of the Mississippi.

For a few days in the spring of 1836, the missionaries Marcus and Narcissa Whitman and Henry and Eliza Spalding stopped at Fort Leavenworth. Narcissa, golden-haired and buxom, riding sidesaddle across the continent, was on her way to eventual martyrdom in distant Oregon.

The arrival of the many guests at the fort in the 1830's had been made possible by the appearance of the steamboat on the Missouri. While hardly luxurious, they were a great improvement over the keelboats and the bullboats that had previously been the only mode of travel on the river.

The *Western Engineer* is said to have been the first steamboat to ascend the Missouri. Of fantastic design, the boat was without a stack, and its bowsprit was shaped like a dragon's head. The steam exhaust pipe was connected with the serpent's open mouth, and when the boat was in motion, the dragon, wheezing loudly, emitted steam, "and appeared to be responsible for the churning of the water by the paddles at the rear." As early as 1829, two crude steamers, the *Liberator* and the *Illinois* were plying the Missouri between St. Louis and Fort Leavenworth. In 1831, the American Fur Company built the *Yellowstone* exclusively for Missouri River travel, and it was on this steamer that Prince Maximillian von Weid made his trips. Small—only 130 feet long with a nineteen-foot beam—she had three decks and a cabin, but no staterooms. A sidewheeler with a wood-burning engine, she required frequent stops for wood. Her two smokestacks continually belched out a cloud of black smoke. The Indians considered her alive and approached her with dread. The *Assinboine,* built the following year, was more of a passenger boat; her stern cabin had ten berths and the fore cabin, twenty-four.

Father de Smet tells of a trip up the river in 1838 on the *Wilmington,* a later, larger, and more luxurious steamboat. Sawyers and half-submerged trees often scraped the boat's keel, and it frequently became stuck on sandbars. Often an entire day would be spent in literally lifting the steamer over the shoals by means of heavy spars. The Jesuit also described the cliffs: "Several hundred feet high, the caverns, the forests and the immense prairies which follow one another in prodigious variety on its shores; its bed strewn with numberless islands one, two, three and even four leagues in length, and filled with every kind of game."

As on all military reservations, there were constant comings and goings of military personnel and their dependents. On each occasion, particularly when those who had served previously on the post returned, they were welcomed with a round of social activities. Newly commissioned young bachelor officers were not quite so popular at first, unless their hosts had eligible daughters. Generally these single men made themselves as inconspicuous as possible until they had become acquainted with their fellow officers.

Such was not the case with Lieutenant Thomas Swords, Jr., when he reported in with a detachment of recruits from Carlisle Barracks, Pennsylvania. By way of Harrisburg, Swords had taken his detail by canalboats to the Alleghenies, and marched them over the mountains to St. Johnsbury where they took a boat to Pittsburgh. From there they embarked on a steamer going down the Ohio to St. Louis. Transferring to another riverboat, they traveled up the Missouri to Fort Leavenworth. Swords carried with him orders to relieve the ailing Lieutenant Gaines P. Kingsbury, and it was not long before the post commander, Colonel Dodge, was informed that an angry young officer had arrived. There was some justification for Swords's wrath. Through an oversight at Carlisle, no provision had been made for medical attention for the enlisted men enroute, nor had he been instructed as to what action should be taken in the event of a medical emergency. At Pittsburgh, nine of his men fell seriously ill with malaria. Advancing his own funds, the young officer not only arranged for medical attention, but contracted with a Dr. Gillsland to accompany him for the rest of the trip. Reporting his actions to his superiors by mail from Pittsburgh, where he had been forced to remain for some time, he had expected a prompt reply. But when he got to Fort Leavenworth, Swords found that there was still no answer. He dispatched a blistering letter to the surgeon general, together with an invoice for the money spent.[8] After some months Swords was finally reimbursed, but he seemed to keep a chip on his shoulder. He was at least consistent, for he was "always mad." The following February, he was placed under arrest for challenging a fellow officer to a duel. Evidently the members of his court-martial did not take the matter too seriously, however, for Swords was not dismissed. He was later appointed quartermaster of the post, and distinguished himself in both the Mexican and Civil wars.

The following February, Swords, Lieutenants James W. Hamilton, Thompson B. Wheelock, and Captain Matthew Duncan, all dragoon officers, occupying adjoining quarters, were in serious difficulty. At mess, the three lieutenants loudly objected to Duncan's "language and conduct toward them." The dispute may have had a Hudson River background, for Swords and Wheelock were both graduates of West Point, and Hamilton had attended the academy for three years, while Captain Duncan had entered the army through the undisciplined Mounted Rangers, the officers of which most of the West Pointers regarded as uncouth. Swords, Hamilton, and Wheelock drew lots to see who should challenge Duncan to a duel. Swords won the dubious distinction, and Hamilton carried the cartel. When Duncan refused to accept the challenge, Hamilton said his conduct only "showed what sort of a captain Colonel Dodge had to depend on to go out against the Indians."

Both Swords and his envoy were arrested and given general courts-martial. They defended their actions by claiming that "Duncan used language in speaking of Hamilton and presumably Swords of an insulting and highly improper character, which (was) . . . derogatory to the character of an officer and a gentleman and . . . expressly unbecoming in a superior officer when speaking of a junior."[9]

Swords and Hamilton were both found guilty and sentenced to be dismissed from the army. Swords's sentence, "due to his good character," was remitted, but Hamilton was actually cashiered. In 1836, however, he was recommissioned in the newly formed 2nd Dragoons. He lost his life on the frontier a year later. Wheelock, who was evidently able to get off scot free, died in 1836. The captain, who apparently had had enough of West Pointers and the army, resigned in 1837; Swords, the only survivor of the fracas, continued his career.

While there had been considerable improvement in the health of the troops since the summers of 1827 and 1828, the post was still considered an unhealthy assignment, and was avoided, if possible, by most travelers during the months of June, July, and August. The fever, as malaria was then called, continued to be a constant threat not only to those on the post, but also to the settlers along the nearby creeks and river bottoms. Fortunately, though, the mortality rate was considerably reduced by the use of "Sappington's

Anti-fever Pills."[10] This preparation, compounded by Dr. John Sappington of central Missouri, had a quinine base, and in the early 1840's was prescribed by both civilian physicians and army surgeons. Sappington was also the author of the *Theory and Treatment of Fevers*,[11] popularly known as "Sappington on Fever."

It had long been illegal to give, sell, or trade liquor to the Indians, but the fur companies, by means of wholesale bribery of Indian agents and other officials, continued to make alcohol their most profitable item of trade. Not only was it used in exchange, but as a lubricant on the Redmen before the bartering began. A drunken Indian was more readily persuaded to part with the products of his months of trappings for less in return. After they had sold their pelts, the Indians would often barter away their horses, blankets, and guns for more liquor. One squaw was reported to have offered her four-year-old boy "for a few bottles."[12] The result of this practice was the complete degeneration of several tribes. The missionaries, including Father de Smet, seeing the evil at first hand, were bitter in their denunciations of the Indian liquor traffic. The problem finally took on the proportions of a scandal and, over the opposition of William Astor and his American Fur Company, Congress enacted a law prohibiting the importation of liquor into the Indian country in 1832.

An unwelcome chore was thus added to the duties of the officers at Fort Leavenworth. No longer would the inspection of steamers heading up the Missouri be made by Indian agents, who were often traders themselves; now the military inspected the boats as they passed the fort. The rigidity of the officers, as stock after stock of alcohol was confiscated, soon aroused the animosity of the traders. In the fall of 1832, one consignment of 1,400 gallons on the steamer *Yellowstone* belonging to Astor's American Fur Company was confiscated. Despite this strict surveillance at the fort, liquor smuggling continued, with large stocks being brought up from Mexico. In an effort to dodge the prohibition, the American Fur Company set up a still at Fort Union, a trading post at the juncture of the Missouri and Yellowstone rivers, buying the necessary corn from the Mandan tribe. The existence of the still was reported to the commandant at Fort Leavenworth, and a detachment of dragoons soon found and destroyed it.

In 1833, an epidemic of cholera and smallpox broke out on the

plains. There were soon a number of cases of cholera at Fort Leavenworth. The assistant surgeon, Dr. Benjamen F. Fellowes, was quite
successful in his treatment of the dreaded disease, and there was
only one death. Nathaniel J. Wyeth, the fur trader, traveling down
the river in a bullboat, stopped at the fort, his principal objective
being to have his son vaccinated for smallpox. Wyeth reported
that he "was received with . . . politeness [and was] offered all
the stores I might require by Lieutenant (Asa) Richardson, the
Officer of the Day . . . I took my boy Baptiste, and the Indian
[guide] to Doctor Benjamen Fellowes' quarters to be vaccinated
and the Doc's wife and another lady happened to be present [and
they were] really beautiful women. Baptiste . . . told the other
boys . . . that he had seen a white squaw, white as snow and
so pretty."

It was at this time that the so-called Missouri-Mormon War
erupted across the river from Fort Leavenworth. Unable to live
in peace with their Eastern neighbors, more and more followers
of Joseph Smith had emigrated to western Missouri, principally
to Jackson and Clay counties. The tide soon became a flood when
their leader reported a revelation from God that Missouri was
truly the land of Zion. By 1833, the Mormons constituted a third
of the population of Jackson County, and almost daily there were
new arrivals.

These devotees of the Angel Moroni, the Latter-Day Saints,
found they were no more popular with their Missouri neighbors
than they had been in the East. Their open contempt for these
who were not the "chosen people," their friendliness with the
Indians, their refusal to touch liquor, tobacco, and even coffee,
their fanatical belief in their own virtue, and, even more important,
their declaration that they intended to take over western Missouri
did not tend to endear them to the rough frontiersmen.

In July, 1833, at an angry meeting held in Independence, Missouri, local citizens demanded that there not only should be no
more emigration of the Saints into Jackson County, but that those
already there should sell their properties and move on. When
the Mormons refused to budge, a howling mob destroyed their
newspaper building, tarred and feathered a few of their members,
including the presiding bishop, gave a lashing to others, and burned
several Mormon homes. At Big Blue River, ten miles west of

Independence, an angry mob of Missourians burned twelve houses and horsewhipped a number of the elders. An attempt was made to obtain redress in the courts, but the "chosen people" found as little justice as they were later to give to non-Mormons in Utah. At the end of the year, there were no more Latter-Day Saints in Jackson County.

Clay County at first welcomed the Mormon refugees but soon found them as intolerable as had their fellow Missourians. At a mass meeting at Liberty, the Mormons were again asked to leave. A temporary solution was found when the Missouri Legislature created a new county, Caldwell, for the Saints, but they soon spread into adjoining counties where they attempted to take over political control. Public feeling was now running high and it soon erupted into bloodshed. Engagements between the antagonists were fought at Crooked River and at Hauns Mill, where a number of Mormons were killed. The warfare between the newcomers and the earlier settlers of Missouri lasted for over three years and did not end until the Mormons decided that Zion was, after all, in the Far West. Fort Leavenworth participated in this strife only as an island of refuge which the Mormons knew as one spot where they could be sure of temporary protection.

Many traveling to Fort Leavenworth found it necessary to use the ferry over the Missouri and the Little Platte rivers and were subjected to the extortions of the operator, Zadock Martin. With his nearest neighbors more than fifteen miles away, Martin had set up a little empire of his own, including a tavern that was a magnet for rowdies. There was always a motley crew of drunks and thugs loitering around the ferry slip, and their chief pleasure seemed to be insulting the passengers. Occasionally, when Martin was busy or when one of the ruffians owed him money, he put them on the payroll, making the trip even more unpleasant. Martin had bought his franchise from Robert Todd in 1828, and successive commanders of the post had received a constant stream of complaints from the law-abiding citizens who had to cross the river. Captain William Wickliff finally took action in 1833; he issued a set of rules governing Martin's operation of the ferry.

Wickliff's regulations provided that all military personnel, all Indians, all official visitors to the fort, and the mail couriers should be carried free, and that a standard fee should be established for civilian passengers. It was also stipulated that Martin should not continue in his employ any persons not sanctioned by the commanding officer of the post. Even more important, with a stroke of his pen, Wickliff abolished Martin's liquor license and directed that he not "be allowed to keep in his house or about the establishment ardent spirits either for his own use or for sales."[13] The complaints soon ended.

In April, 1836, Fort Leavenworth was awaiting a new commanding officer, and Lieutenant Swords was temporarily in charge when his second-in-command, Lieutenant Enoch Steen, reported that a trader had established himself in Indian territory on the east side of the river.[14] The intruder was not only selling whiskey to the Redmen, but his tavern was often frequented by enlisted men who were trading their pistols for liquor. Swords immediately dispatched a sergeant and four men to recover the arms and destroy any buildings. The lieutenant later claimed that he had carefully instructed the sergeant as to the location of the state line and had told him that if the trader's establishment was within the state of Missouri no action should be taken, other than the recovery of the arms. Unfortunately, the sergeant erroneously concluded that the tavern was on Indian lands. He recovered the pistols, burned the log building, and destroyed all the whiskey. Subsequently arrested by the civil authorities, the sergeant and his men were taken to Liberty and charged with arson. Lieutenant Steen, who happened to be in Liberty at the time, had the soldiers admitted to bail and retained a lawyer for their defense. Before the case came to trial, the enlistment term of the men expired, and they were discharged and returned to the East. Unless the matter could be settled, there was bound to be a forfeiture of bail. Swords paid the burned-out trader a hundred dollars and the man withdrew charges. The twenty-five-dollar fee due the lawyer retained by Steen was also settled by Swords. Later the ever-impecunious lieutenant tried, without success, to collect the money from the War Department.[15]

On March 2, 1833, Congress authorized the formation of the 1st Regiment of United States Dragoons, who, although mounted, were trained to fight on both foot and horseback. The regiment was to consist of a colonel, two lieutenant colonels, two majors, an adjutant, the regimental quartermaster, a sergeant-major, a quartermaster-sergeant, a principal musician, two chief buglers, and six hundred troopers. Each of ten companies had a captain, two lieutenants, four sergeants, four corporals, two buglers, one blacksmith, and fifty privates. The regiment was to be a separate branch of the service with a six-pointed star as its insigne and bearing the color orange. Later in 1836, during the Seminole War, a second regiment of dragoons was organized, and in 1846 the Regiment of Mounted Riflemen was formed, with the 1st and 2nd Cavalries established in 1855.

To command the newly created 1st Dragoons, which were being organized at Jefferson Barracks, President Andrew Jackson named Major Henry Dodge. Promoted to colonel while at Fort Gibson, Arkansas, Dodge gave his reasons for recommending Fort Leavenworth as the permanent station for his regiment in a letter to the adjutant general dated February 15, 1834:[16]

> Steamboats could transport the necessary supplies to this place early in the Spring, forage can be secured cheaply on the frontier of the State of Missouri, protection would be afforded to the inhabitants of the State, and this would be the proper point to furnish the necessary escort for the protection of our trade to the Mexican State.

The War Department agreed, instructing the colonel that he would march to Fort Leavenworth with four of his companies, leaving three at Fort Gibson and three at Fort Des Moines.[17] Among the officers accompanying Colonel Dodge and the 1st Dragoons to Fort Leavenworth, was a tall, gangling lieutenant, Philip St George Cooke. Cooke had been born in Leesburg, Virginia, although his father, a surgeon in the Revolutionary War, was a native Philadelphian and a graduate of the University of Pennsylvania Medical School. Commissioned from the military academy in the class of 1827, Cooke had joined the 6th Infantry at Jefferson Barracks. At Cantonment Leavenworth in 1829, after he had returned from Captain Bennett Riley's escort of the Santa Fé traders to the Mexican border, Cooke met and fell in love with Rachel Wilt Hertzog who was visiting her sister, Mary Dougherty, wife of the Indian agent. They were married at the fort on October 28, 1830. Besides being a hardheaded but able officer, Cooke was unusually articulate. During an army career that stretched from 1827 to 1873, he kept voluminous diaries and journals which, unfortunately, were lost after his death in 1895. From this store of personal observations, he extracted information for official reports and articles and three published books. Bernard De Voto described his style as "full of gothic moonlight, sentiments that Fremont would have found noble, and a literary patois hard to associate with as hardbitten an officer as the army had."

When Dodge arrived at the post in the late summer, he found that no stables had been built for his horses and that the quartermaster general had not allotted funds for this purpose. Accordingly, he directed the company commanders to have their men build temporary stables. A number of the troopers refused, claiming that when they enlisted they had been told that they would only be required to care for their horses and perform military duties. Colonel Dodge, although easy-going, considered the incident important and reported to the adjutant general:

> This spirit of insubordination that I have to contend with. The first duties of a soldier is to obey his orders, and I am determined this work shall be done for the preservation of the horses. I regard, however, that this feeling exists, more particularly as the men built their quarters last winter at Fort Gibson and have performed hard service during the summer. I shall pursue a steady and determined course with the insubordinate men until they are brought to a proper sense of duty.[18]

The stables were promptly built.

The quartermaster general had previously allotted funds for the building of new barracks. Constructed of brick and located on the east side of the parade ground, the barracks were built by civilian employees.

When the original boundaries of the territory of Missouri were defined, a large tract of land directly opposite the fort on the east side of the Missouri River had not been included. The eastern boundary of this area extended from north to south along a straight line extending through the mouth of the Kansas River. Various Indian tribes, including the Iowa and the Sac, had frequently

claimed the land, and the government had used it for the temporary
location of other small tribes, including a group of Potawatomie.
The nearby settlers were apprehensive about this use of the tract
and vigorously opposed the proximity of the Indians.

Colonel Dodge agreed with the Missourians, and in recommending that the land be given to the state of Missouri, he suggested
that a natural barrier, such as a river or a range of mountains,
should separate the two races. In June, 1836, Congress conveyed
to Missouri the strip in question, subject to the several Indian
claims' being satisfied. Four months after its decision, officials of
the United States and the state of Missouri, and chiefs of the
Indian tribes concerned held a council at Fort Leavenworth. The
final agreement, known as the Platte Purchase, provided for the
payment of $7,500 to the Indians. In December, Missouri formally
accepted the tract, but the decision was not announced until the
middle of February, 1837. By this time a horde of homesteaders
from all over the nation had gathered in Clay County. When the
news of the approval of the Platte Purchase became known, there
was an invasion by foot, horse, and mule to preempt choice sites.

On July 4, 1836, Colonel Dodge resigned from the army to
accept appointment as governor of the territory of Wisconsin. His
successor in command of the 1st Dragoons and Fort Leavenworth
was one of the most capable officers in the army, Lieutenant Colonel
Stephen Watts Kearny. Of a wealthy New Jersey family, he had
arrived at the fort as a colonel of the dragoons, with his wife, the
former Mary Radford, and a Negro couple. The Negroes, who
were slaves, had been a gift from General William Clark of St.
Louis to his stepdaughter, Kearny's wife.

Making an immediate inspection of the post upon assuming command on the last day of June, Colonel Kearny was appalled at
its condition. The temporary cottonwood stables[19] that Colonel
Dodge had ordered built were beginning to rot away. Not a single
well had been dug, which meant that, should a fire occur, it could
result in the complete destruction of all the buildings on the post.
Equally important, the colonel pointed out in a letter to the War
Department, was that there were no defenses against a possible
Indian attack:

I do not wish to cast any reflections upon my predecessors,
the former commanders of this post, but I cannot refrain from
expressing my astonishment at finding the post in the situation

it is, considering when it was established, and the character
of the Indians around it.[20]

After a considerable struggle with Washington, Kearny was able
to get his well dug, and the blockhouses built by civilian laborers,
but not new stables. As late as November 26, 1841, the post quartermaster, the ever-loquacious Lieutenant Swords, was complaining
to the quartermaster general:

> I would also beg to represent the unfitness of the buildings
> now used as stables and for the workshop of the Quartermasters
> Department they being the old temporary cottonwood log
> stables put up by the Dragoons when they first came to the
> Post, are now in a state of almost entire decay, offering no
> security and but little protection to the public property in
> them.[21]

Colonel Kearny's and Lieutenant Swords's opinions of the stables
were not shared by Colonel Truman Cross, a quartermaster who
made an inspection of the post in June, 1839. He reported:

> There are twelve ranges of stables for Dragoons' horses, two
> of which afford accommodations for the horses of a troop.
> These are constructed of hewn logs, with high lofts for hay,
> and will last a considerable time with care and slight repairs.

The inspector also described the buildings at Fort Leavenworth:

> The old barracks and quarters are [also] constructed of hewn
> logs, one story, with spacious attics, upon light basements
> of stone. They have recently undergone some masonry repairs
> on the flooring etc. and are now in excellent order, affording
> good accommodations for the troops as far as they extend.
> The officers' quarters consist of four blocks—three of these
> have each four good rooms on the second floor, with two
> high basement rooms and two kitchens underneath. All these
> houses have large and airy attics, but only two have been
> finished so that they can be occupied.

> The soldiers' Barracks of this description consists of four blocks
> 52 feet long by 35 feet wide, with an eight foot piazza on

each floor, each building adequate to the accommodation of a company of infantry under late organization but rather scant for the present. There is, besides, an old two-story frame building, formerly used as a hospital but now occupied by unmarried officers. It is still a very good building with a piazza on the West front.

At opposite angles of the square occupied by the buildings, there are two good wooden block houses affording some accommodations for troops in case of need as well as protection. The new buildings which have been completed consist of a very capacious brick hospital, two stories high with every necessary appurtenance—a two story brick house, four rooms on each floor, for the commanding officer's quarters, one range of Brick Barracks for two companies and a capacious stone Storehouse for the Quartermaster and Commissaries Department. [22]

Shortly after Kearny assumed command of the fort and the responsibilities for maintaining order on the Missouri frontier, the so-called Heatherly War erupted, and fear swept the border. In 1831, a Kentucky family, as lawless and evil as could be imagined, settled on the Grand River near the present site of Chillicothe. Later they moved to a dense, trackless forest on the west fork of Medicine Creek where they erected a log fortification. Like the later infamous Benders of Kansas, they engaged in the lucrative practice of killing and robbing travelers. Joining with them from time to time were young men of equally evil dispositions who were fleeing from the law.

On June 19, 1836, the Heatherlys, together with their henchmen, James Dunbar, Alfred Hawkins, and a man named Thomas, stole a number of horses and ponies from a party of Potawatomie. The Indians pursued the thieves, opened fire and retook their horses. One of the Indians was killed and an outlaw wounded. That evening the crestfallen Heatherlys returned to their citadel, but not before they had murdered Dunbar, whom they suspected of treachery. Fearing that the Indians would report the true story of the encounter to the settlers, the Heatherlys quickly circulated the word that they had been attacked by a thousand painted warriors who had killed both Dunbar and Thomas. The alarm spread and the wildest excitement followed, with many settlers fleeing to the towns for protection.

As soon as the affair became known to Colonel Kearny, he dispatched a company of dragoons from Fort Leavenworth, under the command of Captain Matthew Duncan, to ascertain the true facts. Even before the troopers had crossed the river, Governor Daniel Dunklin had raised a force of two hundred militiamen under the command of Colonel Shubael Allen for the purpose of driving all Indians out of the state of Missouri.

Captain Duncan's investigations soon proved beyond doubt that the Indians had shown great restraint when provoked by the outlaws, and Duncan so advised Colonel Kearny. Agent Dougherty immediately sent a message to the unoffending Redmen that they should leave Missouri before they were discovered by Allen's troops. Meanwhile, the Indians involved in the Grand River affair had voluntarily surrendered themselves to Kearny and had been released pending a future demand for their appearance in court. After fruitlessly searching for their prey, the militia finally disbursed and returned to their homes.

The Heatherlys were indicted, but none were found guilty. True to form, they testified that their companion, Hawkins, had murdered Dunbar. Hawkins was sentenced to twenty years in the penitentiary but never served out his term—he died two years after being confined.

The incident had one amusing repercussion. "For more than twenty years afterwards, the Missourians who participated in the war . . . strove to obtain federal military bounty lands as a reward for their services in an Indian War."[23] Their efforts failed, because the War Department refused to recognize the disturbance as having been a war.

That the East was becoming more and more interested in the West was indicated in July, 1836, when Congress appropriated $100,000 for the survey and construction of a military road from Fort Snelling to Fort Towson. The road that would extend for some 850 miles was to be divided into three sections—from Fort Towson to Fort Smith on the Arkansas River; between Forts Smith and Leavenworth; and from Fort Leavenworth to Fort Snelling. By 1839, the 140 miles between Forts Towson and Smith were completed, as was that portion of the road between Marias des

Cygnes above Fort Scott and Fort Leavenworth. The final link
in the southern portion of the road was not finished until 1844.
Attention was also being paid to river transportation, and in 1833,
the army corps of engineers began removing snags, tree trunks,
and sandbars from the Missouri.

When Lieutenant Swords called Kearny's attention to the high cost
of hay and grain on the frontier, the colonel, with the approval
of the Secretary of War, set up a farm program on government
land about a mile from the post. Twelve hundred acres of prairie
lands were fenced and divided into fields to be alternately cultivated
and grazed. An additional plot of one hundred acres was planted
in timothy hay. All of the permanent civilian labor on the post
was used in this project during the spring planting, and were aided
by the troops in the harvest season. It was evident to Colonel
Croghan, when he made his inspection of the post in 1837, that
this program, costing $7,200, was saving the government consider-
ably more than that yearly. By 1839, eight thousand bushels
of oats, twelve thousand bushels of corn, and almost all of the
hay required by the fort were being produced.[24]

In July, 1840, Colonel George Croghan reported on some of
the problems that Colonel Kearny faced. He noted the miserable
condition of the horses after several months on the Arkansas, and
the worn, defaced equipment. "Colonel Kearney (sic)", Croghan
said, "is by no means answerable for this condition of things."
His report went on, "The men themselves are pretty good looking,
though some six or eight are not well-suited to dragoon service,
instance, one man of six feet four and weighing 250 pounds; What
horse could carry such a monster?" Croghan also noted; "Out of
a detachment of recuits consisting of one hundred and ten received
a few weeks ago, there are perhaps twenty who neither understood
or speak a word of English. They are either Dutch or German."[25]

Local affairs and tedious escort and patrol duties along the Sante
Fé and Oregon trails made ever-increasing demands on the troops.
A continuous stream of wagon trains and emigrants passed through
the post in the spring and early summer.

For those who remained on the post, there was always something
to occupy any spare time. They could hunt grouse, race their horses,
participate in theatrical performances, or attend lectures. A round
of social affairs was held on the slightest provocation. Such an occa-

sion was the arrival at the post on May 3, 1843, of the naturalist John J. Audubon and his party, including John G. Bell, taxidermist; Isaac Sprague, artist; Edward Harris, bird specialist; and Lewis M. Squires, secretary. The distinguished visitors were wined and dined and always thereafter spoke glowingly of the post's hospitality. Audubon also noted, "The situation of the Fort is elevated and fine and one has a view of the river up and down for some distance." Harris only noted in his journal that he saw "a number of Carolina parakeets, a species that is long now extinct."

And there was always the irrepressible post quartermaster, Captain Swords. From the vantage point of hindsight, it is almost impossible to understand why reprimands were not constantly being put in his personal file. Probably the answer is that he had considerable ability and was frequently right; besides, he was what enlisted men call a good "guardhouse lawyer." He knew his rights. Nevertheless, he must have often tried the patience of his superiors, for the records of the fort are full of his complaints and objections. The chain of command just did not exist as far as the captain was concerned, and he was always willing to go over anyone's head. On October 4, 1841, he was ordered by Colonel Richard B. Mason, the post commander, to supply immediately the wagons necessary for the removal of manure from the stables. Swords had planned to use all the wagons to unload a steamboat that had arrived from St. Louis with flour, and he insisted that the colonel's order be put in writing. After supplying the wagons and mules for the manure removal, he wrote a seething letter direct to the quartermaster general, Major General Jesup in Washington. He described the incident in detail, pointing out that the manure was the accumulation of many months and could have waited another day, that there were no buildings on the pier to receive the flour, and that it, and not the manure, could have been ruined. To Swords's query as to what should be done in the event the same circumstances again arose, there was no answer from General Jesup.[26]

Swords was not the only young officer whose conduct was a source of gossip on the post (one of the few pastimes that helped to relieve the daily monotony). The romance of a handsome dragoon, Lieutenant Thomas Clark Hammond, a West Point graduate of the class of 1842, was avidly discussed by the army wives at their coffees in late 1845. Hammond, an army brat, and Miss Mary Hughes, daughter of Judge M. M. Hughes of nearby Platte County, Missouri, were madly in love. The judge, having a low opinion of army officers, bitterly opposed their marriage. Taking matters in their own hands, the young couple arranged for a clergyman to meet them at Pilot Knob and were married astride their horses. Shortly thereafter, Hammond left for the Mexican War and was killed at the battle of San Pasquale, never having seen his son, Thomas Hammond, born the previous May 22, 1846. The boy was raised in the home of his grandfather and did not follow in his father's footsteps, but became a prominent physician of Platte County.

The four-year tour of Major Clifton Wharton[27] as commander of Fort Leavenworth set an all-time high for zeal. A member of a prominent and affluent Philadelphia family with many influential friends in Washington, his remaining at the fort must have been of his own choosing. He was to die there of natural causes in August, 1848, leaving a wife and five children. Besides dispatching the usual escorts and discharging the multitudinous duties involved in furnishing supplies and replacements to the Army of the West in New Mexico during the Mexican War, Wharton devoted a good part of his time to preventing the sale of whiskey to the Indians by traders, arresting Oregon emigrants who trespassed on either government or Indian lands, and protecting missionaries and their families from annoyance by drunken Indians.

Not all those professing to be honest Oregon emigrants were what they appeared: the role was an easy way of illegally getting into Indian country. When the major could prove that a professed emigrant was not really Oregon-bound, he sent him back over the Missouri. Wharton got his comeuppance, however, when he tried to intercept absconding debtors from Missouri. There were no laws or regulations that allowed him to stop such defaulters, and if there had been, there were too few troops under his command to carry out such an operation. Finally, he had to settle for turning back only the emigrants who were charged with a felony.

A small tribe of Stockbridge Indians which the government had settled near the fort in the early 1840's, became quite a nuisance to Major Wharton during his second year at the post. It was not that they were hostile; the little group from New York were perhaps the most unwarlike of all Indians. Rather, a religious dispute within the tribe had split it into two factions, one of which refused to recognize the authority of their chief, Hendricks, and carried every small grievance to the post commander for settlement. As Wharton said, he had been forced to "act the part, in some measure, as the chief of the tribe." He finally wrote to department headquarters asking them to take up the matter with the Indian Bureau. An agent soon settled the matter, much to the major's relief.[28]

As Mexico and the United States continued on a collision course and the war clouds gathered, Fort Leavenworth began to conclude its role as guardian of the Santa Fé and Oregon trails. Small parties could travel to Fort Kearny in comparative safety. The fort was now to assume an even greater responsibility. She was to become what David Lavender has aptly described as the army's "spearhead."[29]

CHAPTER SIX

THE OREGON TRAIL

While the mecca of the traders and the commercial caravans continued to be Santa Fé, the goal of most of the emigrants in the 1840's, with the exception of the Mormons, was either California or the Pacific Northwest. Pike's myth of The Great American Desert had had its effect, and the prospective settlers wanted no way-stop. "Oregon or Bust" became their slogan, and the Oregon Trail became the new route west.

The emigrants followed the trail blazed by the "mountain men" who for thirty years had dominated the vast wilderness. The days of flourishing business for these hardy fur trappers and traders were numbered, for almost simultaneously with the great migration, the streams had become exhausted of beaver. Most of the mountain men drifted to other pursuits, but a few like Kit Carson, Joe Meek, Tom Fitzpatrick, and Jim Bridger went on to win fame as guides for both the emigrant trains and the military.

In May, 1841, some of a group known as the Bartleson party became the first to follow the path that would be known as the Oregon Trail. Greenhorns from Peoria, Illinois, they had originally intended to go to California, but had started out with inadequate supplies and little knowledge of what they were facing. Fortunately, before they were well under way, they were overtaken at Council Bluffs by several Oregon-bound Jesuit missionaries led by Father de Smet. The priests had wisely employed an experienced mountain man, Tom Fitzpatrick, whom the Indians called Broken Hand, as their guide, and the two parties joined together for the western trip. Once through the South Pass, the caravan divided, with some heading west to California. They ran into great difficulties, were forced to abandon their wagons, and arrived in the golden land on foot and half-starved. The rest of the Bartleson party and the missionaries with Father de Smet reached Oregon without serious mishap in the fall of 1841.

During the year 1844, over 1,400 emigrants traveled west with their covered wagons. By 1845, the number of settlers annually following the trail had increased to three thousand. In 1848, before the beginning of the California gold rush, three thousand wagons, thirteen thousand persons, and fifty thousand head of stock started westward. During the month of May, 1849, 5,350 wagons, Oregon-bound, crossed the Missouri River. Thereafter, until rails supplanted the prairie schooner, there was seldom a year in which at least five thousand emigrants did not set out toward the sunset.

Generally, the wagon trains formed in early spring at Independence, where civilian supplies could be obtained. Those that passed through Fort Leavenworth crossed a series of rivers—the Kansas, the Vermillion, the Big Blue—then reached the Platte. By way of Fort Laramie, they continued to the South Pass. On the western side of the Rockies, beyond the trading post of the legendary Jim Bridger, the Mormons left the trail and headed south to the Great Salt Lake, while the mainstream of the emigrants continued north, past Soda Springs to Fort Hall on the Snake River. There a subsidiary road, the California Trail, went southwest to San Francisco, while the main route, after passing Fort Boise, terminated at Fort Vancouver on the Columbia.

The farmer-emigrant who followed the trail was often ill-equipped for the western journey. His oxdrawn wagons often began the trek overloaded with household goods that would be abandoned long before they reached the Rocky Mountains. On the rear of his prairie schooner he would lash a chicken coop, and following on an old worn horse, one of his children would drive the milch cow. Often his horses would lose their shoes and become lame. Few men even knew how to shoe their own animals.

A wagon train consisted of anywhere from twenty to a hundred wagons and a few carriages and saddle horses, with many times that number of men, women, and children, as well as the household pets. Dogs were often used as guards against possible lurking Indians.

Nor were the hostiles the only threat the emigrants faced. There was a constant fear that they might run out of water, for many of the water holes were alkaline, poisonous to both humans and animals. The lack of fresh vegetables brought on scurvy, and only a few had the foresight to bring dried fruits to eat on the way.

Occasionally, a thundering herd of buffalo would stampede through a train, overturning wagons and trampling men, women, and children. Weeks would have to be spent in repairing equipment and rounding up the panicked horses, mules, and oxen. And there were wolves—wolves in such numbers as can scarcely be imagined. They were not only a nuisance, but a menace. Their splashing through a shallow stream was often mistaken for approaching horses, and unless the settlers' animals were well guarded, the wolves would drive them off and kill an entire herd. At night they would prowl among the wagons eating any hide or meat they could find. They had even been known to attack and kill careless emigrants, particularly children. The tales of those who traveled the Oregon Trail were always replete with stories of the cunning and skill of those four-footed marauders.

As was true on the Santa Fé Trail, many smaller trains were in constant threat of Indian attack. The army, with three-quarters of its forces already committed and facing a highly mobile and maneuverable foe, found it impossible to police this new route westward. Again from the emigrants, from those who planned to travel west, and from Senator Thomas Hart Benton and other believers in Manifest Destiny, there arose a new demand that something be done by the government. On May 19, 1846, the insistent outcries brought results: Congress passed a bill providing for the "Raising of a Regiment of Mounted Riflemen and for the establishment of military stations on the route to Oregon."

Although the regiment was almost immediately organized, the Mexican War delayed the creating of the posts, and it was not until April, 1848, that the first of these installations, Fort Childs, was established. Located on the Platte River near the present site of Grand Island, Nebraska, and built by Lieutenant Colonel L. E. Powell with a detachment of the Missouri Mounted Volunteers known as the Oregon Battalion, the post was designated Fort Kearny by the War Department.

Seventeen years after the establishment of Fort Leavenworth, two fur trappers, William Sublette and William Campbell, had erected a fort on the North Platte River in southeastern Wyoming. It was named successively Fort Williams, Fort John, and finally Fort Laramie, after a little-known French voyageur who had been killed in the vicinity by Arapaho Indians. A year after the fort's completion, the two trappers had sold their holdings to Astor's American Fur Company, and later, Pierre Chouteau, Jr., and Company, acquired the post. Francis Parkman, Jr., who was there in 1847, wrote an interesting description of Laramie:

> The little Fort is built of bricks dried in the sun, and externally is of an oblong form, with bastions of clay, in the form of ordinary blockhouses, at two of the corners. The walls are about fifteen feet high, and surrounded by a slender palisade. The roofs which are built close against the walls, serve the purpose of a banquette. Within, the fort is divided by a partition: on one side is the square area surrounded by the store rooms, offices and apartments of the inmates; on the other is the corral, a narrow place, encompassed by the high clay walls, where at night, or in the presence of Indians the horses and mules of the Fort are crowded for safekeeping. The main entrance has two gates with an arched passageway intervening. A square window high above the ground, opens laterally from an adjoining chamber into the passage; so that when the inner gate is closed and barred, a person without may still hold communication with those within through this narrow aperture. This obviates the necessity of admitting suspicious Indians for purposes of trading, into the body of the fort, for when danger is apprehended, the inner gate is shut fast, and all traffic is carried on by means of the little window.[1]

In March, 1849, the War Department concluded that one of the new forts should be located at or near the civilian trading post, Fort Laramie.[2] A month later, Major Winslow F. Sanderson was ordered to proceed with a detachment from Fort Leavenworth and locate such a post. He was also authorized, if he deemed it advisable, to negotiate for the purchase of the old fort. Through the owner's agent, Bruce Husbands, a price of $4,000 was agreed upon, and on June 26, 1849, Fort Laramie became a military installation. Major Sanderson set his troops to erecting new quarters. During July, the garrison complement was increased by another rifle company from Leavenworth under the command of Captain Benjamin S. Roberts. On July 23, the first wagon train bringing a miscellaneous collection of brick-making machinery, doors, sashes, nails, glass, and butter churns, arrived from Fort Leavenworth.

In early 1852, several small wagon trains had been attacked by Indians in eastern Kansas on both the Oregon and the Santa Fé trails, and the War Department concluded that a fort must be established, whose garrison would be available for the protection of caravans on either route.[3] Surveys from Fort Leavenworth were accordingly conducted to determine the most desirable site, and on May 17, 1853, at the confluence of the Smoky Hill and the Republican forks of the Kansas River, Fort Center, later to be called Fort Riley, was built.[4] Originally garrisoned by three companies of the 6th and two of the 2nd Infantry, it was reinforced in 1854 by several companies of dragoons transferred from Fort Leavenworth. During the Kansas troubles the new fort, under the command of Colonel Philip St George Cooke came into national prominence. Later, Fort Riley was to achieve fame as the home of the Cavalry School, and it was there that Lt. Colonel George Armstrong Custer organized the 7th Cavalry.

CHAPTER SEVEN

⟫⟫→⤝⟪⟪

THE MEXICAN WAR

Relations between the United States and the newly independent Republic of Mexico were strained from the very start. Joel Poinsette, whose name is perpetuated by the flower he introduced into the United States, was appointed the first American minister. Grudgingly received by the Mexican Government, he was opposed at every turn by the aristocracy, the Church, and the representatives of both Great Britain and France. Poinsette's tour was frustrating and unpleasant, and both he and his successor, Anthony Butler, were finally recalled as *personae non grata* at the request of the Mexican Government.

The dictatorial seizure of power and the creation of a central rather than a federal republic by President Antonio Santa Anna resulted in 1834 in the revolt of Texas. Sympathy in the United States was for the Texas rebels. Were they not, after all, fellow Americans? Were not the Mexicans not only a backward, cruel people, but papists and almost barbarians? Santa Anna's execution of the sole survivor and the burning of the bodies of the defenders, following the battle of the Alamo, served to crystallize this animosity. Pro-Texas meetings were held throughout the western United States. Recruits, arms, and ammunition for the Texas insurgents were openly dispatched south, against all of which the Mexican Government could only protest. The slaughter at Tampico, without trial, of twenty-one Texas-bound Americans intensified the already strained relations and fanned the flames of war.

On April 21, 1836, at San Jacinto, General Sam Houston and

eight hundred Texas troops decisively defeated General Santa Anna's 1,600-man army. After their troops had suffered 910 casualties, both Santa Anna and his second-in-command, General Cos, were captured. While the treaty, signed following the battle by the defeated general as the president of Mexico, was repudiated by the Mexican Congress, Texas had, in fact, achieved its independence. The new republic was promptly recognized by the governments of the United States, Britain, and France.

That Texas should be a part of the Union was not only the desire of most Texans and Americans, but the wish of three successive presidents of the United States—Jackson, Tyler, and Polk. It took ten years, however, for the nation to achieve its goal. The United States could ill-afford to have a weak, small nation on its southern border, a constant temptation to Britain and France. And there was always the interminable question of slavery. There were many Whigs and Free-Soilers who believed that Andy Jackson and Sam Houston had planned the Texas revolution for the sole purpose of adding more slave territories to the Union. When Texas was finally annexed, it had to be by joint resolution of Congress requiring merely a majority vote, rather than by a treaty in which a two-thirds vote in the Senate would have been necessary.

During the war for Texas, there had been a sharp cleavage about it in the nation. Many, particularly in New England, regarded it as a war of aggression, an immoral conflict. But they were more than eager to share the eventual fruits of victory.

President James Polk had believed there would not be a war and that Mexico would agree to sell Texas, New Mexico, and California to the United States with the southern border set at the Rio Grande. Certainly he took few steps to prepare the nation for a conflict. The army of 1845, with a strength of 8,600 men and officers, consisted of eight regiments of infantry, four of artillery, and two companies of dragoons. The United States had apparently learned nothing from the War of 1812. The nation was approaching conflict with the same "penny-pinching shiftlessness, the high-hearted insouciance and the valorous ignorance with which until after 1917 the American people always went to war."[1]

True, the Mexicans did not appear to pose much of a threat. While prior to 1843 its army had numbered 44,000, over half were officers, and when this condition was remedied, it still carried on its rolls over two hundred generals. In spite of their great numbers, the officers of the Mexican army were untrained, incompetent, and often venal. The enlisted men, mainly peons and Indians, poorly clothed, fed, and trained, would later prove they were not lacking in courage. In 1845, the Mexican army was composed of twelve battalions of infantry, twelve regiments of cavalry, and three brigades of artillery. There were French guns, but the gunners completely lacked the technical skills required for their operation. The Mexicans were confident that their army would trounce the troops of the United States, and many expatriate English merchants, who still recalled the American rout at Bladensburg, agreed.

In April, 1846, the United States Congress authorized the raising of fifty thousand troops to be divided into three divisions: the Army of Occupation under Major General Zachary Taylor; the Army of the Center under Brigadier General John E. Wool; and the Army of the West under Colonel Stephen Watts Kearny. The troops of the Army of the West were to be organized at Fort Leavenworth, Kearny was to march to Santa Fé and, after seizing New Mexico, push on westward to California.

In the succeeding days, Fort Leavenworth was a beehive of activity. Captain Swords, as quartermaster, was charged with the responsibility of providing for the recruits that arrived daily, as well as assembling supplies and ammunition for the newly created Army of the West. To accommodate the many wagon trains headed for the fort, seventy-five miles of roadway west of Independence had to be constructed. The road, built through thick timber and over ravines and swamps, was a minor engineering feat. When it was finished, thousands of ox-drawn wagons and mules plodded their way over it to the fort. Daily at the pier on the Missouri, steamboats arrived loaded with supplies and men from St. Louis. Colonel Kearny was so impressed with the achievements of the efficient Swords that he named him quartermaster of the Army of the West.

With the exception of the dragoons and one battalion of regular infantry, Kearny's army of 1,600 men and sixteen pieces of artillery was made up of Missouri volunteers. Undisciplined country boys, they were superb horsemen and crack shots, and accustomed to frontier hardships. They were described by G. F. Ruxton as "the dirtiest, rowdiest crew I have ever seen gathered together."

Second-in-command was Colonel Alexander W. Doniphan, a volunteer, who knew very little and cared less about military science. Doniphan seems to have shared some of the temperament, though not the physical stature—or the politics—of his most famous descendant, Harry S Truman. Years after his stint with the Missouri Volunteers, the colonel, standing back-to-back with Lincoln, proved to be half an inch taller than the President. Born in Kentucky, the youngest of ten children, Doniphan graduated from Augusta College, read law in Lexington, and in 1829 emigrated to Liberty, Missouri. Probably the best known criminal lawyer in the West, he closed his office at the beginning of the Mexican War and enlisted as a private in the 1st Regiment of Missouri Mounted Volunteers. Subsequently he was elected colonel of the regiment.[2]

Preceded by a supply train of over a hundred wagons, escorted by two companies of dragoons, the main body of the army left Leavenworth on June 26, 1846, with Kearny (now a brigadier general) following three days later. Slowly the column wound its way over the six-hundred-mile Santa Fé Trail to Fort Bent. The heat was oppressive, the road rough, and good water so scarce that sixty of the hundred artillery horses died on the trail. The untrained mounts of the Missouri Volunteers, unaccustomed to military discipline or trappings, often broke loose from the column and galloped over the wide expanse of prairie as their riders fought to bring them under control. As the army moved westward, their fuel gave out and they used buffalo chips.[3] Occasionally they had fresh meat from the vast herds of buffalo they sighted. On July 30 the column arrived at Fort Bent, where, after a rest of three days they resumed the march. Sixty men had fallen ill on the way and remained at Fort Bent.

But General Kearny's path into New Mexico was well-planned. James Wiley Magoffin, a Kentuckian of good family, had been trading in New Mexico and Chihuahua since 1828. Magoffin was well-known and liked by almost everyone of importance in those provinces, and Senator Benton, realizing that he could be of great assistance to the United States, arranged an interview for the trader

with President Polk. With a letter from William L. Marcy, the
Secretary of War, Magoffin met with Kearny at Fort Bent on July
31, and the general was quick to avail himself of the merchant's
services. Preceding the army's entrance into New Mexico, Magoffin, by the liberal use of money, flattery, and subtle advice, persuaded the New Mexicans as well as their governor, General
Manuel Armijo, and his second-in-command, Colonel Diego
Archuleta, of the futility of resistance. Furthermore, Magoffin was
able to keep Kearny advised day by day as to the situation his
army faced. Armijo and Archuleta, with a combined force of seven
thousand men, could have made the going rough for Kearny's
1,600, but as a result of Magoffin's efforts, Santa Fé was taken
without the firing of a single shot. In the hope that the merchant
could duplicate his successful feat, Kearny later sent him to
Chihuahua, but Magoffin was captured by the Mexicans and
imprisoned for nine months, and came dangerously close to being
executed as a spy. [4]

In Las Vegas, New Mexico, on August 15, Kearny issued a proclamation calling on the New Mexicans to accept the Americans as
liberators and not conquerors.

If the American force was to be stopped short of Santa Fé,
it would be at Apache Canyon, which Kearny was approaching
on August 18. Word had been received that the pass was heavily
fortified and defended by several thousand Mexicans. But the information was false, as Kearny learned from a "fat and jolly Alcade,"
who reported that the Mexicans had spiked their guns and fled.
James Magoffin had done his work well. The road was now open
to Santa Fé, and General Kearny entered the town unopposed.
The following day, the American flag was raised in the plaza opposite
the governor's palace, and numerous Mexican officers and citizens
took the oath of allegiance to the United States.

After the glowing stories they had heard of Santa Fé, the American soldiers were disappointed to find it a small, squalid village
filled with mud hovels and dingy-walled churches. The governor's
palace, adorned with strings of Indians' ears stretched between
the pillars, the walled houses of the few more affluent Mexicans,
and the filthy jail, were the only large buildings in the town. There
were some planked floors, but most of the inhabitants slept on
the bare ground, and bath facilities were nonexistent. The gringos

quickly decided the town was not a tourist attraction, but they were impressed by the beauty of the women of Santa Fé.

Back at Fort Leavenworth, the post remained in a frenzy. The sound of rumbling wagons, the tramp of feet, the milling of horses and men, the incessant bugle calls continued, for the War Department had ordered the organization of additional men to reinforce the command of General Kearny. Recruits from St. Louis streamed from the steamboat landing. There were long lines of wagon trains arriving at the post daily.

During the remaining months of the war, the post served as a replacement depot, sending recruits south to fill the ranks of the armies of Colonels Doniphan and Price. A battalion of Mormons, recruited at Council Bluffs by Lieutenant James Allen of the 1st Dragoons, was trained at the fort, and after occupational duty in New Mexico, marched westward to California. A regiment of Illinois volunteers were drilled and outfitted at Leavenworth and sent on to relieve Price's men near Santa Fé. A battalion of infantry under Lieutenant Alton Easton was equipped and dispatched south to New Mexico. Among the thousands who left the fort that year for Santa Fé were seventy-six enlistees led by Lieutenant William B. Royall. At Coon Creek,[5] the detail was attacked by a large band of Comanche and Apache Indians, but the recruits gave a good account of themselves and drove off the hostiles.

It was inevitable that some of the volunteer frontier officers would clash with the "copybook" regulars. Major William Gilpin's battalion of five companies of Missouri Mounted Volunteers arrived on October 4, 1847. The major was dissatisfied with the delay in furnishing him with supplies and transportation, and challenged the post commander, Colonel Wharton, to a duel. The two antagonists never met on the field of honor, but the threat had the desired effect. The major left within a few days with his battalion, fifteen wagons of ammunition, two hundred wagons of supplies, and five hundred head of cattle.

Representative Sterling Price of Missouri had resigned his seat in Congress to command this new army. Price's family had moved to Fayette, Missouri, from Virginia, when he was an infant. He returned to the East for college and graduated from Hampden-Sydney. Before becoming active in politics, he had been a lawyer and a successful tobacco commission merchant. Given an appointment as colonel by President Polk, he had returned to Missouri and raised the 2nd Missouri Regiment of Mounted Infantry, which assembled at Fort Leavenworth on August 12, 1848.[6]

Price and his staff left Leavenworth and arrived in Santa Fé in September, but the main body of his troops did not get there until Columbus Day.

Meanwhile General Kearny, after appointing Charles Bent as governor of New Mexico and Francis P. Blair as attorney general, divided the Army of the West into three parts. Colonel Price with 1,200 men, including the Mormon battalion and several pieces of artillery, was designated as the Army of Occupation, with orders to garrison New Mexico. The rest of the Missouri Volunteers he put under the command of Colonel Doniphan with orders to invade the Mexican state of Chihuahua. With the dragoons, the general himself set out for California.

Except for occasional sorties against marauding Indians, Colonel Price faced no serious problems until late January, 1847. The American volunteers had become bored, discipline was nonexistent, and there were continued reports of attacks by American soldiers on New Mexicans. The native population, fearing both for their lives and their property, became restive. At Taos, fifteen Americans, including Governor Bent, were murdered. Colonel Price quickly restored order by rounding up the dissidents. Fifteen men were tried and hanged for murder; the rest were charged with treason. President Polk pardoned the latter on their plea that as citizens of Mexico they could not be guilty of treason against the United States.

Colonel Doniphan's departure was delayed when he had to send a force to quell an uprising of the Navajo Indians in northern New Mexico, but his army was under way by December, 1846. After decisively defeating superior forces at Brazito[7] and Sacramento, and taking the towns of Chihuahua and Saltillo, the colonel marched eastward. The one-year term of the soldiers had expired, and the army was loaded on ships at Matamoras and transported to New Orleans where on May 15, 1847, the Missouri Volunteers were discharged. Over plains, desert, and mountains, Doniphan's little army had marched 3,600 miles since leaving Fort Leavenworth, and in every encounter his men had successfully put the enemy to rout.

Eleven days after leaving Santa Fé, Kearny, with his three hundred dragoons and a couple of mountain howitzers, arrived at Socorro on the Rio Grande. There he met Kit Carson, who was bound for Washington from California with dispatches from Commodore Robert Field Stockton and Major John C. Fremont. Carson told Kearny that the conquest of California had been completed, that all the important towns were in American hands, and that a civil government with Fremont at its head had been established. Kearny accordingly sent two hundred of his men back to Santa Fé, along with his supply wagons and the howitzers. After persuading Carson to entrust his messages to another courier and to accompany the rest of the dragoons westward, Kearny pushed on to California.

Almost as soon as he crossed the California frontier, Kearny learned that the glad tidings forwarded to Washington had been premature—the Americans were being met with increasing opposition. At the pass of San Pasqual, Kearny's dragoons, together with a small detail of sailors and marines that Stockton had sent him, were met by a force of 160 Californians led by a brother of the late Governor Pio Pico. The engagement that ensued between the almost equally numbered forces resulted in the rout of the Mexicans, but Kearny's troops were badly mauled. The general and fourteen enlisted men were wounded. Three of his officers (Captain Abraham R. Johnston, Benjamin D. Moore, and the latter's brother-in-law, Lieutenant Thomas Clark Hammond, of horseback-marriage fame) were killed. The ragged remnants of the band, however, continued on and occupied San Diego in December. From there, Kearny dispatched Major Thomas Swords, Jr., to the Sandwich (Hawaiian) Islands to procure clothing and supplies.[8] Without money, and having to pay for his purchases by drafts on the quartermaster general in Washington, the major was required to engage in "the nicest kind of financing, to make up vouchers that would pass the Treasury auditors."

In San Diego, Kearny was joined by Commodore Stockton, a native of Princeton, New Jersey, and a veteran of the War of 1812. Finding himself commander-in-chief of the Pacific squadron on the eve of the Mexican War, and an early believer in joint operations, Stockton had assumed command of all American forces along the California coast on July 31, 1846. The combined army and navy forces led by Stockton, with Kearny as his executive officer, advanced up the 250-mile road north of Los Angeles. An attempt to stop them at the San Gabriel River was made by forty-five poorly trained and equipped Californians, but they were easily defeated, and two days later, the Americans entered the City of the Angels.

Meanwhile Commander John Drake Sloat had taken Monterey. Fremont had raised the American flag in the San Francisco Bay area, where his force was joined by a California legion from New York City. The Mormon legion, after an overland march from Santa Fé, reached San Diego; Sacramento had been successfully relieved by a corps of volunteer American emigrants under General Ide. The war for California was practically over.

On May 31, General Kearny and the remnants of his dragoons, together with Major Fremont on his way to his court-martial in Washington, and forty men of the topographical corps, left for the return East and arrived at Fort Leavenworth on August 22, 1847.

A vast territory stretching from New Mexico to the Pacific Ocean had been added to the United States. Fort Leavenworth, as "quartermaster" to the Army of the West, had materially contributed to this accomplishment.

CHAPTER EIGHT

⟫⟩→←⟨⟪

THE MORMON WAR

The emigration of the Latter-Day Saints to the distant desert of Utah had not solved the Mormon problem. It had been hoped that the followers of Joseph Smith who had found it impossible to live at peace with their gentile[1] neighbors in the East, would be less troublesome when once settled by themselves in a far distant wilderness. In a spirit of conciliation, their wagon trains westward had received the help and protection of the United States Army; and President Franklin Pierce named their leader, Brigham Young, governor of the Territory of Utah.

A nation with a large dose of puritanism in its background, even though proud of its religious tolerance, found it hard to accept the practice of polygamy within its territorial limits. In 1856, one of the planks in the platform of the recently organized Republican Party opposed "those twin relics of barbarism—polygamy and slavery." Polygamy was an issue that both North and South, both abolitionist and slaveholder could agree upon. Stephen A. Douglas, leader of the Democrats in the Senate, called Mormonism "an ulcer in the body politic that must be cut out if it could not be removed in any other way."

Nor was polygamy the only charge leveled at the "chosen people." Their leaders were accused of debauchery, of holding women against their will, of arousing the Indian tribes against the United States, and of harassing judges and other federal officials to the point where it became impossible for them to perform their duties.[2]

As the flow of emigration pressed ever westward, more and more "gentiles" had stopped off in Salt Lake City. The complete

79

isolation the Mormons had hoped for was ending; the visitors were not loath to send their complaints eastward. The Saints, they wrote to their friends and the newspapers back in the States, had formed a theocracy without distinction between church and state. Territorial courts, they reported, existed solely for the purpose of settling disputes between Mormons, and a jury had never been known to render a verdict for a gentile when the opponent was a member of the faith.

Perhaps the most damning of the many accusations directed at the Mormons was that they were openly disloyal to the United States and absolutely refused to abide by its laws. When there was talk in Washington of removing Brigham Young as governor, he declared: "We have got a Territorial Governor, and I am and will be Governor and no power can hinder it until the Lord Almighty says, Brigham, you need not be Governor any longer, and then I am willing to yield to another Governor."

The intemperate and violent statements of Mormon leaders published in the eastern newspapers were not helpful. In a sermon in 1850, after the death of former President Zachary Taylor, who had not been friendly to the Mormons, Young told his congregation, "Zachary Taylor is dead and gone to Hell, and I am glad of it! I prophesy in the name of Jesus Christ, and by the power of the priesthood that is upon me, that any other President of the United States who shall lift his finger against this people will die an untimely death, and go to Hell."

One of the first actions of President James Buchanan after he took office in March, 1857, was the removal of Brigham Young as governor and the appointment in his stead of the elderly, waddling Alfred Cummings, the roly-poly ex-mayor of Augusta, Georgia. The President then filled the remaining vacant federal posts and directed that a force be assembled at Fort Leavenworth sufficient to quell Young's rebellion and escort the new governor, along with the other federal officials, to Utah. Initially, Colonel William Selby Harney was given command, but at the request of Governor Robert J. Walker, the command, because of the Kansas troubles, was rescinded. Colonel Persifor Smith was next selected, but within a week of his arrival at the post, he became fatally ill. Ultimately the command fell to Colonel Albert Sidney Johnston, but he did not arrive at Fort Leavenworth until September 11, two months after the first contingent of troops had left for Utah.

Once again the fort resounded to the shouts of commands, the cracks of the teamsters' bullwhips, and the piercing shrill of the approaching steamboats.

The 5th and 10th Infantry Regiments, with a battery of the 2nd Artillery, left Leavenworth in stages, the last unit clearing the post on July 18 with Colonel Thomas L. Alexander in command. Colonel Philip St George Cooke, escorting Colonel Johnston, the unwelcome Governor Cummings, the other federal officials, and with six companies of the 2nd Dragoons, moved out on September 17.

With the march having been delayed until so late in the fall, the weather became Colonel Cooke's chief antagonist. For twelve consecutive days it rained steadily. Horses and equipment were never dry, and every depression in the land became filled with water. When the rain ceased, the weather turned freezing cold, and a thick coating of ice covered the countryside. There was plenty of buffalo meat and edible teal ducks, but the buffalo chips, the only source of fuel, had become sodden and would not burn. The dragoons reached Fort Laramie November 1, where they remained four days for re-fitting and re-equipping. There Cooke gave orders "to store all baggage and other things absolutely not necessary, to leave all camp women, and to grind the sabers, which were not to be drawn and not to be trailed, but hooked up whenever the trooper was afoot, so they might not be dulled by contact with the steel scabbard."[3]

From Laramie, Cooke took his detachment up the valley of the Platte and then up the Sweetwater River. There a snowstorm began that lasted five days. During this time he was afraid to halt, as the drifts often reached a depth of fifteen feet. At Pacific Springs, near the summit of the Rocky Mountains, the thermometer registered thirteen below zero, and there was no fuel except the wild sage buried under the deep snow. Descending the mountains, the detachment finally reached Fort Bridger. There Colonel Alexander had arrived more than a month earlier and had set his troops to constructing adobe winter quarters while waiting for Colonel Johnson.

Back in July, at Cottonwood Canyon, Brigham Young had been

holding a large party celebrating the tenth anniversary of the arrival of the Mormons in the Promised Land. It was there that word was brought to him that an army had left Fort Leavenworth for Utah. Young ordered the mobilization of the Utah militia and instructed them that upon:

> ascertaining the locality or route of the troops, proceed at once to annoy them in every way. Use every exertion to stampede their animals and set fire to their trains. Burn the whole country before them and on their flanks. Keep them from sleeping by night surprises. Blockade the road by felling trees, or destroying the fords when you can. Watch for opportunities to set fire to the grass to the windward so far as possible to envelop their trains. . . . Take no life, but destroy their trains, and stampede or drive away their animals at every opportunity.[4]

The bearded Saints of the territorial militia successfully carried out the instructions of their leader, with one exception. They constantly fired upon and killed the troops' guards.

In September, Young issued a proclamation declaring martial law. In his sermons he continued to denounce the government and the army. "They say," he said, "that their Army is legal, and I say that such a statement is false as hell, and that they are as rotten as an old pumpkin that had been frozen seven times and then melted in a harvest sun. Come on with your thousands of illegally ordered troops and I will promise you, in the name of Israel's God, that you shall melt away as the snow before a July sun."

Nor were the other Mormon leaders any less vitriolic. Heber Kimball told a congregation of the Saints, "God Almighty helping me, I will fight until there is not a drop of Blood in my veins, . . . he [Buchanan] has issued orders to send troops to kill Brother Brigham and me, and to take the young women to the States. The woman will be damned that will go: she shall dry up in the fountains of life and be as though she never was. But there ain't any a-going, unless they are whores."

Almost as if to prove that the charges against the Mormons had a solid basis in fact, the Saints in southern Utah staged a massacre that would long be remembered in the annals of infamy.

A longtime landmark in Leavenworth was the Planters Hotel. *(Leavenworth Public Library)*

Fort Leavenworth bridge spanning the Missouri River opened in 1873. (*Fort Leavenworth Museum*)

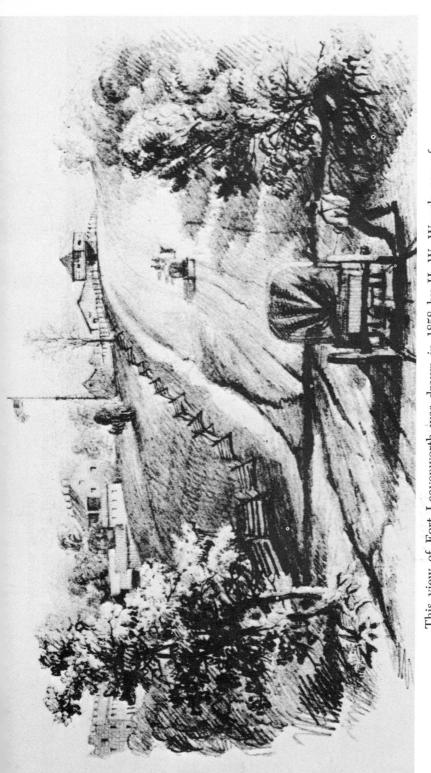

This view of Fort Leavenworth was drawn in 1858 by H. W. Waugh–son of Cincinnati's noted portrait painter Samuel P. Waugh–and is from the old Westport, Missouri approach (now Grant Avenue). (*Fort Leavenworth Museum*)

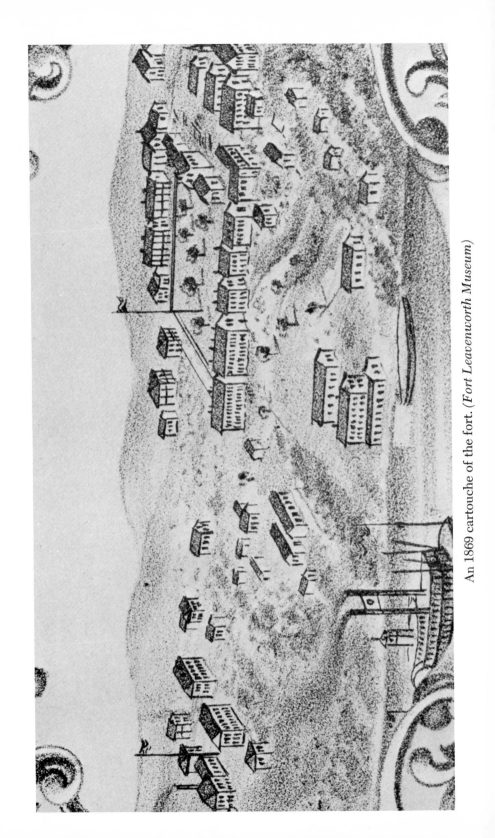

An 1869 cartouche of the fort. (*Fort Leavenworth Museum*)

A bird's-eye view of Fort Leavenworth in 1881. (*National Archives*)

Leavenworth City in the Kansas Territory as represented in an 1856 lithograph. *(Library of Congress)*

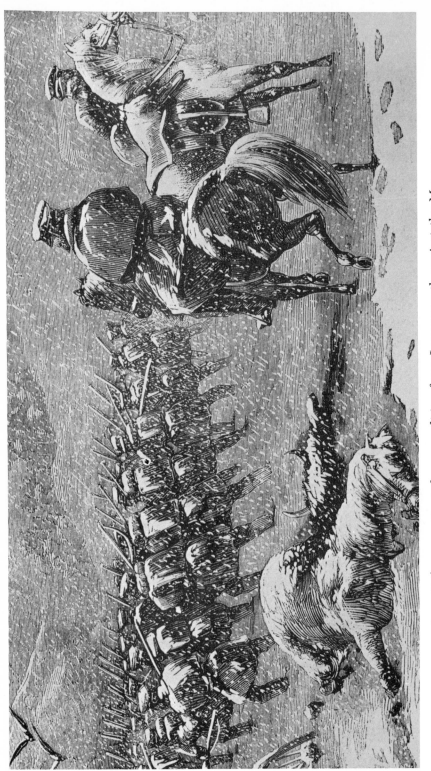

An artist's conception of an expedition from Leavenworth against the Mormons during the Mormon War. (*National Archives*)

Keel boats, such as the vessel depicted by the French artist Felix Achille St. Anlaire in 1832, were a familiar mode of transportation along the Missouri River. *(City Art Museum of St. Louis)*

Following the Civil War, Dougherty Wagons, called "Army Limousines," were a popular form of surface transportation. *(National Archives)*

Travel along the Overland Trail was often in Con-
cord-type stagecoaches. The soldiers shown here were
members of the 10th Cavalry. *(National Archives)*

Steam-powered river boats, like the *Selkirk*, plied the waterways of the area. *(National Archives)*

With the advent of the trolley car, "modern" transportation between Leavenworth City and the fort became available. The trolley station still stands, and has been enlarged to serve as a Post Exchange. (*Fort Leavenworth Museum*)

Fort Leavenworth riflemen are formed for an awards ceremony. *(National Archives)*

In 1856, a group of Arkansas emigrants on their way to California were passing through Utah. Together with Indian allies, the Mormons attacked the train on September 7, at Mountain Meadows. In the initial assault twenty-five of the California-bound travelers were killed. The Mormons then withdrew to the surrounding hills, shooting down on their victims who had barricaded themselves behind the wagons.

After four days of siege, during which the emigrants' water supply had become exhausted, a delegation of Mormons approached under a flag of truce. John D. Lee, the leader of the emissaries, told the frightened emigrants that if they would surrender their arms and ammunition, they would be taken to Cedar City where they would be safe. To this the emigrants acquiesced, and after their weapons had been piled into a wagon and the wounded and children had been loaded in other vehicles, the march was started, with Mormon guards on each side of the column. They had not gone far when the guards turned on the emigrants and slaughtered everyone, including the wounded. Only the children too young to testify against the murderers were spared. As one of the Saints, McCurdy, was killing two of the wounded, he raised his rifle and said, "Oh Lord, my God, receive their Spirits, it is for thy Kingdom that I do this." Before burying the dead, the Mormons allowed their Indian allies to take the victims' scalps.

When Lee gave his report on the massacre to Brigham Young, the leader was at first upset, fearing the reaction not only among some of his people, but also of his enemies in the East. However, after a prayerful consultation with God, he told Lee:

> I have evidence from God that . . . the action was a righteous one and well intended. The brethern acted from pure motives. I sustain you and all the brethern for what they did.

Attempting to justify themselves, the Mormons later charged that the travelers had been contaminating the wells with arsenic, and killing cattle with strychnine, but a subsequent investigation established that no such poisons were included in the caravan's supplies.

When Colonel Johnston learned that the Mormon militia had ambushed and destroyed three supply trains, taken two thousand head of cattle, and fired the grasses so essential to the grazing of the horses and mules, he had no alternative but to remain at Fort Bridger for the rest of the winter. After a request for volunteers, the colonel sent Captain Randolph B. Marcy with a small detail to Fort Massachusetts in New Mexico for new supplies.

The news of the destruction of the army's supply trains, the precarious position of the troops at Fort Bridger, and the Mountain Meadows massacre caused great consternation in Washington. Congress immediately voted an appropriation for four thousand reinforcements, and the War Department directed that they assemble at Fort Leavenworth.

Stressing Brigham Young's disloyalty to the United States Government and the incompatibility of his triple roles as governor of the territory, superintendent of Indian affairs, and head of the church of Latter-Day Saints, President Buchanan explained his actions in the appointment of Cummings and the sending of the force to Utah in a message to Congress in December:

> His power has been therefore absolute over both Church and State. The people of Utah, almost exclusively belong to this Church, and believing with a fanatical spirit that he (Young) is governor of the Territory by divine appointment, they obey his commands as if these were direct revelations from Heaven. If, therefore, he chooses that his government shall come in to collision with the government of the United States, the members of the Mormon Church will yield implicit obedience to his will. Unfortunately existing facts leave but little doubt that such is his determination. Without entering upon a minute history of occurrences, it is sufficient to say that all the officers of the United States, judicial and executive, with the single exception of two Indian agents, have found it necessary for their personal safety to withdraw from the Territory, and there no longer remains any Government in Utah but the despotism of Brigham Young. This being the condition of affairs in the Territory, I could not mistake the path of duty. As Chief Executive Magistrate I was bound to restore the supremacy of the Constitution and have, within the limits. In order to effect this purpose, I appointed a new governor and other federal officers for Utah, and sent with them a military force for their protection, and to aid as a posse comitatus, in case of need, in the execution of the laws.

Brigham Young retorted that he would remain as governor, and that if the troops entered Salt Lake City, he would withdraw his people and burn the buildings. But, realizing that President Buchanan meant business, he reluctantly heeded the urgent advice of a gentile friend, Colonel Thomas L. Kane, and agreed to give up his claim on the governorship, and receive Cummings. The new governor accordingly left Fort Bridger for Salt Lake City. He was escorted most of the way by the territorial militia and, when he arrived, took over the reins of government.

Meanwhile Captain Marcy returned from New Mexico with the desperately needed supplies. The United States troops moved out from Fort Bridger on June 13. The route to Salt Lake City wound through two canyons, Emigration and Echo, where the dust was a foot deep, because the height of the perpendicular walls of the canyons kept the breeze from dispelling it. As the troops emerged from the defile, they could see the buildings and the green fields and orchards of Salt Lake City, and north of it, the waters of the lake.

The column paused long enough to regroup, and then with the American flag flying and the guidons flapping in the breeze, they marched into the city. Brigham Young had carried out part of his threat—save for a few non-Mormon merchants, the city was empty. The Saints had withdrawn to the south. Young did not carry out his second threat—to destroy the city. In fact, he and his followers returned to keep a large contingent of troops near the city until 1859.

The planning for the reinforcement of the Utah expedition continued, and Fort Leavenworth became a staging area once again in May and June of 1858. Not only were several thousand more troops added to the garrison, but a large group of dependents, sharing quarters, remained at the post throughout the Mormon war. This time General Harney was in command.

Congress, now thoroughly aroused at the Mormon arrogance, saw to it that the War Department spared no expense in equipping and supplying a second expedition. Underway by June 11 in Harney's command were two regiments of cavalry and two of artillery. At General Harney's suggestion, the President had wisely named Father de Smet as chaplain of the force. This appointment had taken considerable political courage on the part of Buchanan. Catholicism was suspect to many in the nation, and naming a priest to serve in a campaign to subdue a religious sect was, in the minds of many, a questionable move. The President and Harney had their reasons. They wanted the Jesuit for his influence among the tribes through whose lands the troops would pass. Father de Smet had doubts in his own mind as to the wisdom of the appointment, but he accepted and immediately journeyed to Fort Leavenworth.

Harney, who had been made a brigadier general on June 13, had not reached Fort Bent when a courier brought him word that the Mormons had capitulated. He continued on to Utah with a small detail, sending the main body of troops back to Leavenworth where they remained until 1860.

Brigham Young and his fellow cultists were finally convinced that Utah was not an island, but within the territorial limits of the United States, that the federal laws were supreme within the territory, and that gentiles as well as Mormons were entitled to due process of law. The show of force did not, of course, instill loyalty, for this could develop only after several generations. In the American Civil War three years later, the Mormons took a neutral stand, remaining on the fence until they were sure who would be the winner.

CHAPTER NINE

>>>→>-<-<<<

LIFE ON THE POST

If a young recruit arriving at Fort Leavenworth on a steamer from St. Louis in the fall of 1846 expected to find a raw frontier post, he was quickly disabused after climbing the bluff from the wharf. The orderly brick-and-white-clapboard-covered buildings, the rows of trees, the neat roads, all combined to create the appearance more of a peaceful New England village than a fort in the wilderness. Most of the original log buildings were gone, and the blockhouses, the flagstaff, and an occasional sentry were the only indications that this was a military installation.

The new arrival would have found his quarters quite commodious and comfortable by the standards of the day. In the mess he would receive a plain but ample meal consisting of either a pound of pork or a pound-and-a-half of beef for each man; and in season, there would be fresh vegetables from the post farm. If he wished to take a bath after his long trip, he had access to a number of sawed-off barrels filled with hot water and placed in his company kitchen. That evening, using his issue overcoat as a pillow, he would sleep under an army blanket on a bedsack filled once a month with fresh prairie hay, which his fellow enlisted men called "prairie feathers."

In the days that followed, the young recruit would find that in his off-duty hours there was much to occupy his time. When the weather was good, the men would pitch horseshoes after supper until dark; and thereafter, until tattoo, there would be a continuing poker game in the barracks. If an enlisted man had theatrical inclinations, he could join the Thespian Society. The plays given in the assembly room of the barracks were attended by the entire garrison, and the dramatic ability of the enlisted soldiers, particularly those who took the female leads, was a subject of discussion for weeks. The annual enlisted men's ball took months of preparation and many trips across the river to the nearby town of Weston for the purchase of supplies for decorations. With the number of women quite limited, the troopers were forced to dance with each other in what was often a test of endurance.

A few of the top-grade enlisted soldiers had their families with them. With few exceptions, only commissioned officers were provided with quarters, and an enlisted man with dependents was forced to either build a cabin or buy one from a departing soldier. Even with the extra money their wives earned by doing laundry, an enlisted man could hardly afford a spouse, for infantry privates got only eleven dollars a month; cavalry troopers and artillerymen were given a dollar extra. A corporal was paid thirteen dollars monthly, sergeants seventeen, and orderly sergeants twenty. A second lieutenant got three dollars a month more than an orderly sergeant. The men were supposed to receive their pay every second month, but in the absence of a paymaster it could be in arrears for as long as six months.

Infraction of rules by an enlisted man would often result in a period in the guardhouse, a fine deducted from pay, or as many as fifty lashes for desertion. Less serious offenses were generally taken care of by company punishment rather than by a court-martial.

The officers' quarters at Leavenworth were comfortable, if not spacious. Unlike many of those on the frontier, they had been well-built, but the interiors challenged the ingenuity of the wives. With very little to work with, cupboards and other necessities were made from crates and boxes, the ultimate product being both useful and attractive. In the winter a sheet-iron stove in the middle of the living room furnished the heat, although its radiation extended for only a few feet. On the night of the weekly bath, a tub was put as close to the stove as possible.

One luxury the officers' wives could and did enjoy was a household servant. Usually they were Indian or mestizo women, some of the latter the descendants of early French trappers. White domestics were hard to retain; with the female shortage they would find a husband soon after their arrival. For household help, unattractive young women were preferred, but lack of comeliness was not always a deterrent to marriage. One officer's wife told of deliberately choosing a nursemaid for her homely face. "The girl was almost a grenadier in looks and manners, and although not absolutely hideous, was so far from pleasing that we were confident of retaining her services . . . she had not been in the Fort three days before the man who laid our carpets proposed to her."[1]

Since quarters were not allotted on a first-come first-served basis but according to rank, a newly arrived officer with dependents could force another to move to a less desirable house. Called "the bricks falling," the practice resulted in the shedding of many a feminine tear when a wife was forced to vacate quarters she had spent many hours of hard, loving care in making comfortable. It was particularly annoying when the appropriating officer was of the same rank but held a commission dated a few days earlier than her husband's.

Christmas was, of course, the gala social season of the year, and preparations began weeks in advance. On Christmas morning the wives would call upon each other to view one another's gifts and decorations. Later in the day they would go in a body to "Old Bedlam," the bachelor officers' quarters. Both the officers and their families were required to visit the Christmas mess of the enlisted men, and the ladies were expected to contribute cakes. The dinners in the quarters were sumptuous affairs with courses of antelope, buffalo, ham, prairie hen, canned vegetables, preserves, and an assortment of pies and cakes. Bachelor officers were almost always invited to have dinner in the quarters of their married friends.

In the early days of the fort, Franklin, Missouri (before the town disappeared into the Big Muddy), had been almost a summer resort. The town was cooler and more healthful than the post, and the officers' families often lived there from June to September. Here also was an academy where many an army brat learned the three R's. Later, nearby Weston became the off-duty town, but it never achieved the popularity of Franklin.

Weston was not a mere village, but had several thousand inhabitants. A great many of the wagon trains going west formed there, and it boasted a city club and a Masonic lodge, where a number of the personnel from the post took their degrees. The Rialto, one mile south of Weston, became a bawdy suburb of the post for the enlisted men.

In 1847, a new ferry operated by John Barber was established between the fort and Weston, and this time, with the experience of Zadock Martin fresh in his mind, Lieutenant Colonel Wharton was careful to see that proper regulations were previously agreed upon.[2]

Cholera broke out again at the fort in 1848. It had first appeared in New Orleans and had been carried up the Mississippi by steamer to St. Louis. One boat, the *Mary*, transporting Mormon emigrants, had fifty-eight fatalities out of three hundred passengers and crew. At St. Joseph, the citizens rose en masse to prevent the landing of either passengers or freight. In St. Louis, a group of recruits, Leavenworth-bound, went on the town while waiting for a westbound steamer and contracted the dread disease.

Deaths at the fort were not as numerous as elsewhere, but for years, cases of cholera would recur, adding to the post's reputation as an unhealthy spot. One year the post was almost immobilized by an epidemic of dysentery that strained the resources of the little hospital.

In October, 1848, a council of the Northwestern Confederation of Indian Tribes was held at the fort. Representatives of the Delaware, Shawnee, Wyandot, Ottawa, Potawatomi, Chippewa, Miami, Sac, Fox, Kickapoo, Kansa, and the Peoria were present. Under the Treaty of 1829, it had been agreed that the new reservations given to the tribes would be theirs "in perpetuity," that never would territories nor states be carved out of these lands. Less than twenty years later, the Indians were concerned that the white man was again about to break his promise. Demands had been made that the reservations be opened to white settlement, and Stephen A. Douglas of Illinois had introduced a bill in the Senate creating a new territory to be composed of Kansas and Nebraska. Although the Douglas Bill had yet to pass Congress, the Indians saw the handwriting on the wall and seized the opportunity afforded by the council to enter a vigorous protest. The conference accomplished little, but the Indians did put on quite a spectacular dance near the post that was witnessed by all the officers and ladies.[3]

A young articulate recruit who had enlisted in Boston, arrived at Fort Leavenworth in December, 1849. Percival G. Lowe, brother of Professor T. S. C. Lowe, the first American military aeronaut and organizer of the Army balloon corps that was used so effectively during the Civil War, was a farm boy who had spent three years as a sailor. He concluded that a tour with the dragoons would complete his education. Lowe's path to Leavenworth was not an easy one. He was shepherded, along with seventy-three recruits from Carlisle Barracks, by Lieutenant Charles William Field, a Kentuckian who was to become a major general in the Confederate Army and later a colonel under the khedive of Egypt. The trip was uneventful until the battalion embarked on a western-bound steamer from St. Louis. At Portland, Missouri, some three hundred miles short of Leavenworth, the boat froze in the ice. The troops had no alternative but to march the rest of the way, the trip taking them through snow and over ice. They stopped at inns and plantations where the men slept on floors and in barns. They arrived at the fort on Christmas day. Years later, Lowe was to write a book on his five years' experience as a dragoon.[4]

A West Point graduate and a veteran of both the Black Hawk and Seminole wars, Major Edmund A. Ogden was named quartermaster to succeed the flamboyant Thomas Swords, Jr. In 1850, he got orders from Washington to build a road from Fort Leavenworth to Fort Kearny, and accordingly a survey party was sent out to mark the road. Three years later, Odgen was ordered to construct a road from Leavenworth to Fort Riley. Following the Kaw Valley, the route entailed the construction of bridges over the Stranger, the Grasshopper, Ozawkie, and Soldiers Creek, as well as across the Kansas River.

On a November day in 1854, near the Platte River, the Salt Lake City stage was ambushed by a small Brûlé war party. Three men were killed and one wounded before the hostiles took off with a strong box containing $10,000 in gold. The Secretary of War summoned Colonel Harney home from Paris, where he was on leave, and gave him the assignment of punishing the Sioux. Passing through Fort Leavenworth in April, 1855, the colonel organized his six-hundred-man force at Fort Kearny. At Ash Hollow, near the emigrant road, he met the Indians on October 3 and gave them a sound thrashing. The gold was never recovered, but on October 25, the Sioux leaders, Spotted Tail, Red Leaf, and Long Chin, who had been chiefly responsible for the stage massacre, voluntarily came into Fort Laramie and surrendered. The warriors were moved to Fort Leavenworth where they were tried and condemned to be hanged, but they were pardoned by President Franklin Pierce and released. Their year's stay at the post must have had a salutary effect on the three, for they came to the conclusion that their people could never prevail against the white man, and for the rest of their lives they consistently advocated peace with the paleface. Spotted Tail was over-ruled in tribal council in 1864, and during the Civil War he dutifully took up arms against the federal government; but he did so reluctantly, and only after he had made every effort to convince his people that war against the whites would only result in disaster for the Indians.

That same year, a bearded Virginia aristocrat and West Point graduate, Colonel Robert E. Lee, spent a few weeks at the fort serving on a court-martial board. Another West Point graduate, the blunt and dour William Tecumseh Sherman, having resigned from the army, put out his shingle as an attorney in the nearby city of Leavenworth.

In 1851, the Post Office Department made a contract with a Mormon named Woodson for carrying mail from Leavenworth City to west of the Rockies, but the following year Woodson sublet the western part of the route from Laramie to Salt Lake to the Mormon firm of Little and Hanks. Shortly thereafter a similar contract was made with George Chorpenning for a line from Utah to California. In 1854, Woodson lost his contract and a new one was given to William F. McGraw who planned to carry both passengers and mail. The trip took over a month each way and proved too expensive; McGraw went bankrupt in 1856, and the Mormon firm of Kimball and Young took over the route. With the outbreak of the Mormon war, the contract was rescinded, and the Post Office Department went into the business itself, sending westward a monthly mail mule team, with stops at Forts Kearny and Laramie. Troops from Fort Leavenworth not only escorted the mail train, but sometimes operated the route.

During the fifties, Fort Leavenworth was the quartermaster center for most of the forts and camps from the plains to the Pacific Coast. Supplies were brought to the post from St. Louis by Missouri

steamboats and then transshipped across the plains in covered
wagons, drawn by either oxen or mule teams. All during the Mexican War years, such transportation had been handled by the military, with army officers supervising civilian teamsters or bullwhack-
ers. During this period, huge quantities of supplies had been
abandoned after the oxen and mules dropped dead. Charges were
made that this was due to the officers' lack of knowledge of freighting. Perhaps as a result of this criticism or because of effective
lobbying in Washington, the War Department directed Major
Ogden in the spring of 1848 to contract for the hauling with civilian
freighters. Thereafter, a number of contracts were made for the
transportation of freight to New Mexico, and the system proved
so successful that the War Department adopted the civilian-contract
plan for all freight dispatched westward from Fort Leavenworth.
By early 1855, the newly formed firm of Russell, Majors, and
Waddell was given a monopoly on the transportation of supplies
west of the Missouri River.[5]

Both the firm and its individual partners were to write their
names large in the early history of western transportation. Alexander Majors, a native of Kentucky reared in Independence, Missouri,
was a farmer with a large family, who had been forced to supplement
his income, first as an Indian trader, then by freighting. By 1854,
he was transporting the bulk of the army's supplies over the plains.
Majors was the practical field man of the new firm and was certainly
the most stable of the three partners. William H. Russell, a wheeler-
dealer, spent a good part of his time in Washington where he
had contacts in the government, particularly the War Department. Suave, charming, persuasive, and keen-witted, he was
nevertheless reckless and impulsive, and was ultimately responsible
for the roof crashing down on his partners' heads. William Waddell
was the direct antithesis of Russell. As the financial backer of the
enterprise, Waddell was penny-pinching, cautious, and slow to
reach a decision. A well-to-do merchant of Lexington, Missouri,
he operated as a wholesaler and retailer of various products needed
on the frontier.

When not in use, most of the firm's oxen and mules were kept
in the valley of One-Mile Creek, between the fort and the town
of Leavenworth. Horace Greeley, on his western tour of 1859,
noted in a dispatch to the New York *Tribune:*

Russell, Majors, and Waddell's transportation establishment between the Fort and the city, is a great feature of Leavenworth. Such acres of wagons! Such pyramids of extra axletrees! Such herds of oxen! Such regiments of drivers and other employees! No one who does not see can realize how vast a business this is, nor how immense its outlay as well as income. I presume the great firm has at this hour two millions of dollars invested in stock, mainly oxen, mules, and wagons. (Last year they employed six thousand teamsters and worked 45,000 oxen).[6]

At the same time that Greeley was there, another tourist at the fort was equally impressed; he reported:

Returning to town (from Fort Leavenworth), I passed numbers of the ox trains used in freighting merchandise to New Mexico. They are remarkable, each wagon team consisting of yokes of fine oxen selected and arranged not only for drawing but for picturesque effect, in sets of twenty, either all black, all white, all spotted, or otherwise uniformly marked. Each set of twenty oxen draws from 6500 to 8000 pounds and makes the journey from Leavenworth to Santa Fé at the contract rate of seven miles per day.[7]

At One-Mile Creek, a bright twelve-year-old boy worked for Russell, Majors, and Waddell. He was William Cody, later to win fame as Buffalo Bill.

The stagecoach was, of course, the speediest and most comfortable of western land travel. Within two years after its founding in 1854, the town of Leavenworth had stage networks going in all directions. There was a tri-weekly line of thirty-two miles to Westport, Missouri; daily mail coaches for the eight miles to Weston; a line that carried mail and passengers to Kickapoo and Atchison, where connections could be made for St. Louis; two tri-weekly lines to Lawrence, thirty miles away; daily trips to Lecompton; and a line that ran to Fort Riley, making stops at Salt Creek, Easton, Hardtville, Ozawkie, Indianola, Silver Lake, Louisville, Manhattan, and Ogden.

In 1858, the abortive "Pike's Peak Gold Rush" was responsible for the establishment of a stage line to Denver by Russell, and an equally impractical and over-sanguine partner, John S. Jones. Much against the wishes of his partners, Russell made use of the credit of the Russell, Majors, and Waddell firm to promote the new Leavenworth and Pike's Peak Express Company. There were to be twenty-six way stations with excellent meals and good sleeping accommodations, and the fare was $125. Coaches were to leave Leavenworth and Denver daily, and "the line was equipped with over fifty Concord coaches, built by the Abbott Downing Company of Concord, N.H., the most popular and substantial vehicles of the kind made."[8] Before operations began, the promoters had spent over a quarter of a million dollars, all borrowed money, and the cost of operations daily was estimated to be at least a thousand dollars. The first coach bound for the Rockies left Leavenworth on April 18, 1859. A line to the new gold "diggins" at Golden, Colorado, and one to Salt Lake City were established later the same year. The Pike's Peak Express Company was insolvent from its inception, and by October, the threat of bankruptcy forced the firm of Russell, Majors, and Waddell to take over all its assets and liabilities. During the Civil War, Ben Holiday bought the line and in 1866, sold it to Wells Fargo and Company.

Ben Holiday, one of the great entrepreneurs of the West, arrived in Liberty, Missouri, from Nicholas County, Kentucky, in 1837. He was sixteen years old and without a formal education. Three years later he moved to Weston, where he clerked in a store, started a hotel and later a drugstore. At twenty-three he became the town's postmaster. During the Mexican War, Holiday got contracts from the quartermaster at Fort Leavenworth to supply the troops in Santa Fé with horses, mules and wagons, as well as with bacon and flour, from which he was able to turn a two hundred percent profit. Holiday made still more money after the Civil War by buying surplus government property at the fort and selling it to the western emigrants who were outfitting in Weston. In 1867, he emigrated to Salem, Oregon, built a hotel, went into shipping, and obtained a grant of thousands of acres of the best lands from the legislature. However, the Oregon and California Railroad, which he organized, proved to be his undoing. The interest on the bonds of the railroad, often amounting to thirty percent, came due before the arrival of the emigrants and before the lands could be sold. He attempted to pay it out of his own personal fortune and was soon almost insolvent. The railroad failed, but after his death, his executors were able to pay off his debts, as a result of the increase in the value of his Portland holdings.

On the open plain near the post one day in 1853, a new kind of vehicle was entered in the competition for the traveling public's favor. The covered wagons of the emigrants had long been called prairie schooners, but this contrivance was actually sailing. At its tiller was one Windwagon Thomas, who had arrived in Westport a few months earlier in a light vehicle whose sole motive power was the wind that filled its small sail. To the accompaniment of rearing horses and children scuttling for safety, Thomas brought his apparition to a graceful stop before Yoakum's Tavern, the town's principal gathering place. To the curious citizenry he announced that he had come to enlist their support in building a fleet of prairie ships to carry merchandise to Santa Fé. With the advantage of speed and the savings from not having animals to feed, Windwagon told his new-found friends, a vast profit could be made from the operation of a fleet of such clippers. Furthermore, he said, the Indians would give such a vehicle a wide berth.

When the leading merchants of Westport remained skeptical, Thomas announced that he would sail his small craft the 150 miles to Council Grove and back, perhaps convincing them of the practicality of his project. He returned within nine days, proudly bearing a letter from the blacksmith at Council Grove, proving thereby that he had actually made the trip.

The skeptics of Westport were convinced, and Dr. J. W. Parker, Henry Sager, Indian Agent Benjamin Newsom, J. J. Martin, Thomas M. Adams, and Windwagon Thomas formed the Overland Navigation Company, providing the necessary funds for the construction of the first wind-borne prairie schooner. Rigged like a catboat, the ship was twenty-five feet in length with a seven-foot beam, and had four wheels that were twelve feet in diameter. There was a cabin that rose to the top of the wheels, and above that a deck. The tailgate was in the bow as in a modern LST.

When the ship, or whatever it should be called, was completed, Thomas announced a shakedown run on which each of the directors was invited. All but Dr. J. W. Parker accepted. However, the physician, a conservative soul, did agree to follow the windwagon on a mule. Two yokes of oxen pulled the contraption out to the open prairie where the sail was hoisted, and Windwagon Thomas grasped the tiller. There was a good wind, and the wagon was soon traveling at an alarming rate of speed. Despite the appeals of the directors, Thomas adamantly refused to shorten the sail.

When Thomas tried to come about, it happened. A gust of wind caught the sail and in spite of all the skipper could do, the wagon started to go into reverse, and Dr. Parker on his mule narrowly escaped being run down. The helm locked, and the ship began spinning around and around in a mile-wide circle. One by one, the passengers leaped off, but Captain Thomas, true to the traditions of the sea, remained aboard, clutching the useless tiller but still refusing to reef the sail. The vehicle was finally brought to a halt when it crashed into the bank of Turkey Creek. This initial demonstration was enough for the directors, and negatively settled any possible future investments in the prairie sailing venture. Windwagon Thomas, in his light vehicle, soon left Westport and was never seen in those parts again. [9]

Thomas was not the only one to have built a windwagon. A John Parker, also of Westport, employed a wagonsmith, William Wills, to construct one, and when it was finished it was described as looking like a float depicting the landing of Columbus. One moonlight night, the wagon was hauled out to the prairie from Westport by oxen. Unfortunately the sail was left up, and it took off on its own and was never seen again.

A windwagon was also built by August Rodert, an early merchant of Westport. On the bed of a prairie schooner he erected a windmill —like those in Holland, his native country—from which he ran "a rawhide belt from the shaft of the source of power, to an axle at the rear of his wagon." Hard as it may be to believe, his contraption really worked. The Rodert windwagon is said to have been smashed in an effort to find the Parker wagon.

During the Pike's Peak gold rush, Samuel Peppard of Oskaloosa, Kansas, constructed a windwagon in which he planned to travel to Colorado. Taking an ordinary 350-pound light wagon, he put a sail, nine by eleven feet, over the center of the front axle. Together with Steve Randall, J. T. Forbes, Sid Coldon, and four hundred pounds of supplies and ammunition, Peppard set out in his land schooner for Denver. Peppard reported: "Our best time was two miles in four minutes . . . One day we went fifty miles in three hours and in doing so passed 625 teams. There were, you know, a great many people enroute for the gold fields at that time . . . Many amusing incidents happened along the way and we had no little fun joking with the teamsters as we flew by them."

Some fifty miles northeast of Denver, Peppard's wagon was caught by a whirlwind. The sailing schooner was carried fifty feet into the air and came down, smashing its hind wheels. The ship was beyond repair, and Peppard and his party thumbed a ride into Denver.

At about the same time that Windwagon Thomas was at Westport, another inventor arrived at Fort Leavenworth. His creation was a chunky muzzle-loader fixed to a pack saddle, from which, he informed the commanding officer, it could be fired while on the back of a mule. All that was required was to sight the mule's posterior toward the enemy. Despite skepticism, officers at headquarters provided a mule and granted the inventor permission to conduct a demonstration on a cliff overlooking the Missouri River.

In the presence of most of the officers of the post and many of the enlisted men, the inventor was directed to proceed with his experiment. After strapping the saddle on the mule, he pointed the animal's rear end toward the Missouri bank, loaded the gun, and lighted the fuse. The mule, unaccustomed to the sputtering noise at his rump, craned his neck for a look. Unable to see anything, he began to turn and the spectators hit the dust. When the gun went off, emitting a cloud of smoke, both mule and gun crashed down the bank into the river. Picking themselves up and brushing off their clothes, the ordnance experts advised the demonstrator that his gun would probably not fit into their program.

Almost as fantastic as the windwagon and the mule gun was Russell's scheme for a pony express. The idea was not original; in 1832 a similar line had operated between New York and Washington, D.C. In 1858, riders had carried a St. Louis newspaper containing a message from President Buchanan to California. However, without a liberal government subsidy, it was an extremely impractical idea, for 115 way stations and relay points had to be established between Leavenworth and California, and $75,000 had been spent before a single rider mounted a horse. Only two minutes' time was allowed at each station for the new relay rider to receive the mail sack and be on his way. The Pony Express route across the continent "was as lonesome and weird as it was long and tiresome."[10] The rider first crossed the Kickapoo reservation and over the prairie to Fort Kearny. He was often in sight of large droves of antelope, deer, and huge herds of buffalo. From Kearny, the mail carrier followed the trail along the Platte River to old Julesburg. Fording the south fork, he pressed on northwest to Fort Laramie. By way of the South Pass, he headed for Salt Lake City, and thence through Ruby Valley, Carson City, Placerville, Folsom, and on to Sacramento, where the last pony was replaced by a steamboat for the final lap to San Francisco.

The operation was begun on April 3, 1860, and sliced the mail time between New York and San Francisco from twenty-one to eleven days, the fastest trip being made in March, 1861, when President Lincoln's first inaugural message was carried to Sacramento, California—1,980 miles—in seven days and eighteen hours. However, it was discontinued in October, 1861. Its demise contributed to the eventual folding of the firm of Russell, Majors, and Waddell.

Telegraphy also started to come into its own during this period, and by 1857, the lines of the St. Louis and Missouri River Telegraph Company had reached Boonville, two hundred miles west of St. Louis. The firm proposed[11] to the War Department the extension of the service to Fort Leavenworth. The line was completed in 1859.

The utter disregard for human life that was common on the frontier was forcibly impressed upon Samuel W. Ferguson when he arrived as a brand-new lieutenant at Fort Leavenworth in the summer of 1857. Gently reared in Charleston, South Carolina, Ferguson had graduated the previous June from the military academy and was ill-prepared for his first day on the post. While Ferguson was having a toddy in the quarters of Lieutenant Charles H. Tyler, the officer of the day, the two heard a shot ring out. Shortly thereafter, an orderly reported that "one citizen had killed another near the guardhouse." Tyler said, "Those two men came, together, to my office and one asked protection from the other who he said had threatened to kill him, at the same time stating that they were partners. Whereupon the other coolly said, 'Yes, I do intend to kill him.' " Tyler said he replied that the matter was for the civil authorities and sent them on their way.

The next day, Ferguson took over Tyler's duties, and the two officers reported to General Harney. Tyler related the incident of the murder, and said he would have the man buried, but the general broke in by saying, "No! Let him lie there. I have reported the case to the civil authorities in Leavenworth City, and in this, as in various other matters, they have not taken the slightest notice of my communication."

When Tyler returned to the guardhouse he found that someone had thrown dirt over the body. "This was the only notice taken of the murder."[12]

The city of Leavenworth in 1859, five years after its founding, was no longer a village, but had become a sprawling, brawling, frontier town. In July of that year, James Stephens was robbed and murdered, allegedly by John C. Quarles and W. M. Bayes. A mob gathered before the jail and, despite the remonstrances of Judge Lecomte and the United States marshal, they battered down the door and hanged the two prisoners from an elm tree near the sawmill. Quarles was the first victim, and unfortunately his noose was not properly tightened. For several minutes he was able to grasp the rope and keep himself from strangling. Finally, "a heavy-set brutal ruffian caught him by his feet and threw his whole weight upon him" until he died. Mrs. Bayes, the wife of the second prisoner, fought off the attempt to lynch her husband, "like an infuriated beast."[13] When his turn came, however, the mob was too much for her, and he soon followed his accomplice. Thereafter, the town's authorities often took their prisoners to Fort Leavenworth, with the request that they be lodged in the guardhouse until the date of their trial.

In 1867, the gentle and compassionate Father de Smet was named by the federal government as envoy extraordinary to the Indians of the northern plains. Offered a large salary, all expenses, and the impressive title of major, the Jesuit refused any compensation other than his travel needs. Setting out from the Yankton Agency, 60 miles northwest of Sioux City, his small caravan included a Sioux interpreter, a guide, a horse trader, and a hunter. The priest was greeted warmly by the Indian tribes throughout his travels, and although he sat in council with over fifteen thousand Redmen, he accomplished little other than to write a blistering report of their complaints to the federal authorities. "It is always true," he wrote, "that if the savages sin against the whites it is because the whites have greatly sinned against them. . . . If the Indians become enraged against the whites it is because the whites have made them suffer a long time."[14]

Returning down the Missouri in July, the Jesuit paused for a visit at Fort Leavenworth, where he found a new peace commission recently appointed by President Andrew Johnson. Although weary from his four months of travel, he agreed to accompany this group back to the upper Missouri. Before leaving, however, the priest had to go to St. Louis to replenish his gear and wardrobe. In St. Louis, he was stricken with a fever diagnosed as Bright's disease and was unable to return up the river that year.

During the fifties, the steamboat navigation on the Missouri had kept pace with developments in other means of transportation. St. Louis had become the river hub of the nation, outstripping even New Orleans. After 1855, more steamers operated above St. Louis on the Missouri and Mississippi than between that city and New Orleans. An average of nearly a steamboat a day tied up at Fort Leavenworth in 1858.[15]

If not luxurious, the boats on the Missouri were at least comfortable, and a few rivaled the Mississippi steamers. One of those was the *A. B. Chambers*, whose pilot in 1859 was Mark Twain. Twain often came ashore at Fort Leavenworth and had many friends on the post. A side-wheeler with a low-lying hull, a huge superstructure and two tall, shiny, black smokestacks, the *Chambers* was considered the ultimate in elegance. Vestal describes it as looking like a gilded white wedding cake,[16] and no greater compliment could be paid to a new house in Kansas or Missouri than to say that it was as beautiful as the *Chambers*. The bottom deck was loaded with all types of freight, including horses, mules, Conestoga wagons, hogs, sheep, and coops of squawking chickens. From this deck, other goods were loaded into the hold by a windlass. The cabin, or middle deck, reserved for the passengers, was large and commodious. On the hurricane, or top deck, was the pilot house and the quarters of the ship's officers. Staterooms opened off the long salon on the cabin deck, and the floor was entirely covered with a deep-napped Brussels carpet. The sumptuous oil paintings, the gingerbread cornices, the heavy dark furniture, the gleaming glass prism chandeliers, and the gilded trimming on the walls combined to form an aura of luxury that was rare in America. Ladies were said to "just love" a trip on the *A. B. Chambers*.

The meals served at tables set up in the salon were a gastronomic orgy or, at the very least, an endurance contest. The old menus that have come down to us are beyond belief. At the noonday meal—called dinner—there were at least fifteen courses with numerous side dishes, and no one was given a choice but was served every item. In spite of the luxurious service, the profits for the owners of these boats were said to have been fabulous, equaling in a single season the cost of the steamboat. In some instances just one trip could pay back the original investment. It was on the *Chambers* that former Governor Andrew H. Reeder escaped from Kansas City in June, 1856. In that same year the *Chambers* sank near Atchison. It was raised, however, and continued in service until 1860 when, above the mouth of the Missouri, it again hit a sawyer and this time was a total loss.

Dr. William Lee tells in his journal of a trip from St. Louis to Fort Leavenworth in 1858 on the steamboat *Minnehaha:* "They had a band on board—and a nine-pounder whose business it was to salute every boat it meets. The eating is excellent, but the company bad. I got taken in very nicely at cards by a gentleman sharper who was with others put off the boat about midnight while it was raining cats and dogs after having fleeced the passengers."

On the night before landing at Fort Leavenworth, Dr. Lee noted, "We had a rousing big dinner with wines of all kinds furnished by the boat, in consequence of which everybody got tight and had a free fight towards night."

One of the steamboats that plied the Missouri at the time had a steam vent attached to organ pipes—the steam passing through a large perforated roll similar to that of a pianola. This steam organ played a number of national airs and could be heard for miles. It must have been wearing on the ears of the passengers, but it was considered a great new invention.

In October, 1860, a tall, angular, craggy-faced, homely man spent the night at Leavenworth. He was Abraham Lincoln, an obscure country lawyer, the candidate of the four-year-old Republican Party for President of the United States. The chances of success in his quest for the presidency against the better known Little Giant, Stephen A. Douglas, were not considered favorable. Lincoln's tenure of office would truly be a period that "would try men's souls" and this would nowhere be more true than at the little post in eastern Kansas.

CHAPTER TEN

》》》→←《《《

BLEEDING KANSAS

After five months of acrimonious debate, Congress passed the Kansas-Nebraska Act in May, 1854. On May 30, President Franklin Pierce gave the bill his approval. The Missouri Compromise was, in effect, replaced by popular or squatter sovereignty, for the people of the two newly created territories would themselves determine whether they would enter the Union as free or slave states. The passage of the Kansas-Nebraska Act finally sealed the division of the nation into North and South. Those above the Mason-Dixon line were bitter at what they felt was the betrayal of an agreement on the part of the South. Stephen Douglas, the author of the bill, acknowledged that he could travel from Boston to Chicago in the light of his burning effigies. Southerners knew that Missouri, a slave state, was but a river away from the new territory of Kansas, and could readily seize and control its government. The storm that ensued would plunge the territory of Kansas into a state of anarchy that would last for years—would subject it to a blood bath that would eventually sweep the nation and not end until Appomattox. In the vortex—in the eye of the hurricane—would be a little frontier post on the bank of the Missouri River.

The lands west of Missouri were now about to be opened to white settlement. No matter that by sacred treaty they had been ceded to the Indians, for "as long as the grass grows and the water flows." Promises had been made, but the nation's word had been given to mere savages, and the Great White Father in distant Washington would correct all that. Within a few months, new treaties had been forced upon the Redmen concerned, and hundreds of thousands of rich, loamy acres were now available.

As had been anticipated, the Missourians were not long in taking action. It was only necessary to stake out a plot of 160 acres, file a claim, agree to pay a $1.25 an acre and, after the land was surveyed by the government, erect some sort of an improvement, and the land was yours. Almost before the President's signature was dry, a steady stream of Missourians were streaking across the border and picking choice sites for themselves. Fourteen days after President Pierce approved the act, thirty-nine men at Weston organized the town of Leavenworth four miles from the post. By September, 1854, the village consisted of four tents and a lumber mill, but it had a newspaper which was being published near the levee under an elm. The editors lived in tents, cooked their meals over an open fire, and slept in hay on the ground. As reported in the first issue, September 15, 1854, the paper had been written "sitting on the ground with a big shingle on our knee for a table." Within eight months, Leavenworth could boast that it had a three-story hotel, a sawmill, a tailor shop, two shoemakers, a barber, two blacksmiths, a tin shop, five saloons, two grocery stores, five dry goods shops, a number of lawyers and physicians, and over a hundred houses.[1] The pro-slavery towns of Atchison and Lecompton were to follow.

Nor were the Free-Soilers from the North less active. Emigrants from the Middle West—Illinois, Ohio, and Indiana—began streaming into the new territory. In distant Boston, Eli Thayer founded an emigrant aid society for the purpose of recruiting and sending abolitionist settlers to Kansas, and, as befitted the frugal sons of the rocky soil of New England, at a profit to the association. The Free-Soil squatters settled the towns of Lawrence and Topeka, and later Osawatomie, Manhattan, and Wabaunsee. At first Lawrence was merely a collection of tents. Later these gave way to grass and thatched dwellings and a well-built hotel.

The Kansas-Nebraska Act had designated Fort Leavenworth as the temporary Capitol of the new territory. Already overcrowded, the fort was not impressed by the honor, and the post commander, Captain Franklin E. Hunt, protested to the War Department that there was not a building for such a purpose. Convinced, the Secretary of War, Jefferson Davis, advised the newly appointed Governor, Andrew H. Reeder, that the public buildings at Fort

Leavenworth "are barely sufficient for the wants of the military service, and that . . . no part or portion of them can be spared for the purpose contemplated by the Act. I will remark that this Post is a Depot of great importance to the military service and must continue for some years to come."[2]

The protests of Captain Hunt and Secretary Davis were to no avail, and Governor Reeder arrived by steamer to set up his administration at the post on October 7, 1854. In his entourage were his secretary, G. P. Lowery, and Andrew J. Isacks, the United States Attorney for the territory. He was hospitably received by Captain Hunt, who held a reception for the governor that afternoon, attended not only by the officers of the post but by settlers from Salt Creek Valley.

Andrew Reeder had been a successful lawyer in Easton, Pennsylvania. His father, a second-generation American, had served as a boy in the Revolutionary Army. Although a Democrat, Governor Reeder was violently pro-Free-Soil, but he was nevertheless cordially received by the slavery advocates.

During the fifty days that Reeder remained at Fort Leavenworth, he lived in a suite of rooms in a brick building on the east side of Sumner Place; his executive offices were a large room in a one-story brick building at the northeast corner of the same square, the present site of Pope Hall.[3] John A. Halderman, later to be named the governor's secretary, described the room's furnishing as "consisting of a few chairs, a writing table, some boxes used as bookcases and covered with newspapers for seating visitors, a letter press, a stove and some other rude contrivances."[4]

Governor Reeder had been at the post only a few days when he set out on a tour of the eastern part of the territory. He wanted to inform himself on the topography and population of his domain, map out fair election districts, and name officials for the balloting that would soon take place.

There was now a total of 8,500 white men, women, and children in the territory. Of the 2,900 white males of voting age, over sixty percent had been born in slave states and, accordingly, the pro-slavery forces had a clear majority.

In the first election, held on November 29, 1854, General John W. Whitfield received a decisive majority over his Free-Soil opponent, John A. Wakefield, for election as the territory's first delegate to Congress. There were some pro-slavery Missourians, "border ruffians," as the Free-Soilers called them, who crossed the river and voted in the Kansas election. However, their numbers were insignificant and there were no great protests.

Such was not the case with the election of members of the territorial legislature that followed. Both of the contending groups realized that upon the makeup of this body might depend the decision as to whether Kansas was admitted as a slave or as a free state. Long before the day of election, excitement had reached a fever pitch. There were rallies, processions, and continuous meetings, none of which probably changed a vote.

Unquestionably the Southerners could have won the election fairly, but they were not taking any chances, and they over-reached themselves. Arrangements were made to import thousands of Missourians from across the border and illegally vote them in the election. On election day, "an invading force of 5,000 entered Kansas. They came on horseback, in wagons and carriages—an unkempt, sun-dried, picturesque mob, armed with shotguns, revolvers and bowie knives, and generously supplied with whiskey."[5] General Benjamin F. Stringfellow told a group of the invaders as they were about to leave Missouri, "I advise you one and all to enter every election district in Kansas, in defiance of Reeder and his vile myrmidons and vote at the point of the bowie knife and the revolver."[6] This they did, to the accompaniment of the cocking of pistols and the brandishing of knives in every polling place, except four, in the new territory.

The results were foreordained. A large majority of the representatives elected were pro-slavery, but the outcome was not to be as the Southern Party had anticipated. With a voting registration of 2,900, a total of 6,300 ballots had been cast. An indignant cry of fraud swept the North. There had also been instances of illegal voting on the part of the New England adherents: a group of Free-Soilers had arrived the day before the election and had been allowed to vote, though clearly ineligible. But the great preponderance of fraud had been committed by the Southerners, and the Northern part of the nation girded itself for conflict. The enlistment of Free-Soil emigrants was stepped up. In churches throughout New England and New York, collections were taken to buy weapons for the Northern settlers in Kansas. The offerings raised by the Brooklyn preacher, Henry Ward Beecher, for the purchase of Sharp's rifles, were so large that they were thereafter called "Beecher's Bibles." Bloody warfare in Kansas had become inevitable.

Almost as an anticlimax, protests of fraud were carried to the governor from six of the fourteen districts in which the Missourians had voted. In these precincts, Reeder, after hearings, ordered a new election, but the results could not materially affect the pro-slavery makeup of the legislature. The Free-Soilers answered by refusing even to recognize the *de facto* status of the new governing body.

Meanwhile, Governor Reeder had moved his Capitol from Fort Leavenworth to Shawnee Methodist Mission, where there were more commodious accommodations. He called the legislature to meet at Pawnee, a few miles east of Fort Riley and 125 miles from the Missouri border, where the town company had agreed to erect a stone building for the use of the lawmakers. Before designating Pawnee as the new capital, Reeder had acquired some town lots for himself. These unwise purchases were not only to be used as a vehicle for his ouster, but would haunt him for the rest of his days.

The months between the election and the convening of the legislature were tense. There were a few killings—Cole McCrea, a Free-Soiler, killed Malcolm Clark, a pro-slaver, over a land-claim dispute on Salt Creek. But aside from several such incidents, an uneasy peace prevailed between the two contending groups.

The town of Leavenworth continued to grow. The new hotel was constantly filled to capacity. Russell, Majors, and Waddell, the stagecoach operators, moved their headquarters from Weston to Leavenworth and built a huge blacksmith shop to service their thousands of wagons. The firm was later to employ six thousand teamsters and own forty thousand oxen, and every month trans-port thousands of tons of freight across the Plains. The steamboat trip from St. Louis now took only four days, and each passage brought new emigrants with their trunks and carpetbags. Boxes arrived from the East marked farm machinery or books, and were forwarded to Lawrence, although their contents more often were "Beecher's Bibles."

The legislature which met on July 2, 1855, was as much given to excesses as had been the pro-slavery strategists at the May election. It unseated all of the Free-Soil representatives but two, who resigned. Martin Conway, revealing the strategy of the Free-Soilers, wrote in his letter of resignation that he refused to participate in a legislature "derogatory to the respectability of popular government. I shall yield no submission to this alien legislature. On the contrary I am ready to set its assumed authority at defiance, and shall be prompt to spurn and trample under my feet its insolvent enactments, whenever they conflict with my rights or inclinations."[7]

Accommodations both in Leavenworth and in Lawrence were still primitive. Mrs. Charles Robinson, wife of an agent of the New England Emigrant Aid Society, found a rattlesnake coiled under her stove for warmth, and another pioneer couple found one snuggled between them in bed. At Pawnee, the accommodations were even less desirable. There were only several half-finished shacks, and a legislative hall without windows or doors. The statesmen, living in tents, were forced to cook their meals over open fires, and often slept under the stars. The only things plentiful, reported James Christian, were "rocky mounds and highly rectified whiskey."[8] After four days at Pawnee, during which time they assured themselves of unanimity, they adjourned for ten days, over Governor Reeder's veto, to reconvene at Shawnee Mission. The legislature continued its excesses by enacting a slavery statute that was the most rigorous in America. Residents of the territory could be sent to jail for reading a paper or magazine of pro-Free-Soil sentiment; they could be disenfranchised for refusing to take an oath to support the Fugitive Slave Act; their property could be confiscated for questioning the right of slave holding; and capital punishment was made the penalty for aiding in the escape of a slave. They also memorialized President Pierce to remove Governor Reeder, which he did on July 31.

The new governor, Wilson Shannon, arrived at Fort Leavenworth on September 1, 1855, and went into conference with Colonel Hunt to determine the support he might expect from the military. As governor, Shannon, by trying to remain neutral, would earn the hatred of both factions.

Meeting at Big Springs, a four-cabin trading post on the Oregon Trail west of Lawrence, on September 5, 1885, the Free-Soil Party determined that it would ignore the enactment of what it called an alien legislature, form its own government of the territory, and apply for admission as a state.

The constitutional convention subsequently called by the Free-Soilers, although without legal sanction, met at Topeka on November 11. Andrew Reeder, who had returned to Kansas, was present, as was Dr. Charles Robinson, the agent of the New England Aid Society. The sessions were dominated by James H. Lane, a spellbinder who had recently come to the territory after a political defeat in Indiana.

The constitution prepared at Topeka was submitted to the people of the territory on December 15, in a mock election. With the pro-slavers abstaining, the constitution received 1,731 favorable votes to forty-six opposed. At a later election on January 15, 1856, which the Southerners ignored, Dr. Robinson was named governor and a unanimously Free-Soil legislature was selected. Kansas thus had two governments, with the Free-Soilers in open rebellion against the legally constituted authority.

During the preceding November, in a land dispute at Hickory Point, about ten miles from Lawrence, F. M. Coleman, a pro-slavery adherent, had killed a Free-Soiler, Charles M. Dow. Subsequently, Coleman, claiming self-defense and asking protection, surrendered to the governor at Shawnee Mission. Angered at the killer's supposed escape, a mob from Lawrence, led by Jacob Branson, a friend of the slain man, burned the homes of a number of slavery men in the neighborhood. A warrant was issued for Branson's arrest. Sheriff Samuel J. Jones set out with a posse from Shawnee Mission for Hickory Point and placed Branson under arrest. While returning to the capital, they were met by a group of Jayhawkers armed with Sharp's rifles, who rescued Branson.

There had been open defiance of the law by the Free-Soil Party, not only in the establishment of its own government but in the freeing of Branson. Governor Shannon knew he must take action, that open flouting of the territorial laws would only lead to civil war. He hoped, however, to avoid bloodshed, and believed that a sufficient show of force would result in a capitulation of the Free-Soilers of Lawrence. He accordingly called out the militia to support the sheriff and his posse. Fifteen hundred angry pro-slavery militiamen, mostly Missourians, were soon encamped around Leavenworth and Lecompton, and on the Wakarusa River. Their openly avowed intentions were the capture and destruction of Lawrence.

Shannon was not long in realizing that his militia was but an angry mob, and that he had no control over his own officers. On December 1, he crossed the border to Kansas City, the nearest telegraph office, and sent a wire to President Pierce asking for the authority to call upon Colonel Sumner, then commanding Fort Leavenworth, for the necessary troops to "protect the Sheriff of Douglas County in executing the laws and preserving the peace and good order of the Territory." The governor advised Colonel Sumner of the message.

Unfortunately for Kansas, the wires were down between Lexington and Jefferson City, and a reply was delayed for three days. On December 4, the President advised Governor Shannon that federal troops would be supplied as soon as Secretary of War Davis could issue the necessary orders. Meanwhile, Sumner had put his troops on the alert, but he refused to budge until he had received instructions from the War Department. The orders never came.

Believing that an attack was imminent and that only he might prevent it, Shannon, in the company of Colonel Nathan Boone, a grandson of Daniel Boone, went to Lawrence to talk with the insurgents. His problems there were further complicated by an engagement that had been fought between two small groups of the opposing forces, resulting in the death of Thomas Barber, a popular Free-Soiler. The free-state men refused the governor's request that they give up their Sharp's rifles, but with their fingers crossed, they did promise to respect legal process within Lawrence. This, Shannon felt, was sufficient to justify directing his pro-slavery militia to disperse and go home. Two developments speeded their departure. The whiskey had run out, and the weather was biting cold. The Missourians, in motley array, left their bivouac on the Wakarusa and headed east.

The chilling weather continued. On Christmas day it was thirty degrees below zero, and there were, consequently, a few weeks of comparative quiet. However, on January 15, a Southerner named Cook was killed at Easton, a Free-Soil community eight miles west of Leavenworth, and a few days later at Kickapoo, in retaliation, a New Englander, Reese Brown, was ruthlessly murdered with a hatchet by a group of Missourians calling themselves the Rangers.

It is almost impossible now to sift the facts and arrive at an objective conclusion as to the degree of right and wrong of either side in the reign of terror that swept eastern Kansas after the Brown killing; most of the history of Kansas has been written by scholars with Northern antecedents. The large Eastern newspapers of the day were violently partisan and printed nothing unfavorable to the Free-Soilers. Consequently, those upholding slavery have come down to us as cutthroats and thugs. Both factions had much wrong and some right on their side. The members of the Free-Soil Party, although standing for an ultimately better Kansas, were fanatical, with only contempt for the rule of law. The Pro-Slavery Party, favoring an evil institution, met violence with violence. Murder became a way of life in the territory. An officer returning the short distance to the fort from the town of Leavenworth reported seeing three dead men by the side of the road.

Colonel Sumner finally received the long delayed orders from the War Department authorizing Governor Shannon to use federal troops. They were soon put into effect. Contrary to their promise, the citizens of Lawrence had roughly handled Sheriff Jones and a posse that had gone to arrest Sam Wood and other members of the gang that had freed Branson. From his capital, now at Lecompton, the governor called upon the military for help, and a detachment of ten dragoons under the command of Lieutenant James McIntosh was dispatched to accompany Jones back to Lawrence and then assist him in the performance of his duties. Much to the annoyance of the town's housewives, the troopers spent the day searching house after house for the fugitives. When night fell and it began to rain heavily, they called off the search and bivouacked on the edge of town.

In a woods nearby, a group of Free-Soilers had gathered and the sounds of voices and an occasional shot were heard. At West Point, Lieutenant McIntosh had not been given a course in civil disturbance, and he ignored what he thought were noisy celebrators. He was soon to regret his lack of concern. One of the shots had seriously wounded Sheriff Jones. A chastened lieutenant and his detail returned to Fort Leavenworth with the wounded sheriff.

Former Governor Reeder was the next to make news. In May, a grand jury indicted him "for treason and inciting to riot." With the help of citizens in Lawrence, he twice defied Israel B. Donelson, a United States marshal who had been sent to arrest him. Fearing that the next official might be accompanied by the military, he fled Kansas. In Missouri, he hid in the Kansas City American House for two weeks. Then, donning a dirty shirt and blue denims, pulling a battered straw hat well down over his burnt-cork-smeared face, stuffing a clay pipe in his mouth, and carrying an ax, he was able to elude his pursuers and secure passage on the steamboat *A. B. Chambers*. Brushing the mud of Kansas from his boots, Reeder returned to Easton, Pennsylvania, where he resumed the practice of law.

Violence continued in Kansas; Lawrence was sacked on May 31, 1856. Sheriff Jones, now recovered, with a posse of pro-slavery adherents, destroyed the press and type of the town's newspaper, *The Herald of Freedom*, and burned the Free State Hotel and the home of Dr. Charles Robinson. While only one fatality occurred (when a wall of the burning hotel fell on a Southerner), the attack stirred indignation throughout the country. That Lawrence had defied the federal government for months was conveniently ignored.

John Brown was next to occupy the stage. Following the news of the Lawrence incident, he set out with his sons, Watson, Oliver, and Frederick; his son-in-law, Henry Thompson; and three Free-Soilers, James Townsley, Theodore Wiener, and a man called Bondi. Armed with razor-sharp cutlasses, they headed for Potawatomie Creek where, during the night, they murdered James Doyle; his two sons, William and Drury; and Allen Wilkinson and William Sherman. The bodies, found the next day, had been mutilated. There was indignation in Kansas and Missouri over these senseless murders, but the killings were practically ignored by the Eastern press.

Brown's murders were followed by burnings, lootings, and killings from one end of Kansas to the other. Marauding gangs of both factions ranged the countryside, committing crimes and atrocities. On June 5, the governor alerted Colonel Sumner, advising him that the two contending forces were preparing for combat at Palmyra. Sumner left Fort Leavenworth with a detachment of cavalry and arrived in time to force the two factions to give up their prisoners and return to their homes.

In late June, President Pierce issued a proclamation directing that the Topeka legislature should not be permitted to meet on July 4 as scheduled. The President's message was received with open defiance, and plans for the session continued. On July 3, acting on the governor's orders, Colonel Sumner arrived near Topeka with five companies of dragoons and two pieces of artillery. On the morning of the 4th, he lined up his troops along the street in front of Constitution Hall, where the solons were to meet.[9] Entering the building, he told the assembled members of the legislature, "I am called upon this day to perform the most painful duty of my whole life. God knows that I have no party feeling in this matter and will hold none as long as I occupy my present position. Under the authority of the President's Proclamation I am here to disperse this legislature and therefore to inform you that you cannot meet." In answer to a question from one of the representatives, the colonel replied, "I shall use all the force at my command to carry out my orders."

The Topeka legislature did not meet, but in distant Washington there was a violent reaction. As a result of Sumner's actions, an aroused Northern majority in Congress held up the War Department's Appropriation Act. They would not pass the bill, they said, "unless it carried a proviso that the army should not be used in putting down Free-Soil men in the Territory of Kansas."[10] Facing the prospect of an unpaid army, Secretary Davis made Sumner the goat, although the colonel's orders had come from Washington. Sumner was relieved of his command, and in late August a mollified Congress passed the army's act.

Colonel Persifor F. Smith succeeded Sumner at Fort Leavenworth. A Princeton graduate, a former Louisiana lawyer, and a veteran of the Seminole War, Smith was "a simple, scholarly, unassuming man,"[11] of great ability and clear perception. In July, he refused a request of Governor Shannon to march against a group of four hundred emigrants encamped near Nebraska City. Smith insisted the group was unarmed and peaceful, and he was later proven to be right.

Other violent events now followed in rapid succession. In August, Jim Lane, who had taken the title of general, burned the blockhouse, the post office, and the hotel at Fort Franklin. Fort Titus, a Southern strong-point near Lecompton, was subsequently captured and burned by another group of Free-Soilers.

Governor Shannon finally went to Lawrence in August and bargained with the Free-Soil Party. They agreed to return a cannon captured at the sacking of Lawrence, and to turn over some men they had been holding prisoner since the Fort Franklin attack. The governor promised to release a group of captives taken after the capture of Fort Titus. Upon his return to Lecompton, Shannon wrote to Colonel Smith asking for help, and advising him that eight hundred well-armed men were assembled in Lawrence with the intention of attacking the capital.

But Shannon had had it. He sent in his resignation to the President, and without waiting for a replacement, left the territory. A year later, he wrote, "Govern Kansas in 1855 and 1856! You might as well attempt to govern the Devil in Hell." Daniel Woodson, the secretary of state of the territory, became acting governor and was succeeded on September 9 by John W. Geary.

When the new governor disembarked at Fort Leavenworth, he found the one orderly and peaceful spot he was to see in Kansas. The post was crowded, however, for a number of Free-Soil families from Leavenworth City had sought and received refuge on the post. The next morning, when the new governor left for Lecompton, he was accompanied by Lieutenant Richard Drum and a small detail of enlisted men.

With the help of Colonel Cooke from Fort Riley, Geary was able to avert any attack by Free-Soilers at Lecompton. A pro-slavery body of militia, called to active duty by acting Governor Woodson and about to attack Lawrence again, was persuaded by the governor to disband and return home. A few months of comparative peace followed, but Geary also paid the price of being hated by both factions. After the inauguration of President James Buchanan on March 4, 1857, Geary resigned and left Kansas to be succeeded by Robert J. Walker.

A native Philadelphian and a grandson of Benjamin Franklin (his mother was a Bache), but a resident of Mississippi, Walker had been elected to the United States Senate from that state. He was, with the possible exception of Geary, the ablest of the territorial governors of Kansas. Walker had been assured of President Buchanan's full cooperation. One of his stipulations had been that Brigadier General William S. Harney be put in command of all federal troops in the territory.

Harney, a Tennessee-born officer, had entered the army in 1818 on a direct commission as a lieutenant in the 19th Infantry. During the Seminole War, with the rank of lieutenant colonel, he led the 2nd Dragoons in the deadly Everglade swamps. A giant in strength and standing over six feet tall, Harney was a man of violent disposition who would "brook no nonsense," and while actually feared by many of his subordinates, he nonetheless commanded the grudging admiration of both his officers and his men. Called the "Great White Chief" by the Indians because of his flowing white hair and beard, the general was also greatly respected among the tribes; they said that he and Father de Smet were the "only white men they ever knew who talked sense and told the truth." Harney was an excellent choice for this assignment. He told Governor Walker, "Kansas has been the graveyard of every Governor and General sent there, and I do not intend it to be mine."

In July, at the governor's request, Harney with three hundred dragoons from Fort Leavenworth, went to Lawrence, where Walker said an act of rebellion had been committed in the town's refusal to organize as a city under a charter granted by the legislature. The general found that there was little to be accomplished by force and returned to the fort.

Incidents were to continue throughout the territory, but they became fewer and fewer. The elections that followed were carefully supervised by the military, and there were fewer charges of fraud. The Free-Soilers elected a majority of the legislature, and that signaled the end of the Southerners' hope of a slave-holding Kansas. The curtain was slowly rung down on the territorial prelude to the Civil War.

In spite of the troubles of Bleeding Kansas and the ever-present Indian threats, there were diversions and entertainments for those who lived on the post. Lieutenant George D. Bayard, who six years later was to die in the battle of Fredericksburg, Virginia, wrote in a letter in 1856:

I have enjoyed myself during the holidays very well. There have been balls and parties without number and many pretty ladies from Weston, St. Joseph, and other places. In short, life in Kansas is not so barbarous after all. There were two balls in Leavenworth City on New Year's eve. One was at

the Planter House, and one at McCracken's Hotel, the former
pro-slavery and the latter free-state. Most of the officers went
to both, but as all my lady acquaintances were at the Planter's
House I remained there. We left at five in the morning to
go to reveille. I am told that even at the Planter's House
there were more free-state ladies than there were pro-slavery
ladies. All agree that the ladies from Lawrence fully maintained
their reputation for beauty. The fact is that the free-state settlers outnumber all others five to one, and there is about
as little chance of this being a slave state as there is of my
flying in the air.

Soldiers, whether on the plains of Kansas or in a modern ghetto,
are reluctant to be pitted against their fellow citizens. Those at
Fort Leavenworth had not liked their role in the Kansas troubles,
and this, it would appear, was most unfortunate. Had Governor
Reeder been given the full use of federal troops from the start,
had he thrown out the entire fraudulent election of March, 1855,
and conducted another under military supervision, there might
have been considerably less blood spilled in the territory of Kansas.
It is also true that under such circumstances, Kansas might well
have come into the Union as a slave state, for the Southerners
did, at first, have a majority of the qualified voters. Perhaps the
Kansas blood bath was necessary for the ultimate cleansing of our
body politic—one of the prices that had to be paid for the final
destruction of the evil of slavery.

CHAPTER ELEVEN

>>>>—>—<—<<<

THE CIVIL WAR

The vibrations of the guns at Charleston, South Carolina, that opened fire on Fort Sumter on April 12, 1861, carried almost a thousand miles to the distant fort on the Missouri River. Situated between the predominantly pro-slavery people of eastern Kansas and the Southerners of western Missouri, Fort Leavenworth was an island in a sea of Copperheads. It remained the only hope of denying to the Confederacy the states of Missouri and Kansas and the resources of the West, and preventing the breaching of the Union's overland access to California.

The post at the time was garrisoned by several under-strength companies of the 2nd Infantry and the 2nd Dragoons. Its reduction by a few Confederate regiments maneuvering in friendly country could have been a comparatively simple operation, and would have inevitably resulted in the fall of Forts Riley and Laramie, for which it was a supply center. Besides its strategic importance, its arsenal contained huge stocks of ordnance stores.

Fortunately for the Union, the Confederate government did not move promptly, and General Harney, Commander of the Army of the West at St. Louis, realizing the importance of the post, telegraphed the War Department on April 8: "Under existing conditions and in view of the large amount of public property at Fort Leavenworth, I consider it very important that the garrison should be reinforced, and request authority to order to that Post two companies of artillery from Fort Randall,[1] and two companies of infantry from Fort Kearny."[2] Secretary of War Simon Cameron agreed, and two days later, Harney was able to issue orders to

Colonel Dixon S. Miles of the 2nd Infantry to proceed with his headquarters and two companies of his regiment to Fort Leavenworth. Similarly, orders were dispatched to Forts Randall and Ridgely.[3] Miles and his detachment of 165 officers and men marched from Fort Kearny to Omaha, a distance of 185 miles, in eight-and-a-half days, and there he waited four days for a steamer.[4] Intelligence was received that the boat was to be attacked while passing St. Joseph, but this information proved to be false; Miles arrived at Fort Leavenworth without incident on April 30 and assumed command of the post. With the troops from Fort Randall it was another story. There were no steamers available, and they had to proceed part of the way by rail. A report was current that a plan was afoot to attack the detachment at St. Joseph, so the president of the St. Joseph and Hannibal Railroad refused to allow the troops to be transported over his line.[5] The railroad did finally agree to carry the laundresses, their children, and a few sick to St. Joseph, but the troops were forced to march from Omaha to Marengo, Iowa, a distance of 175 miles, where they took a train west by way of Chicago.[6]

Colonel Miles learned when he arrived at the fort that ten days previously, an armed body of men had seized and looted the ordnance depot at Liberty. There was considerable apprehension, particularly in the city of Leavenworth, that a similar attack would be made on the fort, and Mayor James L. McDowell, although he had previously supported the pro-slavery faction, offered Captain William Steel, then in command, the services of a hundred men to assist in its defense. The offer was accepted and the additional men remained there overnight.

The following morning, Captain Jesse Lee Reno succeeded Captain Peter V. Hagner in the command of the arsenal. A West Point graduate of 1836, Reno was not only a strict disciplinarian but something of a martinet. He was later to be killed in the battle of South Mountain, prior to Antietam, under circumstances that led many to believe that he had been shot by his own troops. When he got to Fort Leavenworth, Reno began to fear that the citizens of Missouri might attack the arsenal, and he persuaded Captain Steel to call upon Governor Robinson of Kansas for assistance. Three companies of 120 militiamen from the nearby town, known as the Leavenworth Light Infantry, the Union Guards and the Shields Guards, and commanded by Captains Powell Clayton, Edward Cozzens, and Daniel McCook, were ordered to the fort, where they remained until the arrival of Colonel Miles. The new commander was somewhat critical of Steel's action and reported to Washington: "This defective organization I instantly disbanded. If I have a necessity for more troops than I now command, I shall accept none but those organized as a present Infantry Company." Miles did, however, have Captain Reno dispatch a courteous letter of thanks to the three militia captains.

Miles himself was to develop considerable apprehension for the safety not only of his own post but for Fort Kearny as well. On May 10, he wrote to Colonel Edward D. Townsend in Washington[7] that the pro-secessionist governor of Missouri had established a permanent camp near St. Joseph where eight companies were being trained. This force was armed with ordnance, including two iron cannons taken from the Liberty arsenal. "Should Missouri secede," he wrote, "not a doubt, but offensive operations against this Post will be attempted—if informed of additional ones [troops at St. Joseph] arriving, I shall without hesitation call on the Governor of the State of Kansas for one or two regiments of infantry to assist in the defense of this place and the towns on the right bank of the Missouri River." The colonel also suggested in his letter that the rebel troops at St. Joseph might be used in "a sudden foray on Fort Kearny, where there were large stores of ordnance supplies."

On May 17, Miles again reported on the camp near St. Joseph, this time to Captain Seth Williams, assistant adjutant general, Department of the West at St. Louis. He wrote that one Captain V. Nichols had advised him that there were seven to eight hundred men at the camp under the command of Colonel Jeff Thompson. Miles recommended that "When the Kansas Regts. are mustered into service [he] be allowed with one or more to take possession of St. Joe and capture this camp, and then [have] the privilege of mustering into service the home guard—giving [them] the necessary arms and munitions of war to enable them to protect themselves, the town, and keep open the Railroad connection at its western terminus."[8]

The installation near St. Joseph had been abandoned, and Colonel Miles had left for the East in late May to be succeeded on June 8

by Major Samuel D. Sturgis before any action was taken.⁹ Sturgis
had arrived with the 1st Cavalry after deactivating Forts Smith,
Gibson, Washita, and Cobb. On the march to Fort Leavenworth,
the troops had barely eluded a large Confederate force.

Short, thickset, and with a head of bushy, curly black hair, Sam
Sturgis was one of the real army characters of the last century.
His famous words a year later when he was given an order that
he thought had originated with his commanding officer, General
John Pope, "I don't give a pinch of owl dung for John Pope,"
was remembered for years in army circles. Pompous and arrogant,
Sturgis was nevertheless a man of action.

Two days after assuming command of the post, he sent Captain
Alfred Sully, with four companies of infantry and two pieces of
artillery, to St. Joseph.¹⁰ The son of America's greatest portrait
painter, Thomas Sully, the captain, a slight sensitive man, was
not only a competent officer but a realist. Traveling by steamboat,
he arrived at St. Joseph on June 9. He was joined the next day
by Captain Francis Armstrong and a company of dragoons which
had ridden overland from the fort. There was much excitement
in the town when the Stars and Stripes were run up in front of
the local hotel.¹¹ Sully was not so sanguine as to the possibility
of the militia's taking over after he left, and successfully defending
the town. He wrote Sturgis, "There are men called 'home guards'
(about 150 of them) who will take their arms and live in their
houses and when the troops are withdrawn the Secesh fellows
will take their arms away. . . . Nothing but a permanent occupation
of St. Joe with force will hold it. The Seceshers have more vim
than the Union men [and] will wipe them out one of these days."¹²

During his short tour, Sturgis also established Camp Union at
Kansas City, which was under the command of Captain William
E. Prince,¹³ a cold and meticulous New Englander. On June
13, learning that a force of eight hundred rebels was encamped
two miles west of Independence, Prince ordered Captain David
F. Stanley, who later in the war as a major general won the Congressional Medal of Honor, on an armed reconnaissance to locate the
enemy. Stanley found them, and while conferring under a flag
of truce, was shot at by the rebels. Colonel Holiday, the Confederate
commander, and two of his officers were killed, but Stanley and
his men effectively withdrew. Captain Prince set out the same

day from Camp Union with three companies of the 1st Infantry, two companies of recruits, riflemen, and dragoons, including a section of artillery; two companies of the 1st Cavalry and a company of the 2nd Dragoons—a total strength of 521 officers and men—to find and destroy the enemy. Upon the approach of the Union troops, the rebels abandoned their camp and withdrew to Independence, followed by Prince. There the captain concluded that the enemy was falling back to meet reinforcements coming from Lexington, so he retraced his steps and returned with his force to Camp Union.[14]

Similar detachments were sent to various other towns in Missouri and southern Kansas. Generally the detail would remain long enough to enroll, arm, and train a home guard, and then return to Fort Leavenworth.

Meanwhile, a group of raw recruits took one matter into their own hands. Their conduct, while not testifying to their discipline, certainly did justice to their zeal, and the fire fight that followed their escapade is considered by some to have been one of the first land engagements of the Civil War.

The 1st Kansas Regiment (infantry) mustered into the army at Fort Leavenworth on May 30, 1861, and went into camp at a spot about halfway between the post and the city. Shortly after they arrived, a group of the enlisted men learned that a company of rebel cavalry was being organized and were flying a Confederate flag across the Missouri River at Iatan, a few miles from Fort Leavenworth. Not having been issued any arms, they could not do much until June 3, when a group of the soldiers secured some minnie rifles and ammunition. That same night, twelve of the enlisted men crossed the river in two skiffs and, as the rebel flag was being raised the next morning, the men seized it and took off. Caught off guard, it was some minutes before the Confederates were in pursuit, and the Union men were well on their way to the Kansas shore. Two of the soldiers from Fort Leavenworth received severe leg wounds from the Iatan sharpshooters.

Magnified many times and with the complexities that civil strife can add, most of the problems of the Mexican War arose again. Fort Leavenworth once more became the staging area and training center of the West. Thousands of volunteers arrived daily from Kansas, were mustered into service, equipped, trained, and sent

East. Camp Lincoln was established on the reservation for the accommodation of these arriving hordes, and in its tents and on its drill fields many a callow farm lad received his first taste of soldiering. Surplus ordnance, supplies, and troops were brought from western posts, whose companies were ordered to the Army of the Potomac by way of Fort Leavenworth.

Persistent demands for aid and protection were coming in constantly from citizens in nearby Missouri. As the hate engendered by the war increased, the predominant Southern sympathizers of that state gave their Union neighbors short shrift.[15] Some of these appeals were met, but there were not enough troops to satisfy them all. Determining which were authentic and which were based on fantasy or rumor became a daily responsibility of the post commander.

The Missouri River steamboats had to be supervised constantly, for often their owners, captains, and pilots were Southern sympathizers, and there were many ways in which their boats could be used to aid the rebel cause. Permits were required for passage both up and down the river and constant inspections of the boats were made.[16]

Senator Jim Lane and Lincoln's first, often corrupt, and always politically minded Secretary of War, Simon Cameron, did not make things any easier for the harassed officers at Fort Leavenworth.[17] Believing that to the victor belong the spoils, they maintained that all civilian employees on the post should be deserving Republicans and arbitrarily named party workers to all the jobs. Clerks, trainmasters, farmers, ordnance keepers, and sutlers with years of experience had to be discharged. Their places were filled by men whose sole competence had been their ability to produce a few additional votes for Lincoln and Hamlin and the other Republican candidates.

Separating the sheep from the goats among the residents of western Missouri and eastern Kansas became a daily problem for Captain Prince, now commanding the post. Just how could one tell who was a loyal Union man and who favored secession? Many citizens seized the opportunity to denounce their enemies as rebels, while others, proclaiming their fervent loyalty to the federal Government, quietly helped the foes of the Republic. Each case had to be considered separately and investigated carefully. There was not always time for adequate inquiries, and many mistakes were made. Affidavits, which were relied upon principally, often proved worthless—their preparation a waste of time.

As more and more civilian arrests were made, the stockade took on the appearance of a camp itself. Those accused of treason or suspected of spying for the rebels in Kansas and Missouri were brought to Leavenworth for safekeeping. Often prisoners were held for months without being brought to trial or even formally charged with a crime. Friends of the accused put constant pressure on the post commander for their release. Thus on September 28, the Masons of Platte City petitioned for the release of Brother John G. Rapp, accused of treason.[18] They maintained he could not possibly be opposing the Union. On October 18, R. A. Ringo and F. B. Moore, M.D., petitioned for the release of Dr. John W. Ringo, whose wife was about to have a baby and being "troubled with another disease, requires the constant attention of a physician."[19]

As in any war, particularly during civil strife, the lack of security often brought disaster. With civilians constantly coming and going at the fort, the rebels were kept informed of the Federals' every move. In July, an important wagon train, carrying much-needed supplies, had to be held up for a considerable time because its proposed routes had been disclosed in the Leavenworth City newspaper, and a rebel force had been sent to intercept it.[20]

Union officers might be convinced in their own minds that certain civilians were Confederate spies, yet be without sufficient evidence for a conviction. Not willing to take chances, they would throw the suspect into the guardhouse and forget him. On September 12, Captain M. P. Berry, a volunteer officer commanding Camp Union, sent a group of prisoners to Fort Leavenworth, "Two of which I have reason to believe are Confederate spies, Van Horn and McAuley, the latter of which I am informed went some time since from the Pike's Peak Gold region to San Antonio, Texas. He now represents himself as having walked from the Rocky Mountains, yet I have no direct proof."

The panic that swept the North after Bull Run on July 21 almost resulted in the death of Fort Leavenworth. The aged and decrepit commander of the army, General Winfield Scott, concluded that the federal government was not capable of fighting a two-front war—could not defend both the East and the West. He recommended that all western posts be abandoned, and that all troops be concentrated in the East. Fortunately for both the nation and the fort, the General's plan was ultimately rejected, but the final decision was made more on political than on military considerations.

Discipline among raw volunteer troops had always been difficult to maintain, and this was never more true than in western Missouri and eastern Kansas in the year 1861. Boys who had been raised since infancy in the belief that pro-slavery sympathizers were the incarnation of the devil were not inclined to show compassion when dealing with their enemies. Many could recall the killings and house-burnings of the Missourians during the days of "Bloody Kansas" only a few years before. In spite of all that the regular officers could do, looting and house-burning became the order of the day with the volunteer Union troops. Often there was little discrimination made between the property of Union and of rebel families. Nor were the German troops from St. Louis, "the wild Dutchmen," any less vindictive against the foes of the Republic.

Captain Prince, while still at Camp Union, was particularly plagued with this problem, which he had anticipated, but "not its extent." Finally when the home of H. S. Storm, of Independence, a former New York resident, a staunch Union man, and a nephew of General Storm, was looted and burned, leaving his family destitute, the captain took action,[21] meteing out stiff punishment to the participants. He was hopeful that the severity of the sentences would act as a deterrent to looting, but it seemed to have little or no effect.

At Fort Leavenworth, the post commander got a steady stream of complaints and demands for reimbursements, the senders all avowing that they were steadfast Union men. On July 29, R. S. Migg, a planter from nearby Independence wrote that in his absence a steamboat, *The White Cloud*, loaded with United States troops —Germans from St. Louis—had approached his landing and been fired upon by "a party of men who had gathered for this purpose, afterwards mounted their horses and made off, but the boat withdrew to the far side of the river and opened fire" on his house with cannon balls and shells. When they were satisfied that the hill was cleared, the Union soldiers "landed and entered the house and carried off such goods as they desired and set fire to the houses and left." Migg charged that the officers were equally involved, and he was probably right.[22] Such acts by both Confederate and Union troops were to continue during the succeeding years of the war, and western Missouri and eastern Kansas came to know total war.

The chaos and confusion along the Missouri was often utilized by criminals as a cloak for their activities. Unorganized bushwhackers from Missouri would cross the river and pillage farms in Kansas. Captain A. W. Williams, a volunteer officer of the 8th Regiment of Kansas Volunteers stationed at Iowa Point, Kansas, reported that on November 24 he had been unable to overtake a party of twenty-four Jayhawkers from Kansas "commanded by one Chandler, who had stolen some twenty-five horses, clothing, silver spoons, etc.", all under the guise of patriotism.

Nor were the Yankees, the rebels, the bushwhackers, or the jayhawkers the only ones that the citizens of the western frontier had to fear. The Indians soon began to take advantage of the chaotic situation. As early as July 29, 1861, Governor Robinson reported to Captain Prince the presence of a large body of hostile Pawnee Indians in Marshall County.[23] This particular group did no great damage, but that could not be said of later uprisings. Even the theretofore quiet Delaware, seeing an opportunity, became restless, and on November 18, the Indian agent F. Johnson appealed for aid. "You will please send me without one moment's delay," he anxiously wrote, "not less than twenty mounted men without waiting for provisions or camp equipage—we have had difficulty here and the Lieutenant in charge of my escort needs an immediate reinforcement."[24] In Colorado territory there was fear that, should the regular army troops be replaced with untrained volunteers, there would be another Indian uprising. The Indian agent there officially advised Captain Elmer Otis in command of Fort Wise that, should the regular troops leave, he would not be responsible for the Indians.[25] In November, twenty-eight citizens of Emporia, Kansas, petitioned Governor Robinson for protection from the Cherokee. "Positive and apparently reliable intelligence has reached this place," their appeal read, "that the Cherokee are meditating a foray upon this sector of Kansas, soon. . . . It is well known to us that many persons who have heretofore lived in this part of the country are now in the Indian country endeavoring to incite the Cherokee to take advantage of our weakness to make a descent upon us at this time."[26] In southern Kansas, they made frequent raids, attacking, robbing, and killing the settlers. The town of Humboldt, after such a foray, was burned to the ground.[27]

Brigadier General Sterling Price of Mexican War fame almost —but not quite—saved Missouri for the Confederacy in the indecisive battle at Wilson's Creek, southwest of Springfield, Missouri. The rebel force of 11,600 men was attacked early in the morning of August 10, 1861, by Brigadier General Nathaniel Lyon's army of 5,600. A fiery little redheaded West Point graduate, Lyon was an extremely able officer but, unfortunately for the Union cause, he was killed in midmorning of the battle. General Sherman was later to blame "the next four years of strife and pillage in Missouri" on Lyon's death.[28] The federal troops on a promontory called Oak Hill had repulsed two Confederate attacks before Lyon was killed. A third attack also failed, and the rebels retired down the hill. Major Sam Sturgis, who had succeeded Lyon, then ordered a Union withdrawal. His decision was later to be sharply criticized, although the order was probably prompted by the weary condition of his troops and their consequent inability to withstand another attack. Neither side could claim a decisive victory.[29] The federal army had not been destroyed. Price went on to occupy Springfield and, on September 20, captured a federal brigade at Lexington, Missouri; but by early November he withdrew to the southern end of the state. In eastern Kansas and at Fort Leavenworth itself, there was considerable anxiety when news of the result of the battle at Wilson's Creek was received. Price was on the loose, and a sizable effort was made to bring in all available troops to meet any threat to the post. Apprehension turned to relief, however, when on November 11 it was learned that the Confederate general had retraced his steps to Arkansas.

As in the Mexican War, friction had frequently existed between the volunteer and the regular officers. During the period when General Price was a threat to Kansas, a controversy arose between General Lane and Governor Robinson, with Captain Prince at Fort Leavenworth and General Fremont at St. Louis squarely in the middle. Lane, besides being a brigadier general of volunteers, was also United States senator from Kansas and, as such, had influence with the administration in Washington. Commanding a motley brigade of untrained and undisciplined Kansas volunteers, whose depredations were a constant cause of complaints, Robinson insisted that the government stores at Fort Scott be removed to Fort Leavenworth and Lane's brigade relieved. Lane, for his part, insisted that Fort Leavenworth could best be defended in Missouri and southern Kansas. The regulars were of the opinion that there were too many small detached units of insufficient strength to meet an enemy threat. General Fremont finally agreed with Robinson and ordered Lane to withdraw to Fort Leavenworth.

Prince, now a major, the last of the regular-army officers to command Fort Leavenworth during the Civil War, was relieved of command to join the 3rd Infantry Regiment in June of 1862, and he was succeeded by Lieutenant Colonel John T. Burris of the 10th Kansas Infantry.

Jayhawkers in small groups of unauthorized looters, "red legs" (so-called because of their maroon leggings—Buffalo Bill was said to be one), and detachments of General Lane's troops continued their pillaging raids into Missouri, burning farm after farm. However, it remained for the Missouri bushwhackers, or guerrillas, to bring irregular warfare to a science. The best known of these desperadoes was William Clark Quantrill, whose deeds would be remembered with horror for generations. Born in Canal Dover, Ohio, he was a thickset man of medium height with a large head, white hair, a round face, a bull neck, and a high forehead. He had originally been a Kansas free-stater but had changed sides and shifted his operations to Missouri in late 1860. With some semblance of Confederate legitimacy (he held a commission from Sterling Price), Quantrill organized a band of about one hundred men, including Jesse and Frank James. Ruthless, cruel, venal, and given to killing his prisoners, he remained a thorn in the side of the troops at Fort Leavenworth during the rest of the war. "Bloody Bill" Anderson, another guerrilla leader as bloodthirsty as Quantrill, was said to have carried the scalps of two women dangling from his bridle. He was famous for butchering large groups of people all at one time. Other guerrilla leaders included Cole Younger, later of bank robbery fame, the son of Colonel Henry Younger, a well-known planter, judge, and legislator; and George Todd, who came from a respectable Kansas City family.

A guerrilla named Jim Vaughan, disguised as a Union soldier, was captured in May, 1863, by federal troops while getting a shave and a haircut in a Kansas City barber shop. The irregulars had been outlawed, and Vaughan, by wearing the blue uniform, made himself doubly subject to execution as a spy. On the scaffold, he told the spectators, "We can be killed but we cannot be conquered. Taking my life today will cost you one hundred lives, and this debt my friends will pay in a very short time." His words were to prove prophetic.

Less than two weeks later, a band of guerrillas seeking revenge for Vaughan's death saw a company of troops from Fort Leavenworth moving toward Westport. Entering the town from the south, they concealed themselves behind stone walls on opposite sides of a lane they knew the Federals would have to travel. Carelessly led by their captain, the Union detachment moved into the lane and was met by a murderous crossfire. Before they could reorganize and withdraw, thirty-three of the troopers had been killed, as against only three irregulars. Those from the fort had been taught a hard lesson in guerrilla warfare.

The troops at Camp Union had been able to stop supplies of ammunition from reaching the bushwhackers from Kansas City, but a number of women and young girls, mostly relatives of the guerrillas, were still getting through the blockade with not only information for the irregulars but supplies of food as well. Finally a number of these young women were arrested, and as there was no room in the Union Hotel where female prisoners were generally kept, they were put in the two top floors of a three-story building that had been rented from George Caleb Bingham, the artist. (Bingham had recently added the third floor to the house for a studio.) The girls were treated well by the sergeant in charge of the prisoners, and when he saw cracks in the foundation, he reported to his superiors that he did not believe the building was safe. However, an inspector general sent from Fort Leavenwoth gave the structure a clean bill of health. On August 13, 1863, the building collapsed with a mighty roar and many of the women were buried in the ruins and had to be dug out. Four of the victims, relatives of the guerrillas, were killed and several others seriously injured. One of those who died, Josephine Anderson, was the sister of Bloody Bill; another, Charity Kerr, was a cousin of Cole Younger and the sister of Quantrill's chief scout, John

McCorkle. There is no doubt that the added weight of the studio and gross negligence caused the collapse of the building, and not a deliberate plan to murder the girls, as was rumored throughout the town, and as the guerrillas believed. Thereafter, Bloody Bill carried with him a silken cord in which he made knots for each victim it had been used to hang. There were eventually fifty-three knots. Other bushwhackers began hanging scalps from their saddles. Along the Missouri, the conflict became a war of extermination between the irregulars and the federal troops, with no prisoners taken and no mercy shown.

Probably the most infamous of all the bushwhacker exploits was the raid on August 21, 1863, of the often-sacked town of Lawrence. Led by Quantrill, the guerrilla bands joined together to number some two hundred men. They literally carried out their leader's orders "to kill every man and burn every house"; over two hundred people were ruthlessly slaughtered. When Quantrill's men left that night, all that remained of the town were ruins and a tall black column of smoke.

Two months after the holocaust at Lawrence, the Kansas general, James G. Blunt, was on an inspection tour in southern Kansas near the Missouri border. Riding in a carriage, the general was escorted by two hundred mounted men. In the vicinity of Baxter Springs, the detachment was suddenly attacked by Quantrill with a hundred of his cohorts. Without time to organize a defense, the general's force beat a hasty retreat and the rout became a pursuit. Blunt successfully evaded capture, but 125 of the troopers were killed while Quantrill had only four casualties.

On the morning of September 27, 1864, Bloody Bill stopped a train at Centralia, Missouri, by putting railroad ties on the tracks. Twenty-three unarmed federal soldiers on furlough were among the passengers, and he executed twenty-two, keeping only a sergeant for the purpose of exchange. Riding into Centralia, the band looted two stores and burned a building, then left to join Quantrill and his men three miles from town. The combined bands now numbered 264 men.

Major A. V. E. Johnson of the 39th Missouri Infantry arrived in Centralia two hours later and immediately set out in pursuit of what he believed to be Anderson's eighty bushwhackers. Arriving in full view of the enemy, the Union officer dismounted his men and placed them along the ridge of a hill. There they were charged by the guerrillas, who were spread out in a line three-quarters of a mile long. Johnson's force was able to fire only one volley, which went over the heads of the attacking irregulars, and only two of the enemy were hit. Fourteen of the Federals were able to escape; the others were killed to a man, while Quantrill and Anderson suffered only three casualties.

Against such an elusive foe who nearly always struck in small bands and was soon gone, the troops at Fort Leavenworth were rarely effective. The deployment of infantry to combat the guerrillas was useless. By the time word of their whereabouts was received at the post and a detachment detailed, the trail was cold and the bandits had long since vanished. More by luck than good management, troops from the fort would occasionally stumble onto a group of the renegades, but not often.[29]

With federal troops withdrawn not only from the Texas posts, but also from Forts Smith, Towson, Washita, Arbuckle, and Cobb, the Confederates achieved considerable success in their efforts to enlist the support of the Western Indians, many of whom felt they had been abandoned by the government in Washington. This was particularly true of the five civilized tribes, to whom the rebels promised a separate state, equal rights, and suffrage, after the conclusion of hostilities. Thus the Confederacy secured allies among the Creek, many of the Cherokee, the Choctaw (some of whom were slaveholders themselves), and the Chickasaw. It was not until 1862 that the North made any real effort to solicit the cooperation of any Indian tribe. In that year at Fort Gibson, which had been retaken after being occupied by Chief Stand Watie of the Lower Cherokee, a Union regiment was formed of Cherokee warriors from the upper branch of the tribe.[30] At Fort Leavenworth, the conciliatory policy toward Indians that dated back to Isaac McCoy paid dividends, and the Delaware furnished almost all of the scouts needed by the army.[31]

Also mustered into federal service were a number of Negro units including the 1st Kansas Colored Volunteers, who were stationed at the post during 1864. There were thus red, white, and black troops fighting side by side for the Union in the West.

Meanwhile, the usual military routine at Fort Leavenworth continued. Secretary of War Stanton himself was called on to perform the important task of naming a bugler for the post; the laxity of discipline of the Kansas volunteers was again evidenced when a large group of drunken soldiers shot up the city of Leavenworth; and the department surgeon, Dr. S. B. Davis, became quite concerned over a number of prostitutes who were living on the reservation, half a mile south of the barracks. "They are," he wrote, "unquestionably lewd women of the lowest kind and their camp is a resort for soldiers from the Post. In order to prevent the spread of loathsome disease among the latter, it will be necessary to send the former away, at once."[32]

In September, 1864, the Union cause was almost at its lowest ebb. The draft riots that made the Vietnamese War's card-burnings seem like child's play had been suppressed, but conscription was still bitterly resented. Abraham Lincoln's campaign for reelection against the popular "dove" of his day, General George B. McClellan, had not gone well, and the President himself was reconciled to defeat.

Acceptable draft subsitutes were hard to find, and the nation was at the bottom of the manpower barrel when the President was approached by Lieutenant Colonel Henry S. Huidekoper and Judge S. Newton Pettis, both of Meadville, Pennsylvania, with the suggestion that the states be permitted to recruit Confederate prisoners of war to fill their quotas.[33] Lincoln was impressed and gave the colonel a note to the authorities at the Rock Island, Illinois, prisoner-of-war installation. The plan was opposed by both Secretary of War Stanton and General Ulysses S. Grant, but Lincoln insisted that the program proceed.

This was not the first time that the use of Southern prisoners had been suggested; early in 1864, General Benjamin Butler had quietly been sent by Lincoln and Stanton to the POW camp at Point Lookout, Maryland, where he organized a regiment of former Confederates who were willing to take the oath of allegiance to the United States. Grant, however, had refused to use the regiment for anything other than guard duty.

With the request by the President that the program proposed by Huidekoper and Pettis proceed, Grant finally and reluctantly acquiesced, but suggested that the ex-rebels be confined to one regiment and be used either on the northern frontier of the United States or in New Mexico. Grant's recommendation was ignored,

134

and 1,197 men were recruited at Rock Island, organized into two regiments, and assigned to General Pope, who desperately needed troops in his western command. Eventually there were six regiments, or a total of some five thousand former Confederate soldiers, recruited from the prisoner-of-war installations at Rock Island, Point Lookout, Alton, and Camps Douglas, Chase, and Morton. Of a variety of names they were given, "Galvanized Yankee," implying that these ex-Confederates had a thin coating of Yankeeism just as iron may have an outer layer of zinc, was the designation for these ex-rebels that stuck.

Fort Leavenworth was selected as the staging area for two of the new regiments, and by February, 1865, the post was bulging. The officers in charge of organizing and drilling the Galvanized Yankees were Northerners, with one exception—Captain John T. Shanks, an opportunist, who was probably the worst scoundrel in either regiment.

Among the men who had turned their backs on the Stars and Bars, there were many who had sincerely become disenchanted with the Southern cause, and there were others who despaired of ultimate Confederate victory and only wanted to get the war over. To the vast bulk, however, enlistment had been motivated by a hope of survival. Rations in the northern POW camps had been reduced to less than subsistence, and the prospect of a decent meal was a patent bribe for a change of colors. One of the few Galvanized Yankees to achieve later fame is remembered for the words, "Dr. Livingston, I presume." He was Henry M. Stanley, the newspaper correspondent and African explorer.

The welcome mat was not put out for the new arrivals. To the troops of the permanent party[34] at Leavenworth, they were worse than rebels—they were turncoats who had deserted their cause and their comrades. While the officers of the Galvanized Yankees were for the most part Northerners, they, too, were coolly received. The feeling was that a decent man would not consent to command double traitors. As for Captain Shanks, he was completely ignored by the entire permanent party.

Despite a greater desertion rate than any other volunteer unit, the Galvanized Yankees justified Lincoln's confidence in the program. After leaving Leavenworth they served at a score of lonely frontier posts. Stage and telegraph lines were kept in operation thanks to their presence; they participated in numerous engage-

ments with the Indians; many died in battle; hundreds more suc-
cumbed to the ravages of scurvy, dysentery, and fever.

Nearly all of the Galvanized Yankees were discharged from Fort
Leavenworth in late 1866 and were soon forgotten. Theirs was
not a record of service that they could boast about on their return
home. And, in spite of a federal service record, they were not
eligible for membership in the Grand Army of the Republic. The
story of these men who had changed sides has been conveniently
ignored by the historians of the former states of the Confederacy.
The men of these regiments became a lost legion, but there are
many members of the societies of the Sons and of the Daughters
of the Confederacy who are descended from them; when they
returned home they also conveniently forgot that period of their
life. Those killed in service became a part of the history of the
West.

In mid-September, 1864, word reached Fort Leavenworth that
General Price was again moving north through Missouri. This time
he brought with him ten thousand seasoned cavalrymen, eight
twenty-five-pound guns, a number of twelve-pound howitzers, and
a five-hundred-wagon baggage train. In southern Missouri he was
able to procure an additional six thousand men, not all of whom
were mounted. It was the largest force he had yet commanded.

Another northward thrust by Price had not been anticipated,
and most of the troops from the fort were in the West pursuing
Indians. There was not enough time for their recall, and the post
urgently requested additional men from the new governor of Kansas, Thomas Carney. The request was promptly granted, and all
able-bodied males were called out. Major General Samuel R. Curtis,
a volunteer officer who was on temporary duty on the plains,
was sent for; and Major Franklin E. Hunt, a West Point graduate
and paymaster at the fort, was given the defense of the city of
Leavenworth. On the western side of the fort, overlooking the
city, an earthwork with gun positions called Fort Sully was erected.
Within the town, a long line of defensive positions were dug along
what is now Michigan Avenue. General Curtis, in command of
both Kansas City and the fort, had the citizens of the former and
of Westport called out to dig breastworks before the two towns.
The general was able to assemble fifteen thousand men, but many
were armed only with shotguns.

General Price's objective when he entered Missouri had been

the state capital, Jefferson City, located on the banks of the Missouri River in the center of the state. He had hoped to set up there the state government in exile that was accompanying him, but he found the city too strongly held and accordingly by-passed the capital and moved westward toward Kansas City, which was an excellent base for an attack on Fort Leavenworth. Price had not been gone from the vicinity of Jefferson City very long when Major Alfred Pleasonton set out in pursuit with 6,500 men. The Confederates were thus advancing toward a large Union army with a formidable force on their rear.

On the Little Blue River, eight miles east of Independence, on October 21, 1864, Curtis, with a delaying force, met Price's oncoming Confederates. The rebels easily drove back the Union advance guard and took Independence. The next day Price crossed the Big Blue between Independence and Kansas City, the Yankees withdrawing to their main defense breastworks. Price's problems were complicated, however, when Pleasonton's forces struck his rear guard at Independence.

On the morning of the 23rd, Curtis and a force composed mostly of Kansans attacked the rebels in a timber on the south side of Brush Creek, where Curtis successfully turned Price's left flank and forced the Confederates to withdraw from the timber. Meanwhile, Pleasonton's troops were engaged with the enemy's rear along the Big Blue. After several hours of desultory small-arms fire, they forced a crossing of the river and advanced to high ground that put them in a position to join with the forces of Curtis. Price, with his army whittled down to nine thousand men, was facing a combined Union force of twenty thousand. The engagement, which would be known as the Battle of Westport, was now as good as won for the Union, and while a few hours of stiff resistance on the part of the Confederates remained, they were gradually forced back. Price was able to extricate his troops from the battlefield, but two days later at Mound City, Kansas, they were overtaken by the federal army and forced to burn their wagon trains and explode their reserve ammunition. A few hours later, on Mine Creek, eight hundred rebel prisoners were taken. Thereafter Price's army rapidly disintegrated and was able to avoid complete annihilation only by fleeing in small separate units. Price himself escaped capture by virtue of the speed of a good horse.

The battle of Westport also rang down the curtain on the Missouri guerrillas. Bloody Bill Anderson was killed during a skirmish in Ray County, and Captain George Todd was shot at Independence. Quantrill, who escaped, died a month later during a raid into Kentucky.

Westport, sometimes called the "Gettysburg of the West," was the most decisive battle fought beyond the Mississippi during the Civil War. Had the tide of battle been other than it was, had Price been victorious, the effect would have been incalculable. Fort Leavenworth would unquestionably have fallen, along with all the other posts of the West, including Jefferson Barracks at St. Louis. California, without land access to the East, would have been neutralized for the duration of the war; Missouri, Kansas, and Nebraska would have been lost to the North; the pro-Union Indians would have been forced to come to terms with the rebels; and the Mormons would probably have abandoned their neutrality and joined forces with the rebels. A rich Western empire with all its resources would have fallen into the lap of the Confederacy, and the war would have been prolonged for months, if not years. But with Price's defeat, the war had been contained to the East, and Fort Leavenworth remained the mighty fortress of the West.

CHAPTER TWELVE

>>>→←<<<

THE BUFFALO SOLDIERS

On July 28, 1866, a little over a year after Appomattox and the end of the war, Congress passed an act providing for the formation of six regiments of Negro troops, of which two were to be cavalry and four infantry. The act further provided that the new troops should be commanded by white officers with at least two years of active field service in the Civil War. Chaplains to be appointed for each of the regiments would, in addition to their spiritual duties, teach reading and writing to the former slave recruits.

Negro soldiers in militia units were not an entirely new development—they had fought side by side with whites in the French and Indian War. At Bunker Hill, Peter Salem, a Negro soldier, stopped an attack of British marines when he shot their leader, Major Pitcairn. Salem Poor, also a Negro, was recommended to the Continental Congress for outstanding bravery in the battle of Charleston. Pompey Lamb, a former slave, by securing the British countersign at Stony Point, was chiefly responsible for the capture of that citadel without the firing of a single shot. Austin Darney, a slave who had served as a substitute for his master in the Revolution, was voted 112 acres of land by the Georgia legislature for his bravery and fortitude in several engagements. In addition to the many integrated units raised by the rebellious colonies, Rhode Island supplied General Washington with a Negro regiment that distinguished itself at both Monmouth and Red Bank. Connecticut and New York also furnished the Continental Army with Negro units. Black troops froze in the snow at Valley Forge, and were present at the surrender of Cornwallis at Yorktown.

In the War of 1812, the use of nonwhite troops was generally opposed. However, there were two Negro regiments raised in New York State, and three battalions of "free men of color" materially contributed to General Andrew Jackson's victory at New Orleans.[1]

Although at first Lincoln and his advisers were reluctant to make use of Negro troops, the Civil War saw their widest deployment. Nineteen months after the firing on Fort Sumter, the 1st Regiment of South Carolina Volunteers, composed entirely of former slaves, was organized, with Colonel T. W. Higginson of Massachusetts as its commander.[2] A number of other units of Negro troops were subsequently formed, but it was not until three months after the Emancipation Proclamation in March, 1863, that a serious effort was made to enlist blacks. Negroes fought and died for the Union at Fort Wagner, South Carolina; Millikens Bend, Louisiana; Fort Pillow, Tennessee; Baxter Springs, Kansas; Cold Harbor, Virginia; and on numerous other battlefields of the war. If proof of the courage of these black soldiers is needed, their charge into the crater at Petersburg provides it. During the Civil War, Negroes had participated in 440 engagements; 180,000 wore the Union blue, and of those, 33,380 gave their lives to the nation.

In spite of this record, there were many in the War Department and in the military who were convinced that Negroes would panic in combat and would be unable to withstand the rigors of an arduous campaign. Today, over a hundred years later, there are still men mouthing such patent absurdities. How wrong they were would be proved by the "Buffalo Soldiers" of the 9th and 10th Regiments of the United States Cavalry.[3] In early August, 1866, General Grant named Colonel Benjamin Grierson to the command of the 10th Cavalry, and Fort Leavenworth was selected as its staging area.

Tall, dark, and bearded, Colonel Grierson had carved for himself one of the most flamboyant and distinguished careers of the many volunteers who had served in the Union army. Formerly a music teacher in a small Illinois town, he had been an ardent Republican and had known and admired Abraham Lincoln. As a result of a fall from a mare when he was a boy of eight, he was afraid of horses, and when Sumter was fired upon, he applied for a commission in the infantry. When his appointment arrived, he found himself a major in the 6th Illinois Volunteer Cavalry. Soon given command of the regiment and promoted to colonel, Grierson was selected by Grant in 1863 to lead one of the most daring and imaginative exploits of the Civil War. With three regiments of cavalry, the colonel conducted a diversionary six-hundred-mile, sixteen-day raid through Mississippi and gained himself a brevet and a national reputation. Discharged from the army at the war's end, and reluctant to return to his mild pre-war vocation, he eagerly accepted the appointment to command the 10th (all-black) Cavalry.

Racial prejudice posed a formidable obstacle to the new commander in organizing the 10th at Fort Leavenworth. There was no dearth of those wanting to enlist. To a former slave, thirteen dollars a month, plus board and clothing, was affluence indeed, and the recruiting stations were crowded with prospective enlistees. Officer procurement was another story. In spite of the Negroes' battlefield record, most officers refused to believe that they would make good soldiers. Many preferred a lower rank in a white regiment, no matter what caliber of enlisted men it might contain. By January, 1867, only seven officers had joined the regiment.

Grierson's biggest problem was not officer procurement, however, but Colonel William Hoffman, who commanded both the 3rd Regiment and Fort Leavenworth. Hoffman, a West Point graduate, had been commissary general of prisoners during the Civil War and was unalterably opposed to the introduction of Negro soldiers into the army. Every conceivable obstacle was thrown in Grierson's path, and no incident was so slight that it was not used for the harassment of the commander of the 10th.

Hoffman quartered the Negro troops in a swampy area, the only low ground on the post, and many of the men were soon in the hospital with fever and pneumonia. Grierson received daily admonishments that his men were untidy and unclean, that their quarters were a shambles, and that they didn't salute properly. Hoffman charged that the Grierson training program was poor, that he was not following channels, and that his officers were incompetent. At parades, the troops of the 10th were not allowed to pass in review, and were kept at least fifteen feet from any white troops.

Grierson fought back as best he could, but there was little he could do when Hoffman was refusing to receive any of his complaints. When charges were brought against Grierson, however, they were quashed by higher authorities.

A cavalry regiment is only as good as its mounts, and the horses assigned to the Negro troops were old and crippled relics of the Civil War. Grierson took the matter up with departmental headquarters, but even after leaving Leavenworth, he was not able to solve the problem.

Grierson organized his companies as quickly as possible, and sent them west to Forts Riley and Gibson, sometimes without a full complement. Company A left in February and, two months later, C started west. Company D left Fort Leavenworth in May, 1867, before it was fully organized, and in August Grierson moved his headquarters to Fort Riley, where the rest of the regiment was assembled and trained.

Almost before their organization was completed, and certainly before their officer complement had been filled, the companies of the 10th saw action in the field. By late May, 1867, Company C was sent in pursuit of hostile Sioux and Cheyenne between the Arkansas and the Platte rivers.

Contrary to the predictions of skeptical white officers, the Negro soldiers soon proved that they could stand up under fire. On August 2, Captain George A. Armes and a detachment of thirty-four men of F Company fought a six-hour engagement with eighty Cheyenne, and the troopers gave a good account of themselves. By late fall, all companies of the regiment had seen action in the field and had acquitted themselves with distinction. Never once in its entire history did one of the units, or even a detail of the 10th, panic in combat.

Nor did the troopers of the 10th, when under the command of their own Negro noncommissioned officers, fail to show their mettle. On September 15, 1867, Sergeant Edward Davis and a detail of nine men were guarding a railroad construction crew fifty miles west of Fort Hays. Two civilian hunters and Private John Randall left camp to get some fresh meat for the workers, and the detail had not gone far when they were attacked by seventy Cheyenne. The civilians were killed immediately, and Randall crawled into a railroad culvert which the Indians probed with their lances, inflicting eleven wounds on the already seriously wounded soldier. Davis and his detail, although outnumbered almost seven to one, immediately went into action, attacking the hostiles. The Indians finally broke off action and withdrew after suffering thirteen warriors killed or wounded, four more than in Davis's entire force. Randall was rescued from his narrow prison and he eventually recovered. The Cheyenne must have felt they had tangled with a buzz saw.

One could go on almost indefinitely listing individual acts of bravery of the Negro soldiers, most of whom received no recognition. Stories were commonplace of men who had died in rescuing wounded comrades under murderous fire, and of soldiers individually attacking and dispersing large groups of hostiles. In one of the last skirmishes in the Apache war, Sergeant William McBrayar, a North Carolinian of Company K, won for himself and the regiment the Congressional Medal of Honor.

The soldiers of the 10th developed an esprit de corps that has seldom been equaled in the United States Army. They not only wanted to be soldiers, they wanted to be in the 10th Regiment of Cavalry. The desertion rate, always an index of morale, became the lowest in American military history. In 1877, there were eighteen desertions in the 10th, compared with 184 in Mackenzie's famous 4th. Two years later, only five men went AWOL, during a period of fourteen months.

Not always were those of the 10th charged with "going over the hill" actually deserters. One trooper sent with mail from Fort Arbuckle to Gibson, in the dead of winter, never arrived there and was listed as a deserter. Months later his body was discovered in some willows along the Canadian River. "Still strapped to his back was the mail pouch, for which he had given his life in an attempt to cross an icy stream near Fort Gibson."

The 10th went on to become one of the great frontier regiments. The troops fought with bravery and distinction on the plains of Kansas, in the Indian territory, in the arid deserts of the Southwest, and in the mountains of New Mexico, Colorado, and the Dakotas. In the Apache wars, they became experts in guerrilla warfare. Denying their wily foe access to water and food, they outfought and outmarched the Apache. Defeating Victorio, they drove him into Mexico and to his ultimate destruction.

Nor were the enlisted men of the 10th the only ones who brought distinction to the regiment. Both General John J. Pershing and

Major General Wesley Merritt saw combat service as young officers with the 10th Cavalry. General Pershing's nickname "Black Jack" was given him by officers of other units during his service with the Buffalo Soldiers.

The Indians developed a grudging but healthy respect for the 10th. Seeing a similarity between the hair of the Negro troops and that of their sacred animal, the buffalo, the Redmen bestowed the name of "Buffalo Soldiers" upon their adversaries, a name the black troopers bore proudly. A buffalo became the outstanding feature of the regimental coat of arms; when a Negro division was organized in World War I, it adopted the bison as its symbol, and this emblem was continued through World War II.[4]

The first Negro officer of both the regular army and of the 10th Cavalry was Henry Ossian Flipper, a Georgian born in slavery in 1856. Although he was the sixth black appointee to West Point, Flipper was the first to graduate and stood fiftieth in the seventy-six-member class of 1877. The resoluteness and fortitude that he displayed in his four-year ordeal at the racially oriented military academy are beyond belief. Given the silent treatment almost from the first day by his fellow cadets, Flipper's existence was rarely even acknowledged by anyone other than members of the faculty. Years later, he wrote in his memoirs, "I had not from October 1875 'till May 1876 spoken to a female of any age. There was no society for me to enjoy—no friends, male or female, so absolute was my isolation."[5]

While with the 10th Cavalry, Lieutenant Flipper was responsible for draining the malaria-infested ponds at Fort Sill; building a military road from Fort Sill to Gainesville, Texas; and installing telegraph lines from Fort Elliott to Fort Supply, Indian territory. He also participated in the campaign against Victorio and the Apache Indians. In 1882, on flimsy and questionable charges, he was railroaded out of the army.

On the premise that certain funds in the amount of $3,791.07, for which Flipper was responsible, had not been received by the chief commissary of the Department of Texas, the obese and vitriolic post commander, Colonel William Shafter, at Fort Davis, Texas, on August 13, 1881, charged the lieutenant with embezzlement. Less than three weeks later, on August 29, 1881, the colonel wrote the adjutant general that Flipper had made good on all monies with which he was charged, but Shafter nevertheless insisted on going ahead with the court-martial. The court subsequently acquitted Flipper of embezzling public funds; but on the theory that he had been less than frank when accused of the crime, found him guilty of conduct unbecoming an officer and a gentleman. He was sentenced to be dismissed from the service, and the findings of the court were upheld by the reviewing authority.

On Columbus Day, October 12, 1931, the 10th Cavalry, less its 2nd Squadron and the machine-gun troop, returned to Fort Leavenworth as garrison troops, remaining there until the unit's deactivation.

Although during the first half of the twentieth century, many Negro officers had attended and graduated from the Command and General Staff College at Fort Leavenworth, ugly segregation was to continue in the army until January 16, 1950.[6] Over eighty years before that date, the Buffalo Soldiers had, by their bravery and devotion to duty, demonstrated the stupidity of such a policy.

Brigadier General Henry Leavenworth. *(Fort Leavenworth Museum)*

Reverend Father Pierre Jean de Smet, S.J. *(Library of Congress)*

Chief Joseph—In-Matuyah-Lat-Cut, Thunder Cloud
Traveling Over the Mountain—of the Nez Perces
tribe. (Portrait painted by Cyrenius Hall at Fort
Leavenworth in June 1868.) *(Fort Leavenworth
Museum)*

Colonel Benjamin Grierson, Commanding Officer, 10th Cavalry. *(National Archives)*

The first School of Application for Infantry and Cavalry at Fort Leavenworth was housed in this building. It is now occupied by the Army National Bank (1st Floor) and offices of the S. J. A. *(Fort Leavenworth Museum)*

Light Battery of the 2nd Artillery at Fort Leavenworth. (*National Archives*)

Class of 1883, U.S. Infantry and Cavalry School, Fort Leavenworth. (*National Archives*)

Sherman Hall, constructed circa 1855-1860, was first an arsenal storehouse, later became an academic building used by the General Staff School. (*Fort Leavenworth Museum*)

The present Headquarters complex has also served academic purposes at Leavenworth in the past. (*U.S. Army Photograph*)

Bell Hall, the new academic building which opened January 1, 1959, is now the hub of Leavenworth's school activity. *(Fort Leavenworth Museum)*

World War II classroom scene at Fort Leavenworth.
(U.S. Army Photograph)

Officers from Denmark, Belgium and Greece participate in a map reading exercise at Fort Leavenworth instructed by U.S. Army faculty member. (*U.S. Army Photograph*)

International array of military headgear reflects the cosmopolitan flavor at the Command and General Staff College during the 1954-55 academic year, when 35 Allied Nations were represented in the student body. (*U.S. Army Photograph*)

The Command and General Staff College provided the men who played a determining part in the American military effort of 1918

Later on the basis for the successful campaigns in Europe and the Pacific during the last war and in the present Korean campaign was laid down at Fort Leavenworth.

Most of our great commanders were developed on the heights overlooking the Missouri River at this old frontier post in the heart of America.

July 3, 1951

General George C. Marshall's letter salutes Leaven-worth's role in developing "great commanders." *(Fort Leavenworth Museum)*

SHAPE.
France.
July 4, 1951.

DDE

Dear McBride:

I have so often and so enthusiastically testified to the contributions made by Leavenworth to the professional competence of the United States Army that I shall not here repeat those statements. The record of two World Wars speaks eloquently of the worth of this college to the nation.

In Leavenworth the tradition is hard work — hard work at the most serious of all military tasks,— that of preserving American interests against aggressive foes. In Leavenworth's class rooms war is reduced to fundamentals, learned so exhaustively by the student that they come to him thereafter as second nature. So equipped in battle, the graduate is free for the fullest exercise of inspirational leadership. In peace this is no less vital.

Today Leavenworth's graduates — a national asset of incalculable value — are a prime force in shaping armies of the free world that may some day stand as civilization's last, but sure, defense.

With best wishes

Dwight D. Eisenhower

General Dwight D. Eisenhower's letter praises graduates as "a national asset of incalculable value." (*Fort Leavenworth Museum*)

Major General John H. Hay, Jr., Commandant of the
Command and General Staff School and Post Com-
mander of Fort Leavenworth. *(Fort Leavenworth
Museum)*

CHAPTER THIRTEEN

>>> > < <<<

THE POST AFTER THE CIVIL WAR

The Civil War had not come to a grinding halt in the West as it had in the East. The Indians who had supported the Confederacy continued their depredations, still making war on the federal government, attacking wagon trains and outlying settlements, and harassing the workers building the Kansas Pacific Railroad. Western-bound travel came to a virtual standstill. In the years 1865-1867, Fort Leavenworth became the nerve center of hostilities.

During this same period, the post was also a separation center for the volunteer soldiers of Kansas and Missouri. Many of the troops it had trained and sent forth to fight for the Union returned to be discharged and sent home.

One unfortunate consequence of the Indians' activities was the necessity of retaining a number of veteran volunteer regiments that had fought long and valiantly for the Union. They felt they had done their duty and should go home rather than be sent to the western plains. But regular troops that could be spared for the frontier service were not sufficient to cope with the widespread Indian disorders. One disgruntled unit, the 6th West Virginia Volunteers, commanded by Lieutenant Colonel Rufus E. Fleming, was most displeased at being ordered west. The discontent of these West Virginians increased when their troop train collided head-on with an eastbound freight at Carlyle, Illinois, with one man killed and five seriously injured, and seventy-five horses killed.[1] By the time the troops reached Fort Leavenworth, the dissatisfaction of both officers and men had reached a mutinous pitch.

On July 14, Colonel Fleming received orders to proceed

to Fort Kearny the following day. The temper of the men at the post had deteriorated to almost open mutiny, and Fleming, with his captains—John W. Kidwell, Robert F. Lindsey, Eli L. Parker, Michael Donohue, James B. Smith, and D. J. M. Williamson—gave the troopers the option of either going with the regiment or remaining at Fort Leavenworth. Williamson went even further, suggesting to the men of his company that they desert. The captain was alleged to have told them, "Boys the order is to march. Those that want to go, saddle up, those that don't want to go remain in camp and keep quiet—all those who—[are] going home—cross the river —tonight for if—[you] do not—[you will] not get over by morning."[2]

A large number of the troopers, given the option, elected to remain at Fort Leavenworth, and a decimated regiment left for Fort Kearny. A group of about twenty-five crossed the river that night and headed back home.

The West Virginia mutiny not only shocked Fort Leavenworth, but rocked the entire military establishment. Carlos John Stolbrand, a volunteer brigadier general, was appointed to investigate the case, and charges were filed against Fleming and his captains. No actions were taken against the enlisted men, and even the deserters who were apprehended were not brought to trial. The officers themselves could not be tried immediately, as they were at Fort Laramie with their regiment. Perhaps the leniency of the sentence that Fleming and his subordinates later received at courts-martial, a mere dismissal from the army, took into account their services on November 11, 1865, near Alkali, Colorado, where the troops rescued a wagon train being attacked by a band of four hundred Indians. The remainder of the 6th West Virginia Volunteers returned to Fort Leavenworth in late September and were mustered out of the service.

Dissatisfaction and the low morale of many of the volunteer soldiers retained on duty spread to the regular troops, and the desertion rate rose alarmingly at Fort Leavenworth and other posts throughout the country. In the twenty-five years following the Civil War, one-third of all men recruited became deserters. There were many letters to the editor of the *Army and Navy Journal* proposing solutions to the problem.[3] It was suggested that an increase in pay and better living conditions for the enlisted men might help army morale. Others took a harder line and recommended severe punishment for the AWOLs, with an increase of from twenty to a hundred dollars in the bounty paid for the apprehension of deserters.

Living conditions had improved at the fort. The water had previously been drawn from the Big Muddy and delivered in barrels to the officers' quarters and the barracks, where it was allowed to stand and clear. In 1865, a well was drilled near the wharf and, while the water was still delivered in wagons, it contained much less silt.

Lieutenant Colonel Gustan Heinrichs, of the 40th Missouri Volunteer Infantry, during his short tenure as commander, did much to improve the appearance of the post. New and more commodious barracks and quarters were built, sidewalks were laid, and a number of mud roads paved. In May, 1865, the colonel suggested to the Reverend Hiram Stone, the post chaplain, that he call the ladies together and ask them to give the streets, squares, and public places on the post suitable names. His only other recommendation, which incidentally was ignored by the ladies, was that "one of the most public avenues be named in honor of that noble American soldier, Nathaniel Lyon—who left this place [Fort Leavenworth] in 1865 [and] who took command of the Volunteers at St. Louis, and led them there to the bloody field on which he fell fighting for our glorious cause."[4]

By 1867, the post was almost back to its peacetime routine. Early in February, the post commander, Colonel Hoffman, learned that a drunken brawl had taken place in the city of Leavenworth between officers from the post. He saw to it that the men in question were duly reprimanded. In March, the mysterious disappearance of Lieutenant William D. F. Landon caused considerable conjecture. He had been drinking heavily, was in arrest, and had appeared to be depressed. It was at first thought that he had deserted, although why an officer who could resign his commission would go AWOL remained a question. Finally his fully clothed body was found nine miles down river and it was concluded that he had died by accidental drowning.[5]

The shortage of females in the West continued through the seventies. A domestic upon her arrival at the post was immediately courted, and within a few weeks would have married either a soldier or a bachelor from the nearby city of Leavenworth. The army was finally forced to recognize the problem, and in 1876 instructed the employment agencies in Chicago to send west as domestics only the ugliest girls obtainable. The next consignment of maids dispatched were pockmarked, buck-toothed, and cross-eyed, but within sixty days they had all acquired husbands.

The laundresses, most of whom were married to enlisted men, were a source of constant irritation to the officers and their wives. *The Army and Navy Journal* commented on August 12, 1871, that "every officer who has commanded a Post will agree. . . . that one laundress is more trouble and annoyance than a company of men. . . ." It added, "This is true especially at Frontier Post —[for] they know no officer would have the inhumanity to [discharge and] order [women] into the uninhabited wilds that surround the garrison." The laundresses were given rations by the company to which they were attached and were allowed compensation for the washing they did on an agreed scale, but they often refused to work when they were indisposed or unless a larger charge was allowed. A story was told at Fort Leavenworth of a laundress, a Mrs. Riley, who, when she was sent some soiled linen by a bachelor officer, returned it saying that she had a maid herself and "didn't wash for nobody."

In the spring of 1867, a plague of grasshoppers invaded the post. They came in great dark clouds sometimes a hundred miles long, hitting against the barracks and quarters like hailstones. Within a few minutes they could riddle a housewife's laundry hanging on the line, and between dawn and dusk, destroy a forty-acre field of corn. The pests would literally cover the ground, sometimes in heaps several feet high, and when they died in such piles the odor of putrefaction was sickening. However, the plague apparently did provide the officers some amusement; Colonel Grierson wrote in a letter to his wife:

> . . . they [grasshoppers] were impolite and unceremonious enough to hop up, get up, or in some way make their merry way up under the hoops and skirts of the ladies who are bold enough to promenade among them. From the motions I am of the opinion that they were being tickled almost to death by grasshoppers—and even in some instances their wiggling

was most excruciating—even enough to drive a man with a heart of stone to the rescue . . . should the grasshoppers remain here very long, I have no doubt but what some Yankee will invent some new pattern for the relief of the ladies in the way of solid drawers.[6]

Besides grasshoppers, there were other pests that not only made a nuisance of themselves but were costly to the government. On every military post where horses and cattle were stabled, there was a constant fight to keep down the rodent population that yearly destroyed hundreds of bushels of grain. This was particularly true at Fort Leavenworth, as the steamboats, their holds teeming with rats, were discharging cargo daily at the wharf. Once a year, several large cages of mewing cats, requisitioned from Jefferson barracks, would arrive at the landing to be turned loose on the pests.

Nor were rats the only menace to health brought to the post by steamboat. Passengers who had been exposed in New Orleans or St. Louis would come down with cholera or smallpox, and the steamer would soon become a floating dispensary without a physician. At the Fort Leavenworth wharf, many of the boats would leave their sick, and the post, with a hospital and surgeon, could not refuse to receive them. The garrison paid a stiff price for this humanity—there were periodic outbreaks there of these virulent diseases.

In spite of the problems of family life in the West, both officers and enlisted men, and their respective dependents, had their lighter moments. The arrival of the headquarters and four troops of the 7th Cavalry in December, 1869, resulted in a series of hops, balls, and social events during their year-and-a-half tour at Fort Leavenworth. The most recherché of these affairs was a ball given by the noncommissioned officers soon after their arrival. With many months of accumulated pay burning holes in their pockets, the enlisted men went to town. The decoration, the food, and drinks were almost too elaborate, but the affair was remembered by officers, their ladies, and the enlisted personnel as the most enjoyable affair that had ever been held on the post.

Since 1845, the Thespian Society of the enlisted men had been the sole theatrical entertainment until an officers' society was formed in 1872 for the purpose of putting on plays. By 1875, these performances had become very popular with the garrison, and the productions were both ambitious and well done. On December 30 of that year the comedy "Home" was presented, and the next month, "Still Waters Run Deep." Among the cast for the latter play whose names appeared on the program, were Major Dunn, Lieutenants Pope and Whitten, and the Madames Borden, Lewis, and Carter. [7]

It was during this period that another determined effort was made to improve the general appearance of the fort. Trees were planted along the various roads, and officers were encouraged to plant "currant, raspberry and blackberry bushes around their quarters." These efforts led to many of cries of anguish when the landscaped homes were taken over by a newly arrived officer whose date of rank was senior to the occupant's.

Fort Leavenworth was the focus of national attention when in mid-September, 1867, it was the scene of the court-martial of that "tarnished hero," Lieutenant Colonel George Armstrong Custer. [8] Always indifferent to the sufferings of other men and a believer in discipline for everyone but himself, Custer was leading a detachment of six companies of the 7th Cavalry on a hunt for hostile Sioux and Cheyenne in the summer of that year. The Indians seemed to have evaporated, the water was alkaline, the food poor, most of the men were suffering from dysentery and scurvy, and the horses were jaded, but Custer relentlessly marched his troops as much as sixty-five miles a day. On July 5, Custer received orders directing that he and his troops should march to Fort Wallace by way of Republican Forks.

The command had almost reached a state of mutiny when, on July 7, only a half day's march from the Platte River, it rested for a noonday break. In broad daylight, seven men on horseback and five on foot took off. Custer, beside himself with rage, shouted to the officer of the day, Lieutenant Henry Jackson, an order to pursue the fugitives and "bring in none alive." The lieutenant's horse was not saddled, but Major Joel Elliott and Lieutenant William W. Cooke took off after the deserters. The mounted men escaped, but three of the men on foot were ruthlessly shot, and the other two saved themselves only by shamming death. The wounded men were thrown into a wagon and given no immediate medical attention. Private Charles Johnson died ten days later at Fort Wallace. [9]

When Custer arrived at Wallace on July 14, he was given orders from General Hancock to remain there and to keep the 7th Cavalry constantly engaged in harassing the Indians. He also heard a rumor that there was an epidemic of cholera at Fort Riley, where his wife, Libby, whom he had not seen for two months, was staying. Disregarding his orders, he selected an escort of seventy-five tired troopers and as many equally exhausted horses. With Captain Lewis McL. Hamilton, grandson of Alexander Hamilton, the Canadian Lieutenant Cooke, and his brother Tom Custer for companions, he set out for Riley by way of Forts Hays and Harker. At Downer's Station, the rear of his column was attacked by Indians and a trooper was killed. Custer neither paused to pursue the fleeing Indians nor to bury his dead, but pressed on. Covering a distance of 156 miles in fifty-five hours, of which only six were allowed for rest and sleep, Custer left his escort at Hays, and with his brother Tom, Cooke, and two orderlies pushed on toward Fort Riley. "He seemed to have cast away along with Hancock's orders, all mercy and sense of duty."[10] From Fort Harker, after a brief stop to report to Colonel Smith, he continued the journey to Riley.

In late July, Custer, by order of General Hancock, was arrested and charged with ordering soldiers of his command to be shot without a trial; that after such men had been shot and wounded, they were placed by his order in a wagon and hauled eighteen miles without medical treatment; that by his orders he had caused the death of Trooper Johnson; that on his eastward dash, contrary to orders, and on personal business, he had damaged government horses; and finally that he had neither pursued the Indians that had attacked his escort nor buried his dead. He was ordered to stand trial at Fort Leavenworth on September 15.[11]

Custer and his wife gave the impression of taking the entire matter lightly. They charged that the whole thing was a frame-up on the part of General Hancock; that the principal witnesses for the prosecution, Captains Robert M. West and Frederick Benteen, were drunks; that Custer was being made a scapegoat; and finally that the court, which included Colonels Hoffman and Grierson, was stacked against him.

The defense, which was composed equally of hindsight and fabrication, did not impress the court, and Custer was found guilty on all counts. The sentence was light: suspension from rank and command for one year and forfeiture of all pay and allowances for the same period. General Grant, in approving the conclusions of the court-martial, remarked on the "leniency of the sentence."

(It is interesting that a study of the medical records of Fort Riley for the summer of 1867 disclose that no cases of cholera were reported at that post.)

Custer's tribulations were not quite over. In reviewing the records of the case, the Bureau of Military Justice suggested that he might be brought to trial in a civil court for the murder of Private Johnson. On January 3, 1868, Custer and Lieutenant Cooke were arrested for murder. But Judge Henry J. Adams of Leavenworth City dismissed the charges.[12]

While it was in no way comparable to the days of the Civil War, violence in western Missouri and eastern Kansas continued during the late sixties and early seventies as a way of life for many. Ex-guerrillas as well as former soldiers found themselves unable to readjust to a more peaceful existence and became bandits and outlaws. Jesse James and Cole Younger, who were later to extend their operations, were probably the most notorious of these highwaymen. Paymasters traveling to the various ports required a strong escort, and if pay on a post was a day or two late, the enlisted men began humming the old army ditty, "We Fear Some Disaster Has Befell The Paymaster."

By January, 1868, the situation around Lawrence had become so intolerable that Secretary of the Treasury Hugh McCulloch wrote to the War Department requesting troops for the purpose of guarding government funds collected by the receiver of the land office: "A band of robbers has obtained such a foothold in the section of the country between Humboldt and Lawrence, Kansas," he wrote, "committing depredations upon travellers both by public and private conveyance that the safety of the public money—requires that it should be guarded."[13] Civil authorities were simply not able to control the brigands, and, once again, the military as represented by Fort Leavenworth stepped into the breach.

In August, 1869, Major Marcus A. Reno, newly assigned to the 7th Cavalry, reported at Fort Leavenworth for duty with that regiment. He was accompanied by his wife, Mary Hannah, and his son, Ross. Bearing the laurels of not only a distinguished Civil

War record, but also one of able service with the Freedmen's Bureau in New Orleans, Reno was destined to become one of the tragic figures of the American army. Unfairly blamed for the defeat of Lieutenant Colonel Custer at the Battle of the Little Big Horn, Reno would ultimately leave the army in disgrace.

In spite of the trouble with Indians and highwaymen, the seventies were the most tranquil years that the fort had yet known. The luxuries of civilization were reaching the post. A few of the high-ranking officers actually had bathrooms in their quarters. Young ladies from the post were attending classes in German taught by Albert Pulitzer, the emigrant brother of the famous Joseph.[14] Professional theatrical troupes often performed in the nearby towns and, occasionally, singers and actors of international fame appeared there. Leavenworth had grown, and the designation "City" no longer seemed ridiculous. Within a few years it could boast of having two hundred saloons, one for every thirty families—the largest and most luxurious was the Saratoga.[15]

A track with a grandstand for the ladies was built in the bottoms on the fort's reservation; the races were well-attended not only by the military but by the local citizens as well. A national hero, General William Tecumseh Sherman, was a frequent guest at the quarters of his cousin, the well-connected Major William McK. Dunn. Dunn's wife was the daughter of the former governor of Maine, Senator Lot P. Morrill, who also visited the fort often.[16] In 1871, a Catholic church, and in 1878, the first post chapel were erected. The officers' club was organized in 1877, and an assignment at Fort Leavenworth was no longer considered one into exile.

On August 14, 1877, Fort Leavenworth was again the focus of national attention when the remains of Captains Tom Custer and George W. Yates, and Lieutenants Algernon E. Smith, James Calhoun, and Donald MacIntosh—victims of Custer's mad stand at Little Big Horn the previous year—were brought to the post for re-interment. After a short service in the chapel, they were buried in the fort's cemetery.

Chief Joseph and his band of four hundred Nez Percé Indians, who had led the army a merry chase in one of the most masterly retreats in military history, were confined at the post from November, 1877, to July, 1878, and the chief's camp became a popular point of interest. A call on the venerable old man was a must for the guests.[17] There were also many others incarcerated at the post, for in 1874, the first military prison had been established there.

For years the headquarters of the Department of Missouri seesawed back and forth between Jefferson Barracks and Fort Leavenworth, but in April, 1870, it was removed to the latter post, where it remained for twenty years. Until 1883, General John Pope commanded the department from there, and troops of the states of Missouri, Kansas, Illinois, and Colorado, as well as of the Indian and New Mexico territories, put a severe strain on the facilities of the post. This was not eased when, during the winter of 1870, the headquarters and five troops of the 7th Cavalry were also stationed at the fort.

The shortage of living quarters brought about one particularly ludicrous situation, although the officers concerned, Lieutenants John B. Rodman and William P. Vose, both military-academy graduates, were quite serious about it. They were assigned "severally" and not as "tenants in common" a single house as their quarters. Over the objection of Rodman, Vose carpeted the hallway and placed furniture in it. He also set up sleeping quarters for his two servants in the attic and basement halls. In Vose's absence, Rodman removed the carpeting and furniture to Vose's part of the house. The dispute was soon carried to the commanding officer. The CO ruled that, thereafter, Lieutenant Vose was to occupy the southern half of the house, and Rodman the northern half, and that the division of the house "was to be a line passing longitudinally through the center of the house from cellar to roof." The hallways were to be used only as passageways.

Morale among both officers and the enlisted men during the late sixties and early seventies was probably at the lowest ebb that it had ever been or ever would be. One officer, First Lieutenant Charles Bunzhaf of the 10th Cavalry,[18] was reported to have remarked in the Continental Hotel in the city of Leavenworth on March 14, 1870, "God damn the American Army to hell! It is the God damnedest army that ever was. It is the worst demoralized army today in the world. The American Army is nothing but a mob, and the worst one ever organized. It is composed of nothing but a God damned set of thieves and cutthroats from beginning to end. An officer cannot go anywhere without being insulted by a Buck soldier."[19]

The politically-inspired officer appointments that Secretary of War Stanton had made in the army following the Civil War were having their effects. Incompetent, uneducated, and frequently drunkards, these men were unable either to lead or to handle troops. Unfortunately, many of the pre-war regular officers of the caliber of George Custer were also indifferent to the needs, and often callous in their treatment, of the enlisted men.

To understand man's "inhumanity to man" as exemplified by many of the army officers of a hundred years ago, it is necessary to project oneself back into the nineteenth century. They were not out of tune with the age in which they lived, for it was not a gentle era. It was a time when, during periods of economic depressions, laboring men and their families were allowed to die of starvation; when the Astors and other landlords could lease flats at exorbitant rentals in rotting tenements that were firetraps and avoid the consequences of their greed; when men like Gould and Vanderbilt could wreck railroads and ruin other men without compunction if it were to their advantage; when the elderly poor were sent to poorhouses or county farms when they were no longer able to work; and when allegedly respectable businessmen founded their fortunes on wages far below a living standard, on child labor, and on keeping their employees eternally in debt to the company store.

On October 1, 1869, Captain David Hillhouse Buel, a West Point graduate of 1861, became the commanding officer of the arsenal at Fort Leavenworth. A tall, lanky martinet, Buel had ably served as a cavalry officer in the early days of the Civil War. Subsequently, he had been the ordnance officer of the Army of the Tennessee, and thereafter transferred to the ordnance corps. He found his new detachment riddled with insubordination and in an almost mutinous state. Unfortunately, in the months that followed, he met the problem by assuming a dictatorial attitude, and he bore down mercilessly on his enlisted men.

On July 19, 1870, Private James M. Malone, who claimed illness, committed a minor infraction of rules and Buel, as punishment, directed that he saw a cord of wood.

After completing about half his task, Malone covered up the

rest of the wood with the part he had cut and returned to his barracks. His ruse was discovered, and Buel sent for him and ordered him not only to finish the job, but to saw another half cord. That night, Malone deserted.

Three days later, on the night of the 23rd, Buel, his wife, Georgie, and two of their children attended a charity fair at the quarters of Colonel Sturgis, commander of the 7th Cavalry. The bazaar was given by the post children for the benefit of a Leavenworth blind widow and her children. At about 10:00 P.M., the Buels, returning to their quarters, had alighted from their carriage and were strolling up the walk when a shot rang out and the captain fell to the ground with a bullet in his back. Within a matter of minutes, Buel died in his wife's arms, but not before saying, "Who shot me? Georgie I'm dying. Good bye."[20]

It was quickly determined that the murderer had been the deserter, Malone. A search was soon underway by both civilians and military, and every lead was immediately followed. Successfully eluding his pursuers for three days, Malone was spotted by Richard Morrison, a civilian in the quartermasters office, on July 26, attempting to cross the river in a small boat. Morrison demanded that Malone put up his hands and surrender. When Malone started to bring up his gun, Morrison shot and wounded him with his pistol. That night in the guardhouse, in the presence of Major David L. Magruder, the post surgeon, and Lieutenant John P. Walker, the officer of the day, Malone made a deathbed confession of the murder of Buel. When she learned that her husband's assailant was dying, Mrs. Buel is said to have visited him and granted her forgiveness. Civilian Morrison received a five-hundred-dollar reward for the capture of the fugitive.[21]

It was the general consensus that others were involved in the murder of Buel, and as Lieutenant Cullen Bryant, the dead officer's executive assistant, was an inexperienced newcomer to the fort, General Pope ordered an infantry officer, Captain Simon Snyder, with a detail of twenty-five men to take over the arsenal. This, in turn, aroused the ire of one of the chief ranking ordnance officers in Washington, Major Stephen Vincent Benét, father of the poet. Benét registered a vigorous protest, not because of the presence of the new enlisted detachment, but because an infantry officer should presume to command an arsenal. The problem was resolved on August 10, when Captain Alfred Mordecai, a brilliant young officer who had formerly been with the topogs, but was now in ordnance, took command of the arsenal. An academy classmate of Buel, he had previously commanded Rock Island.

Following the Civil War, the population of the city of Leavenworth reached eighteen thousand, with Kansas City having only 3,500 people, but the future of the two cities depended upon which town would be the first to get a branch of the railroad that ran across northern Missouri from Hannibal to St. Joseph. Using both fair means and foul, the people of Kansas City were successful in inducing the federal government to build a bridge across the Missouri River connecting their town with the state of Kansas. By 1869, when it was completed, there were three railroad lines on both sides of the river converging at Kansas City by way of the new bridge. In that same year, the Atchison, Topeka, and Santa Fé reached Topeka, and the golden spike was driven joining the rails of the first transcontinental line. On September 1, 1870, seven years after the work had begun at the Kansas state line at Wyandott, the Kansas Pacific Railroad to Denver was completed. From Denver it would later turn north and connect with the Union Pacific at the new town of Cheyenne, Wyoming. Leavenworth City had lost; it had been bypassed by all the major railroad lines.

The new channels of communication also affected Fort Leavenworth, for it was no longer needed as the army's western supply center. Consequently it played only a small role in the Indian wars of the seventies. The expeditions against the hostiles were organized at and marched from the more recently established posts farther west. With supplies and ordnance no longer routed through the fort, its arsenal was discontinued in February, 1874, and the stores moved to Rock Island.

An epoch in the long history of Fort Leavenworth had come to an end, but the post would now begin an era during which its renown would eventually spread throughout the world.

CHAPTER FOURTEEN

>>>>-><-<<<

THE SCHOOLS

The Civil War had demonstrated that strong personal qualities of leadership in an officer were not enough. To this minimal requirement there had to be added a basic education and some knowledge of military tactics. It was understandable that in the hectic days of the war, officers commissioned directly from civilian life or elected by the men of their regiments would fail to meet such criteria, but unfortunately, many of the regular officers, particularly in the infantry and cavalry, were equally unqualified for command. During the war, men had died unnecessarily because of their officers' tactical deficiencies and inability to give an understandable order.

Following the cessation of hostilities in 1865, the problem had been doubly compounded by the politically inspired appointments that Secretary of War Stanton had made in the expanded regular army. A belief in the principles of the radical faction of the Republican Party seemed to be the only qualification Stanton required to justify the granting of a commission. Ineffectuals, drunkards, and foreign adventurers with questionable antecedents, often lacking even a grade-school education, were added to the officer corps. Within a few years the incompetence of many of the officers had become an open scandal, and the term "army bum" began to be used to describe men holding an army commission. Congress was forced to act. It directed the War Department to set up committees authorized to weed out the incompetents. Nicknamed "Benzine Boards" for their cleansing properties, the committees relieved hundreds of officers from active duty.

161

The officer corps had reached such a low point in public esteem that friends of the army felt called upon to come to its defense. Thus the editor of the *Leavenworth Times* wrote in an editorial on December 18, 1881:

> It seems a gay thing to be an officer and be stationed at Fort Leavenworth and at home in these fine quarters, and ride or drive to and from the city, but there is a reverse to this picture . . . At any time these carefully dressed, daintily booted and gloved young gentlemen may be ordered to some desolate spot . . . to pass months . . . surrounded by skulking savages . . . a transfer may mean death in some defile and mutilation afterwards . . . Some good people grumble about the expense of the Army and military Posts but our little Army serves to keep alive the military traditions and spirit of the country and the sight of blue uniforms, and the flag that does not come down until sunset, and the voice of the sunset gun, all remind young people that they have a country and that it has brave defenders.

Since engineering, ordnance, and artillery officers require at the very least some knowledge of basic mathematics for the performance of their duties, Stanton had been a little more discriminating in his selections for those more technical branches of the army. Ever since 1824, the artillery corps had maintained a school at Fortress Monroe, but the infantry school, founded by Colonel Leavenworth in 1826, had been discontinued two years later.

No one had a greater understanding of the weaknesses of the officer personnel of both the infantry and the cavalry than did Generals Grant, Sherman, and Sheridan. All three separately arrived at the conclusion that a determined effort should be made to improve the educational qualifications of the officers. In 1881, their combined efforts were to result in the establishment of a school of application for infantry and cavalry, similar to the one then in operation for the artillery at Fortress Monroe. The school was to consist of a commander, a staff composed of the next five officers in order of rank, and a student body of lieutenants, "preferably such as have no families or who have not had previously the benefit of other instruction," to be detailed from each regiment of infantry and cavalry. Troop units of the school would consist of not less than four companies of infantry, four troops of cavalry, and a battery of light artillery.[1] The order creating the new institution read:

> The school will habitually consist of three field officers of cavalry or infantry, with not less than four companies of infantry, four troops of cavalry, one light battery of artillery and the officers attached for instruction as hereinafter described. These companies may be changed from time to time according to the exigencies of service. The officers detailed for *instruction* will be *one* lieutenant of each regiment of cavalry and infantry, preferably such as have no families or who have not had previously the benefit of other instruction, who will be nominated by the commanding officer of the regiment and announced in general orders by the Adjutant General of the Army, by or before the 1st of July of each alternate year beginning with July, 1881, for the next term of two years. The officers so detailed will be attached to the companies composing the school, and will perform all the duties of company officers in addition to those of instruction.

That General Sherman, the army commander, was giving considerable thought to the projected academy is indicated by his letter of November 22, 1881 to General Philip Henry Sheridan who commanded the Division of Missouri[2]:

> I want this new school to start out with the doctrine that service with troops in the field, in time of peace, is the most honorable of all, and the best possible preparation for high command when war does come, as it always does, suddenly.

> I don't want to meddle with this new school or have it the subject of legislation, because if this is done, like West Point, it will be made political and taken out of control.

> The school should form a model post, like Gibraltar with duty done as though in actual war, and instruction by books be made secondary to drill, guard duty, and the usual forms of a well regulated garrison.

Fort Leavenworth in 1882 was an ideal location for the school. It was one of the army's largest permanent posts, it was centrally located, there were quarters available for the faculty and student officers, and it was considered an attractive place to live. The correspondent of the *Army and Navy Journal* in the March 25, 1882, issue wrote that the fort in the spring of the year "appears in all its beauty. The lawn in front of the quarters of Colonel Otis is being neatly sodded. Southwest of the Post Headquarters the grounds are being graded and the ravine filled up. . . . On pleasant days the Lieutenants are to be seen signalling out of doors. Nearly all of them expert wig-waggers. . . . Many officers have handsome private turnouts," and the ". . . fine road to the city was a favorite drive. The citizens of Leavenworth (City) drive out in great numbers to witness daily drills and surround the parade ground on Sundays, when the band plays for two hours."

The organizer of the school and its first commandant was a Maryland-born-non-West-Point infantry officer, Colonel Elwell S. Otis. He was assigned five officers who were to constitute the staff of the school: Majors John J. Upham, 5th Cavalry, John S. Poland, 18th Infantry, Captains Edward B. Williston, 2nd Artillery, Samuel B. M. Young, 8th Cavalry, and John S. McNaught, 20th Infantry. Upham and Poland were both graduates of the military academy; Williston held the Congressional Medal of Honor; McNaught had risen from the ranks; while Young, a brilliant scholar, was, after retirement, to distinguish himself as an historian and author.

The school was officially designated as established by the War Department on January 26, 1882.[3] The order formally creating the new institution read in part:

> . . . Colonel Elwell S. Otis, 20th Infantry, commands the school . . . and is charged with the practical instruction of every soldier and officer of his command in everything which pertains to army organization, tactics, discipline, equipment, drill, care of men, care of horses, public property, accountability, etc., and generally of everything which is provided for in Army Regulations. These must be his first care and the second is "theoretical instruction," which ought to precede a commission, but is not always the case, *viz:* reading, geometry, and trigonometry sufficient for the measurement and delineation of ground, and such history as every young gentleman should be presumed to know; and third, the "science and practice of war," so far as they can be acquired from books.

. . . The subjects for the schools are the lieutenants . . . making about fifty in all. These will, on reporting, be examined by the staff at the school and divided into two classes, the first only requiring the higher instruction, as defined above, and the second the whole course of two years.

The course of instructions and the textbooks for the first class were:

Mahan's Outposts.
Meyer's Signaling.
Mahan's (Wheeler's) Field Fortifications.
Woolsey's International Law and Laws of War.
Ive's Military Law.
Operation of War (Hamley).
The Lessons of War as taught by the great masters, Colonel France J. Soady.
Lectures by professors and essays prepared by the students from general reading.
Practical instruction in surveying and reconnoitering by itineraries and field notes as prescribed for the use of the Army.

The course of instructions and the textbooks for the second class were:

Correct reading aloud, with care and precision, with proper accent and pauses, to be heard and understood.

Writing—a plain hand, easy to read, designed for the use of the party receiving and not an exhibition of the haste and negligence of the writer, especially the signature.

Grammar (Bingham).
Arithmetic (Hagar).
Geometry (Chauvenit).
Trigonometry (Chauvenit).
General Sketch of History (Freeman).
History of the United States (Seavey, Goodrich).

Officially designated The United States Infantry and Cavalry

School in 1886, the college in its formative years became a laboratory of military instruction, and staff, faculty, and students were encouraged to make recommendations for the improvement of the curriculum.

The growth and development of the school continued, and in 1888 there were seven departments.[4] A Department of Military Art taught military policy, strategy, tactics, operations of a mixed character, military geography, military administration, and didactic study of campaigns and battles. A Department of Law was divided into military law, constitutional law, and international law. A Department of Engineering offered courses in topography and mathematics, fortifications, field engineering, signaling, and telegraphy. The students were instructed in tactics, field service, equitation, and hippology in the Department of Cavalry, while in the Department of Infantry, tactics and infantry field service were the important courses offered. Ordnance and gunnery were taught in the Department of Artillery, and courses in hygiene and early aid to the injured were given in the Department of Military Hygiene. By 1890, the practical exercises in military art, which later became such an important feature of the school, had been instituted, and two years later seminars replaced daily recitations.

The year 1890 also saw the interruption of cavalry instruction when the two troops stationed at the post were ordered to duty against the Indians in the Dakotas. This problem, the interruption of the school by the troops being sent elsewhere for duty, was not solved until 1895 when, after another experience in the departure of infantry companies, the school and the fort were separated. With the assignment of all instructor personnel to the school rather than the fort, a major obstacle was eliminated.

In the early years of the school's development, Captain Arthur Lockwood Wagner, an instructor in the Department of Military Art, made more of an imprint on the Infantry and Calvary School than any of its other early commandants or teachers. Born in Illinois, Wagner had been an indifferent cadet at West Point, graduating fortieth out of a class of forty-three. Thereafter, however, by tours as professor of Military Science and Tactics at several schools in the South, his interest in military teaching was stimulated. Coming to Leavenworth in 1886 and remaining eleven years, he was not only responsible for much of its progressive development, but was also the author of several texts. By 1893, he had become the head of the Department of Military Art and, in that year, was singled out by the commandant, Colonel Edwin F. Townsend, in his annual report as having "brought untiring zeal to the accomplishment of the work in his department and with the help of his able assistant instructors has been remarkably successful in the instruction of the Classes."[5]

The captain's own report for 1893 indicates the progressive influence that he had exerted in the development of the school:

The instruction has been by recitation, by lecture, by practical tactical exercises in the field, and tactical exercises indoors by means of the map. Only the first has been made the subject of examination, though marks have been recorded in the third and fourth methods of instruction which will have suitable weight in determining the relative merits of the members of the class on graduation.

The practical tactical exercises in the field consisted of exercises with and exercises without troops.

The terrain rides, or field exercises without troops, are a feature of instruction here. They are based upon similar methods of instruction in the European staff school, with such modifications as are required by the altered conditions found here.

The instruction in *Kriegspiel* [war game] has had in view not only the generally recognized object of that game—namely map reading, correct estimation of the designs of an adversary and the rapid accommodation of the player to the changing tactical conditions presented in the course of the game—but also instructions in the issuing of orders.

In 1895, Captain Wagner instituted the use of map problems that required written solutions, a form of instruction that has continued to this day.

Leaving Fort Leavenworth in March, 1897, to serve on the staff of Major General Nelson A. Miles, Captain Wagner had the satisfaction of seeing most of his recommendations for the courses at the school adopted by the War Department.[6] In a new revision of the curriculum, emphasis was placed on a practical approach, and the new instruction was divided as follows:

1. Department of Tactics,— Part I, Infantry Drill Regulations; II, Small Arms Firing Regulations; III, Infantry Fire and use in Battle; IV, Cavalry Drill Regulations; V, Equitation and Hippology; VI, Field Artillery Drill Regulations; VII, Manual of Guard Duty; VIII, Troops in Campaign; IX, Security and Information; X, Organization and Tactics; XI, Practical Work in the study and application of the principles of minor tactics.

2. Department of Strategy,—Part I, Military Policy and Institutions; II, Military Geography; III, Logistics; IV, Staff Duties; V, The Conduct of War; VI, Maneuvers on Map and War Game; VII, Military History; VIII, Graduation Essay.

3. Department of Engineering,—Part I, Military Topography and Sketching; II, Field Fortifications; III, Field Engineering; IV, Signaling and Telegraphy; V, Photography.

4. Department of Law,—Part I, Military Law; II, Constitutional Law; III, International Law; IV, Administration.

5. Department of Hygiene,— Studies in textbook on military hygiene.

Wagner, now a lieutenant colonel, was recalled for duty at the school for a short period in 1904 when he again prepared a reorganized program of instruction. Thereafter he served in Washington on the newly created General Staff.

For the four years during the Spanish American War and the Philippine insurrection, the school was closed, there not being enough regular officers to meet the pressing military needs. It was also unfortunate that during this period the men who had graduated as lieutenants had not achieved sufficient rank to make the influence of the school felt under battlefield conditions.

While the school was closed, the post was used as a staging area, and subsequently as a separation center. It was at the fort in March, 1901, that the 14th Cavalry was organized.

It was during this period that the hatchet-wielding temperance crusader, Carry Nation, visited the Leavenworth area. An inmate of the Old Soldiers' Home had written her protesting the sale of beer on government land and suggesting that she bring her "hatchet and clear out the canteen in the Home. —We are to be paid in one week. Over seventy half-barrels of beer are sold in one day at the Home after Pension Day."

Carry arrived in the city of Leavenworth on March 26, 1901, marching her broad, bouncing form down the street to a weed-covered lot, where, with a tirade of epithets, she delivered to a group of onlookers her lecture on the evils of drink. Always enterprising, she concluded her speech by selling small replicas of her famous hatchet. Informed by the town's authorities that she would not be allowed to cause any trouble, she was escorted to the Old Soldiers' Home by a detachment of policemen.

The fondness of the aged soldiers for their beer for once deterred the embattled Carry; she had barely entered the canteen, when several of its occupants grabbed her and tossed her into the street. Bruised and shaken, she beat a hasty retreat to Leavenworth City and headed for one of the bars.

It was not Carry's day. At the National Hotel she allowed herself to be hoodwinked by the owner, Ferdinand Mella. Brandishing her hatchet and shouting, "Look out for me, you hellbound, rum-soaked rummies," she was grabbed by the arm by Mella who, in a conciliatory manner, asked her to join him in prayer.

"Have you been converted?" she asked.

"I want to be," Mella replied.

For almost an hour, while kneeling on the sawdust-covered floor of the bar, Carry struggled with Satan for the soul of the saloon-keeper. Finally, convinced that Mella was contrite for his past wrong-doings and that she had achieved a signal victory over the devil, she agreed to sell the publican a hatchet, a button, a photograph, and several tracts. After Mella had locked the door of the saloon and formally announced that he was through with the liquor traffic, he accompanied Carry to the station where she took the train for St. Louis. Mella thereafter reopened his saloon to a much expanded clientele.

Carry Nation returned to Leavenworth City a decade later, but this time a broken and sick woman. There in the Evergreen Hospital she died on June 2, 1911.

The school reopened in the fall of 1902 with the War Department directing that the preliminary basic instruction that had formerly taken place at Leavenworth be included in schools to be established on various other posts. Leavenworth was converted to a post-graduate institution, and its term of instruction was reduced to one year. Its new designation was the General Service and Staff College.

The happy combination in 1903 of Elihu Root as Secretary of War and Brigadier General J. Franklin Bell as commandant did much to increase the prestige of the school at Fort Leavenworth. A firm believer in the general staff concept, Root, who is ranked as America's greatest Secretary of War, was also an articulate advocate of military education. Bell, who had graduated from the military academy in 1878, had been a professor of Military Science and Tactics at Southern Illinois University from 1886 to 1889, and had seen considerable combat in both the Spanish American War and the Philippines, was to remain as commandant until 1906 and was later army chief of staff. The combined efforts of these two men resulted in the school's ultimately reaching college and graduate level.

A general staff, under a chief of staff, for which Secretary Root had so long labored, was created by Congress in 1903, and the demand for educated professional officers became even more urgent. Fortunately, the schools at Fort Leavenworth, with their emphasis on staff training, were able to fill the breach.

In 1904, the student's tour was again increased to two years, the first year being designated the Infantry and Cavalry School, and the second the Staff College. In that year a Signal School was also established at Leavenworth.[7] In 1905, the name of the school was again changed—to the United States Infantry and Cavalry School—and in 1907 it became known as the Army School of the Line. In the same year, General Bell acknowledged that the detailing of lieutenants as students at Leavenworth had been a mistake, and announced that thereafter only senior captains and young ranking majors would be assigned there. Reserve officers as well as militiamen were admitted as students in 1905.

Brigadier General Frederick Funston, the hero of the Philippine insurrection and the captor of Emilio Aguinaldo, became commandant of the school in August, 1908, and remained in the position until January, 1911. During his administration, a selected course of three months for field-grade officers was established. The course was almost entirely composed of instruction in military tactics, and was so planned that its students took part in tactical problems and exercises with the Staff College class. In 1910, an Army Field Engineering School was included, and a year later there was added the Army Field Service School for Medical Officers. Both were terminated with the advent of World War II.

Classes at Fort Leavenworth were again suspended with the outbreak of World War I, but it was in that conflict that the impact of the school's instruction was first felt. The foresight of Grant, Sherman, Sheridan, and Root, and the labors of Wagner, Bell, and the other officers who had staffed its faculty, finally reaped dividends. Former students of the school, qualified professional officers commanded regiments, brigades, and divisions, and served in high staff positions. Their performance in combat justified the years of effort that had gone into the formation of the school and its curriculum. Both General John J. Pershing and Marshal Ferdinand Foch, on separate visits to Fort Leavenworth, paid high tribute to the character of its graduates and the value of its instruction. (It is interesting to note that in the party accompanying General Pershing there was an obscure major named George C. Marshall.) Marshal Foch, in his address, told the student officers:

> The services rendered by you in the war have plainly shown the character and the value of the instruction of this school. . . . not only must one have a precise and accurate tactical knowledge of up to date military matters, but [also]—a general development of [the] brain—a general culture exceedingly vast.

With the post serving both as an induction and training center during the months of World War I, Fort Leavenworth was again a beehive of activity. The first class of provisional lieutenants—or "ninety-day wonders" as they were soon to be called by the enlisted men—was graduated before war was declared on Germany. In a period of weeks, raw young men from civilian life, sixty percent of whom had never had any previous military training, were given the training that would make them into soldiers capable of chalking up a record in combat that was more than creditable.

It wasn't all work, however: on April 2, 1917, the *Army and Navy Journal* reported that the officers of the provisional battalion of lieutenants gave a ball in the Fort Leavenworth gymnasium, which, for the occasion, had been converted into a beautiful Japanese garden. The affair was attended by five hundred guests from Leavenworth and other surrounding cities. The *Journal* described the ball as "brilliant."

After the declaration of war, the signal corps upped the number of men in training on the post from one hundred to 350, and with the signal officer reserve training, the post had more soldiers of that branch than any other fort in the country. A reporter wrote: "Fort Leavenworth has probably the best facilities of any post in the United States for the education of men for this particular arm of the service."

In the July 7, 1917, issue of the *Army and Navy Journal*, its correspondent described the scene at Fort Leavenworth:

> On the hillsides of the parade ground are squads of men noting the topographical features of the country by small sketches which will be later elaborated into maps. The men scattered over the landscape in khaki colored groups each party intent on his own lessons give an impression of life and activity long missed on the reservation. On the north end of the west end parade grounds, troops of Cavalry are rapidly changing the soft turf into a field of dust as the horses walk, trot, gallop, wheel and charge. Nearby is the plot where the horsemen learn the use of their sabres. In another direction a detachment of the Signal Corps soldiers can be seen stringing a concealed telegraph wire from one spot to another—laying it along the ground or beneath the surface. One of the most interesting tasks of the officers is trench building. Over the hill south of Merritt Lake are a series of barbed-wire barricades reinforced by rows of sharpened stakes. Behind these are the trenches exactly as those used in France. The main fighting trenches are connected by passageways . . . permitting [safe] retreat or [the] bringing up of supplies.

Reopened as the School of the Line and the General Staff School in 1919, the tour was again reduced to one year. Between the World Wars, four thousand regular and five hundred national guard and reserve officers were graduated. Assignment to, and graduation from the school had now become a prerequisite for the professional advancement of regular officers.

Between the two World Wars, the faculty at the college produced a complete series of texts based on American military practice. Leavenworth thus became the recognized source of army doctrine and procedure.

As the clouds of World War II began to gather, plans were made for the continuation of the school during wartime, with a greater expansion of student enrollment. Shorter courses were initiated and by January, 1942, the post was ready to accommodate classes totaling 1,400 student officers. During the forty-two months that World War II continued, there were twenty-seven classes and nineteen thousand regular army, reserve, national guard, navy, marine corps, and allied officers graduated.

World War II fully established the importance of the Command and General Staff College in the defensive structure of the United States. George C. Marshall and Dwight D. Eisenhower had respectively headed their classes when they graduated from the school. Virtually every senior army commander, including Generals Omar N. Bradley, Alexander Patch, Matthew B. Ridgway, Mark Clark, and Maxwell Taylor, was a Leavenworth man. Almost without exception, their staffs had been manned by alumni of the school.

General George C. Marshall, chief of staff of the army, said in a speech in Kansas City on November 18, 1945:

Leavenworth provided the leaders who played a determining part . . . in the liberation of Europe and Asia in 1945. . . . The land battles of Europe and the Pacific were first won in the heart of America. MacArthur, Eisenhower, Arnold, Bradley, and a long list of our great commanders were developed on the heights overlooking the Missouri River at Fort Leavenworth.

And Secretary of War Robert C. Patterson, told the student body at the college in May, 1947:

The longer I serve with the War Department the more I appreciate what Leavenworth has done for the Nation's safety in the past and its great value to the service for the future. It is no exaggeration to say that our victories in World War II were won right here at Leavenworth, perhaps with the aid of a Gettysburg map. Here our great war leaders learned the art of combined arms, the handling of large bodies of troops.

Besides its principal role—support of the schools and college—the garrison at Fort Leavenworth performed other duties. Between 1940 and 1946, 318,000 men were processed through its induction center; 452,000 went through its reception center, and the separation center discharged 147,000 men.

On May 29, 1946, the start of the first year of postwar operations, the school was renamed the Command and General Staff College, and the War Department directed that it should "provide instructions in the light of war lessons and modern development to insure

a . Research and study to improve methods of personnel, intelligence, tactical, and logistical procedures.
b . Efficient, administrative, intelligence, and logistical support of the fighting forces.
c . Effective development and employment of all field forces within the framework of the Army group.
d . Coordinated employment of army units with air and naval forces.

The War Department directive also stipulated that a regular course of approximately ten months and an associate course of approximately four months' duration were to be conducted yearly. The stated purpose of the two courses was identical: "To prepare officers for duty as commanders and staff officers at the division and higher levels."

Members of the 1963-64 class of the Command and General Staff Officers' course were the first student officers to be given an opportunity to participate in a voluntary program officially known as the Masters Program, leading to a master's degree. Designed to complement the regular course, it required a thesis describing a research study of a significant problem within the scope of the

Command and General Staff Officers' course, with comprehensive written and oral examinations.

The Army War College that had been established in Washington was closed during World War II, and when it reopened in 1950 it was located at Fort Leavenworth. It remained there for only a year, and was then moved to Carlisle Barracks, Pennsylvania.

The Korean action had less impact on the college than any previous conflict. The curriculum, which had been expanded to include the many military aspects of World War II, required few modifications to accommodate the situation in Korea. Mobilization of trained officers did increase, however, and the school was called upon to accommodate the expansion. One regular course (proper name: Command and General Staff Officers' Course) has been held each year starting in 1946–1947. One associate class was held in 1947, 1948, 1949, 1950, 1952, and 1953; two associate classes were held in 1951, 1954, 1955, 1956, and one in 1967.

Any enumeration of the schools at Fort Leavenworth would be incomplete without mentioning the United States Disciplinary Barracks, as distinguished from the federal prison, which is a civilian institution and not a part of the post. Prior to 1875, military prisoners, both long-term and minor offenders, had been confined in local post stockades and in various state penitentiaries. This proved unwise both from administrative and housing standpoints. In that year, the first United States military prison was established at Leavenworth. In 1915, the name of the prison was changed to the United States Disciplinary Barracks, and greater emphasis was placed on rehabilitation and the restoration to duty of inmates with records of good conduct. Today the barracks is, in effect, a school, with a special plan of rehabilitation for each of its students, looking toward either their restoration to duty or their return to civilian life as good citizens. Prisoners are taught such trades as photo-tag, printing, agriculture, floriculture, mechanics, barbering, furniture construction, shoe repair, and automatic data processing.

Beginning with Lieutenant Henry C. Lecomte of the Swiss army in 1894 and two Mexican officers in 1908, a succession of foreign students have attended the college. Following World War II, the numbers of these allied officers have greatly increased, and thousands have graduated to carry the institutions' seventy-six doctrines to the four corners of the world. During the academic year of 1955–1956, there were seventy-six allied officers from thirty-nine nations in attendance. In the 1968–1969 session, there were ninety-six allied officers from fifty-one countries. Of the 3,500 foreign officers from seventy-eight countries who have graduated from the United States Army Command and General Staff College, fourteen have become heads of state; one hundred and fourteen have gained minister, cabinet or ambassador status; eighty-three have served as commanding generals of their countries' armed forces; and 977 have attained general-officer rank.

Instructions in the tactical employment of nuclear weapons was first presented by the college in 1952, and by 1956, had developed into two courses. A five-week course was presented to non-Leavenworth students selected army-wide, and three-and-a-half weeks of study was given to selected students of both the regular and associate courses. Both courses continued until 1958, when the shorter one was dropped. Responsibility for the five-week course was transferred to the Artillery and Missile School in July, 1962. The tactical employment of nuclear weapons per se, however, is still a part of the regular program.

With the increased complexities of modern warfare, the Command and General Staff College has remained abreast of the times. The academic standards are high, and the course is grueling. Unlike the National War College, the Army War College, and the Industrial College of the Armed Forces, each of whose atmosphere is informal, the Command and General Staff College gives detailed examinations, and there is formal grading.

It is at the Command and General Staff College that the Leavenworth stamp is put upon an officer, whether he be from West Point, the reserve officer training corps, officer candidate school, or civilian life. At his branch school, he may have been given more detailed information on his specialty, but only at Fort Leavenworth will he be prepared for combat command and staff responsibilities.

Officers who attain the rank of major or lieutenant colonel are not automatically admitted to Fort Leavenworth. Students are selected from those officers who have not yet reached the age of forty-nine, have at least eight years of commissioned service, and have exhibited potential for assignment to high command or staff positions. Only half of those eligible are assigned to the school. For most of those who do attend, it is their last formal military educational opportunity.

Since April, 1968, the principal mission of the Command and General Staff College has been defined by the Department of the Army as:

To prepare officers—
a. For duty as commanders of divisions, corps, armies, and comparable commands in the communications zone.
b. For duty on the general staff of divisions, corps, armies, and comparable commands in the communications zone.

To provide instruction in the light of modern developments and war lessons to ensure—
a. Effective development and employment of all field forces within the framework of the field army and the communications zone.
b. Efficient personnel, intelligence, and logistical support of the fighting forces.

Leavenworth uses a variety of teaching methods. There are lectures, seminars, map, and terrain studies. These exercises are generally followed by a critique in which the school's solution is presented. The case system of teaching, as developed by law schools, is also employed.

Major General Michael S. Davison, the college commandant and a former combat commander with the 45th Division in World War II, announced in 1967 that, starting with the fall term of that year, the number of students in the regular course would be increased from 756 to almost 1,300 and that the associate course would be discontinued. This increase in enrollment from August 1966 to September 1968 created a housing problem, but since 1969 four hundred sets of quarters have been built. Now almost all student officers are quartered on the post.

In February 1972, Major General John J. Hennessey, who had become the commander at Fort Leavenworth the previous year, announced a number of sweeping changes in both the curriculum and in the instructional methods of the college. Thereafter, the number of required courses would be considerably reduced to allow an expanded elective program of studies that would be more nearly geared to the particular professional interest of the student; there would be a lower student-teacher ratio, smaller classes, and the increased use of seminars. The move toward less reliance on required courses of study accords with the Army's current trend toward increased specialization among officers.

The Command and General Staff College also publishes a monthly magazine, *The Military Review*, containing digests of articles from foreign military journals; original articles on strategy, tactics, leadership, command and ordnance; and book reviews. This periodical has a widespread influence not only in the United States, but within the military establishment of its allies as well.

With its Command and Staff College and *The Military Review*, Fort Leavenworth has become a principal center for the formulation of army doctrine. Many of the policies put into effect by the Pentagon had their inception at the fort on the banks of the Missouri River.

Fort Leavenworth is today a busy but peaceful spot. Strolling along its tree-shaded roads, past the frame-and-brick quarters, some of which go back to the middle of the last century, with the neatly landscaped grounds, and finally past the huge and beautiful academic buildings, one cannot help remembering the intrepid men who first arrived there almost a century and a half ago: Colonel Leavenworth, whose personal life was unhappy and whose military career was distinguished; Major Belknap, whose son caused him much grief and finally tarnished his name; Dougherty, the Indian agent, who unlike so many of his peers, had thought first of his savage wards rather than himself; and the legions of stalwart enlisted men who gave so much and asked so little in return. Perhaps if they could see the panorama of today's Fort Leavenworth and could know of its place in the history of the nation and of the free world, they would rest easy.

Throughout its 143 years of existence, Fort Leavenworth has remained a faithful sentinel of the plains. Originally the guardian of the American West—it has entered the last half of the twentieth century as the vital proving ground for soldiers who would lead the defense of Western civilization.

NOTES

CHAPTER ONE   The Road to Santa Fé

1. Benjamin Smith Barton, naturalist, physician, and lecturer at the University of Pennsylvania; Casper Wister, professor of Anatomy at the University of Pennsylvania and for whom the Wister Institute of Anatomy is named; Benjamin Rush, probably the leading physician of the United States, professor of Medicine of the University of Pennsylvania and a signer of the Declaration of Independence.

2. "A bullboat was an open-work basket made of willow sticks lashed together with strips of green rawhide and covered with a single buffalo skin." See Vestal, Stanley, *The Missouri*, New York, 1945, Page 158.

3. Goetzmann, William H., *Exploration and Empire*, New York, 1966, Page 8.

4. Jacobs, James, *Tarnished Warrior*, New York, 1918.

5. Smith, Elbert B., *Magnificent Missourian*, Philadelphia, 1958.

CHAPTER TWO   Cantonment Leavenworth

1. Orders NO. 14, Adjutant General's Office, Washington, D.C., March 7, 1827; National Archives.

2. Vestal, Stanley, *The Missouri*, New York, 1945, Page 11.

3. Hunt, Elvid, *History of Fort Leavenworth, 1827-1927*, Fort Leavenworth, Kansas, 1926.

4. According to Henry Shindler, local historian, a daughter was born to one of the officers on the post in 1827. Kansas State Historical Society Transactions, Vol. 12; Early Settlers XII.

5. A brevet was a commission conferred upon an officer a grade in the Army additional to and higher than that which he holds by virtue of his commission in a particular corps of a legally established military organization. See bibliography, Fry, James Barnett.

6. Fort Atkinson, located on Council Bluffs on the Missouri fourteen miles above the present-day city of Omaha, was established in September, 1819, by Colonel Henry Atkinson.

7. Caesar, Gene, *King of the Mountain Men, the Life of Jim Bridger*, New York, 1961, Page 42.

8. Colonel Leavenworth's Report to Departmental Headquarters, May 8, 1827; National Archives.

9. War Department Orders, NO. 56, September 19, 1827; National Archives.

10. Letter from General Leavenworth to Brigadier General Thomas S. Jesup, June 8, 1828; National Archives.

11. Ashburn, Percy M., *A History of the Medical Department of the United States Army*, Boston, 1929, Page 48.

12. Croghan, Colonel George; Prucha, Francis Paul, Editor, *Army Life on the Western Frontier*, Norman, Oklahoma, 1958, Page 10.

13. Fort Gibson, located where the Grand, Verdigris, and Arkansas rivers join, was established April 21, 1824, by Colonel Matthew Arbuckle. There, in June, 1834, was a great council of Cherokee, Osage, and Choctaw tribes. To impress the Indians, Colonel Leavenworth reviewed the 1st Dragoons.

CHAPTER THREE   Neighboring Indians

1. Swanton, John R., *The Indian Tribes of North America* (Smithsonian Institution) Washington, D.C., 1952, Pages 48-55.

2. Swanton, *Supra*, Pages 252–254. See also, Wissler, Clark, *Indians of the United States*, Garden City, N.Y., 1966, Pages 90–95; 98–99.

3. Swanton, *Supra*, Pages 225–230.

CHAPTER FOUR   The Expeditions

1. Croghan, Colonel George, *Supra*, Page 24.

2. Hunt, *Supra*, Page 34.

3. See *Annual Report of the Secretary of War, 1835*.

4. Nadeau, Remi, *Fort Laramie and the Sioux Indians*, Englewood Cliffs, N.J., 1967, Page 59.

5. Bent's Fort, a trading post built in 1833–34 by two brothers, Charles and William Bent, and their partner Ceran St. Vrain, was near the present site of La Junta, Colorado. It was one of adobe construction, and was large and commodious. See Lavender, David, *Bent's Fort*, Garden City, N.Y., 1954.

6. Of the seventy-five officers who served in the topographical corps, all but eight were West Point graduates. The formal creation of the corps was achieved by the Act of July 5, 1803. The War of 1812 saw the corps full-fledged, consisting of sixteen officers holding the rank of brevet captains and majors. Isaac Roberdeau and John James Abert served as leaders of the corps during most of its lifetime, 1803–1863.

It was a complex institution having a political, a military, a scientific, and even a romantic significance that the corps of topographical engineers entered the West. Its officers were a new type of explorer, carrying the burden and lessons of civilization to the wilderness. Goetzmann, William H., *Army Explorations in the American West, 1803*–1863. New Haven, Conn., 1959, Pages 18–20.

7. Fort Bridger, an Indian Trading Post on the Oregon Trail on the far slope

of the Rockies. Established about 1842 or 1843, it was of primitive construction. It was abandoned and burned in 1853.

8. Seabrook, S. L., *Expedition of Col. E. V. Sumner Against the Cheyenne Indians, 1857*. Kansas State Historical Society Transactions, 16, 305–315. See also *Report of Colonel Sumner*, August 15, 1857; National Archives.

CHAPTER FIVE   Fort Leavenworth

1. Parker, Rev. Samuel, *Journal of an Exploring Tour Beyond the Rocky Mountains*, New York, 1838.

2. Hunt, *Supra*, Page 46.

3. De Voto, Bernard, *Across the Wide Missouri*, Boston, 1947, Page 393.

4. Catlin, George, *Manners, Customs and Conditions of the North American Indian*, London, 1857; see also Kent, Ruth, *Great Day in the West; Forts, Posts, and Rendezvous Beyond the Mississippi*, Norman, Oklahoma, 1956, Page 72.

5. Shindler, Henry, *Fort Leavenworth; Its Churches and Schools*, Fort Leavenworth, Kansas, 1912, Page 4; See also Hunt, *Supra*, Page 57.

6. Terrell, John Upton, *Black Robe*, Garden City, N.Y., 1964, Page 7.

7. Shindler, *Supra*, Page 6.

8. Letter, Thomas Swords, lieutenant, dragoons, Fort Leavenworth, to Dr. Joseph Lovell, surgeon general, U.S. Army, Washington, D.C. August 25, 1825, National Archives.

9. Proceedings of court-martial of Lieutenant Thomas Swords, Jr., August, 1826; National Archives.

10. Magoffin, Susan Shelby; Drum, Stella M., editor; *Down the Santa Fé Trail and into New Mexico; The Diary of Susan Shelby Magoffin, 1846–1847*, New Haven, Connecticut, 1926, Page 147.

11. Arrow Rock, Missouri, 1844.

12. Nadeau, *Supra*, Page 35.

13. Wickliff, Captain William N., *Rules for the Government of the Fort Leavenworth Ferry*, Fort Leavenworth, N.D. (probably 1833), National Archives.

14. Land later ceded to Missouri.

15. Letter, Lieutenant Thomas Swords, Jr., to the adjutant general, November 22, 1836; National Archives.

16. National Archives.

17. War Department General Orders, NO. 41, 1834.

18. Letter, Colonel Henry Dodge to the adjutant general, October 20, 1834; National Archives.

19. As early as August 26, 1836, Colonel George Croghan on an inspection tour had reported, "The stables (at Fort Leavenworth) are execrable, worse than the worst stables at the worst country taverns that I have yet seen, added to which their location is bad." Croghan, *Supra*, Page 45.

20. Letter, Colonel S. W. Kearny, Fort Leavenworth, to Major Thomas F. Hunt, acting quartermaster, Washington, D.C., August 9, 1836; National Archives.

21. Letter, Lieutenant Thomas Swords, Jr., Fort Leavenworth, to Major Thomas F. Hunt, acting quartermaster, Washington, D.C., November 26, 1841.

22. Cross, Thomas, Report, June 1839; National Archives.

23. Croghan, *Supra*, Page 84.

24. Croghan, *Supra*, Pages 147–148.

25. From 1820 to the Civil War, a large proportion of the soldiers in the United States Army were of foreign birth, as a result of the difficulty in procuring suitable recruits from among the native born. In 1822 and 1823, roughly one-fourth of the men who enlisted were of foreign birth; in 1836 and 1837, the proportion was approximately 40 percent. Of 5,000 recruits entering the service in 1850 and 1851, over 70 percent were Europeans; Irish and Germans predominated among these foreign recruits. Registers of Enlistment, Adjutant General's Office, National Archives; Surgeon General's Office, Statistical Report from January 1839 to January 1855, 626–28. Croghan, *Supra*, Page 142.

26. Letter, Lieutenant Thomas Swords, Jr., to Major General Jessup, quartermaster general, Washington, D.C., October 4, 1841; National Archives.

27. In Powell, Colonel William H., *List of Officers of the U.S. Army from 1779 to 1900*, New York, 1900, Wharton is listed as having died July 13, 1847. This is incorrect, for there are letters written by him in the National Archives dated thereafter. See Letter, C. Wharton, Lt. Col., Commanding (Fort Leavenworth), to General Arbuckle, Fort Smith, dated August 14, 1847; National Archives.

28. Letter, Wharton, Colonel C., July 1845; National Archives.

29. Lavender, *Bent's Fort, Supra*, Page 155.

CHAPTER SIX   The Oregon Trail

1. Parkman, Francis, Jr., *The California and Oregon Trail*, New York, 1847, Page 85.

2. General Orders NO. 19, Headquarters of the Army.

3. General Orders NO. 38, Headquarters 6th Military District, October 2, 1852.

4. War Department General Orders NO. 17, June 27, 1853.

CHAPTER SEVEN   The Mexican War

1. Bill, Alfred Hoyt, *Rehearsal for Conflict, the War with Mexico 1846–1848*, New York, 1947, Page 58.

2. Magoffin, *Supra*, Pages 121–122.

3. On the treeless plains, the dried droppings of the buffalo were often used for fuel.

4. Magoffin, *Supra*, Introduction XIV; Page 264. See also letter, Major Philip St George Cooke to J. W. Magoffin, Esquire, Philadelphia, February 21, 1849; National Archives.

5. Near the present site of Kinsley, Kansas.

6. Boatner, Mark M., III, *The Civil War Dictionary*, New York, 1959, Page 932.

7. The battle was fought on Christmas day, 1846.

8. Magoffin, *Supra*, Page 119, note.

CHAPTER EIGHT   The Mormon War

1. Gentile: A term used by Mormons to describe a non-Mormon.
2. Unquestionably many of these federal officials left much to be desired, for their personal life in Utah was often justifiably open to criticism.
3. Ferguson, Brigadier General Samuel, *With Albert Sidney Johnson's Expedition to Utah in 1857*, Kansas State Historical Society Transactions, XII, 304–312.
4. Mullen, Robert, *The Latter Day Saints*, Garden City, N.Y., 1966.

CHAPTER NINE   Life on the Post

1. Boyd, Mrs. Orsemus B., *Cavalry Life in Tent and Field*, New York, 1894, Page 197.
2. Letter, Colonel Roger Jones, adjutant general, Washington, D.C., to Lt. Colonel C. Wharton, Fort Leavenworth, July 9, 1847; National Archives.
3. *Kansas Historical Quarterly*, 1965, 31, Page 187.
4. Lowe, Percival G., *Five Years a Dragoon*, Norman, Oklahoma, 1965.
5. Moody, Ralph, *Stagecoach West*, New York, 1967, Page 139.
6. Hunt, *Supra*, Page 98.
7. Hunt, *Supra*, Page 97.
8. Root, Frank A., and Connelley, William E., *The Overland Stage to California*, Topeka, Kansas, 1901. See also Moody, *Supra*, Page 158.
9. *Kansas City Star*, August 6, 1905. For an interesting account of the windwagon, see Vestal, Stanley, *The Old Santa Fé Trail*, Boston, 1939, Pages 3–9.
10. Root and Connelley, *Supra*, Page 113.
11. Letter, Charles M. Stebbins, president, St. Louis and Missouri River Telegraph Company, St. Louis, to Lt. Colonel George H. Cross, department quartermaster general, July 29, 1857; National Archives.
12. Ferguson, *Supra*, XII, Page 304.
13. Kansas State Historical Transactions (note), XII, Page 305.
14. Letter, Fr. Pierre de Smet, to Adjutant General, July 18, 1867; National Archives.
15. Hawgood, John A., *America's Western Frontiers*, New York, 1967, Page 241.
16. Vestal, *The Missouri, Supra*, Page 38.

CHAPTER TEN   Bleeding Kansas

1. Dick, Everett, *The Sod House Frontier; 1857–1890*, New York, 1943, Page 41.
2. Letter, Jefferson Davis, Washington, D.C., to A. H. Reeder, Washington, D.C., July 8, 1854; National Archives.
3. Hunt, *Supra*, Page 109.
4. Hunt, *Supra*, Page 110.
5. Prentis, Noble L., *A History of Kansas*, Topeka, Kansas, 1909.
6. Quoted in Prentis, *Supra*, Page 81.
7. Nichols, Alice, *Bleeding Kansas*, New York, 1954, Page 35.
8. Nichols, *Supra*, Page 34.
9. Kansas State Historical Society Transactions, XVI, Page 310.

10. Nichols, *Supra,* Page 133.
11. Herr, Major General John K., *The Story of the U. S. Cavalry,* Boston, 1953, Page 52.

CHAPTER ELEVEN   The Civil War

1. Fort Randall established in August, 1856, near Long Lake, South Dakota. It was named in honor of Colonel Daniel Randall, deputy paymaster of the army.
2. Telegram, General William S. Harney to the Secretary of War, April 8, 1861; National Archives. See also Hunt, *Supra,* Page 127.
3. Fort Ridgely in Minnesota, established in March, 1856, by troops of the 6th Infantry.
4. Letter, Colonel D. S. Miles, Fort Leavenworth, to the adjutant general, Washington, D.C., April 30, 1861; National Archives.
5. Letter, Colonel D. S. Miles, Fort Leavenworth, to the adjutant general, Washington, D.C., April 30, 1861; National Archives.
6. Letter, Colonel D. S. Miles, Fort Leavenworth, to the adjutant general, Department of the West, St. Louis, Missouri, August 30, 1861; National Archives.
7. Letter, Colonel D. S. Miles, Fort Leavenworth, to Colonel E. D. Townsend, Washington, D.C., May 10, 1861; National Archives.
8. Letter, Colonel D. S. Miles, Fort Leavenworth, to Captain Seth Williams, St. Louis, May 17, 1861; National Archives.
9. Letter, Major S. D. Sturgis, Fort Leavenworth, to General N. Lyon, commander of the Department of the West, St. Louis, June 8, 1861; National Archives.
10. Letter, 1st Lieutenant A. V. Colburn, adjutant, Fort Leavenworth, to Captain Alfred Sully, Fort Leavenworth, June 10, 1861; National Archives.
11. Letter, Captain Alfred Sully, Camp St. Joseph, to Major S. D. Sturgis, Fort Leavenworth, June 11, 1861; National Archives.
12. Letter, Captain Alfred Sully, Camp St. Joseph, to Major S. D. Sturgis, Fort Leavenworth, June 12, 1861; National Archives.
13. Letter, A. V. Colburn, Fort Leavenworth, to Captain W. E. Prince, Fort Leavenworth, June 10, 1861; National Archives.
14. Letter, Captain W. E. Prince, Camp Union, Kansas City, to Lieutenant A. V. Colburn, adjutant, 1st Cavalry and Post, Fort Leavenworth, June 15, 1861; and letter, to Captain D. F. Stanley, Kansas City, to Captain W. E. Prince, June 13, 1861; National Archives.
15. Letter, W. G. Nugent, Austin, Missouri, to Captain W. E. Prince, Fort Leavenworth, June 25, 1861; National Archives. (There were hundreds of similar letters received at Fort Leavenworth.)
16. Permit issued by Brigadier General N. Lyon, St. Louis, to steamer *Sioux City,* June 28, 1861; National Archives.
17. Letter, J. H. Lane, Washington, D.C., to Hon. Simon Cameron, Secretary of War, July 3, 1861. See also letter, L. C. Easton, quartermaster, Fort Leavenworth, to Brigadier General M. C. Meigs, Washington, D.C., August 20, 1861; National Archives.
18. Letter, W. M. Paxton, secretary, Hall of Platte Lodge, No. 56, F & AM, Fort Leavenworth, September 28, 1861; National Archives.
19. Affidavit, R. A. Ringo and F. B. Moore, M.D., Clay County, Mo., October 18, 1861; National Archives.

20. Letter, Captain W. E. Prince, Fort Leavenworth, to General N. Lyon, Springfield, Missouri, July 27, 1861; National Archives.

21. Report, Captain W. E. Prince, Fort Leavenworth, June 28, 1861; National Archives.

22. Letter, R. S. Migg, Independence, Missouri, to Captain W. E. Prince, Fort Leavenworth, July 29, 1861; National Archives.

23. Letter, Captain W. E. Prince, Fort Leavenworth, to Governor G. Robinson, July 31, 1861; National Archives.

24. Letter, F. Johnson, Indian agent, Delaware Council House, to Captain W. E. Prince, Fort Leavenworth, November 18, 1861; National Archives.

25. Letter, Captain Elmer Otis, Fort Wise, Colorado Territory, to Captain J. C. Kelton AAG, Western Department, St. Louis, Mo., October, 1861; National Archives.

26. Petition from citizens of Emporia, Kansas, to Governor Charles Robinson, November 28, 1861; National Archives.

27. Letter, Wm. R. Judson, Colonel commanding 6th Regiment, Fort Scott, to Major General Hunter, November 20, 1861; National Archives.

28. Boatner, *Supra*, Page 935.

29. Report, Lt. J. M. Vance, Independence, Missouri, to Adjutant Frank F. Preble, June 19, 1862; National Archives.

30. Report, Major W. A. Philip, 1st Indian Regiment, to Colonel William Weir, July 13, 1862; National Archives.

31. Letter, Henry C. Hodges, Depart QM, to Chief of the Delaware, May 12, 1864; and letter, 1st Lt. H. . . . (?) AAAG, Department of the Border, Kansas City, to commanding officer, September 30, 1863; National Archives.

32. Letter, S. B. Davis, surgeon, U.S. Volunteers, Fort Leavenworth, to Major S. J. McKenny, inspector general, Department of Kansas City, August 11, 1864; National Archives.

33. Brown, D. Alexander, *The Galvanized Yankees*, Urbana, Illinois, 1965.

34. Permanent party: personnel permanently stationed on a post generally engaged in housekeeping duties.

CHAPTER TWELVE The Buffalo Soldiers

1. Schoenfeld, Seymour J., *The Negro in the Armed Forces*, Washington, D.C., 1945.

2. Leckie, William H., *The Buffalo Soldiers*, Norman, Oklahoma, 1967.

3. Bernardo, C. Joseph, and Bacon, Eugene H., *American Military Policy, Its Development Since 1775*, Harrisburg, Pennsylvania, 1955.

4. American Battle Monument Commission, *92nd Division, Summary of Operation in the World War*, Washington, D.C., 1944; and see Kahn, Ely J. Jr., and McLemore, Henry, *Fighting Divisions*, Washington, D.C., 1946.

5. Flipper, Henry O., Harris, Theodore D., editor, *The Western Memoirs of Henry O. Flipper*, El Paso, Texas, 1963. See also Jackson, Sara D., *The Colored Cadet at West Point*, unpublished manuscript, Washington, D.C., 1968.

6. The author is proud of his part in the desegregation of the army. In 1947, as a delegate to the New Jersey Constitutional Convention together with the late William Randolph, a Newark attorney and the grandson of a slave, he introduced an amendment to the New Jersey Bill of Rights ending segregation

in the militia or national guard. President Truman and Secretary of Defense James Forrestal, were accordingly forced to permit the desegregation of the New Jersey Guard. New York and other northern states subsequently took the same course of action. The desegregation of the army soon followed.

CHAPTER THIRTEEN   The Post After the Civil War

1. Report, Lieutenant Colonel R. E. Fleming, East St. Louis, to Major J. W. Barnis, June 23, 1865; National Archives.

2. Letter and attached charges, C. J. Stolbrand, Brigadier General Volts, Fort Leavenworth, to Captain J. E. Jacobs AAG, August 29, 1865; National Archives.

3. *Army and Navy Journal*, May 26, 1866, Page 652; June 2, 1866, Page 650; and June 16, 1866, Page 681.

4. Letter, Lieutenant G. Dodge, post adjutant, Fort Leavenworth, to Reverend Hiram Stone, post chaplain, May 1, 1885; National Archives.

5. Letter, Colonel W. Hoffman, Fort Leavenworth, to Mrs. B. F. Landon, Rutland, Vermont, March 18, 1867; National Archives.

6. Quoted from Leckie, *Supra*, Page 13.

7. *Army and Navy Journal*, January 20, 1876.

8. See Transcript of the Court-Martial of Lieutenant Colonel George A. Custer, 1867; National Archives.

9. Fort Wallace, at the juncture of Pond Creek with the south fork of the Smoky Hill River in Kansas. The post was first established on October 26, 1865, but thereafter moved several times. It was named for Brigadier General W. H. L. Wallace, killed at the battle of Shiloh. It was abandoned May 31, 1882.

10. Van de Water, Frederic F., *Glory Hunter, A Life of General Custer*, Indianapolis, 1934, Page 174.

11. Chandler, Lieutenant Colonel Melbourne C., *Of GaryOwen in Glory*, Washington, D.C., 1960, Page 4.

12. Kinsley, D.A., *Favor the Bold*, New York, 1968, Page 74. Kansas State Historical Society Collections, XVII, Page 221.

13. The Secretary of the Treasury to the Secretary of War, Washington, D.C., 1868; National Archives.

14. Swanberg, W. A., *Pulitzer*, New York, 1967.

15. *The Leavenworth Times*, February 4, 1887.

16. Goodale, Ephriam, Goodale, Roy, editor, "A Civilian at Fort Leavenworth and Fort Hays, 1874–1879," *The Kansas Historical Quarterly*, Summer 1867, Page 143.

17. Goodale, *Supra*, Page 138.

18. Army records disclose no such officer. The officer was probably using an alias.

19. Letter, M. J. Martin, Leavenworth, Kansas, to commanding officer, Fort Leavenworth, March 15, 1870; National Archives.

20. *Army and Navy Journal*, August 6, 1870.

21. Letter, Major James W. Moore, department quartermaster, Fort Leavenworth, to the acting assistant adjutant general, Department of the Missouri, Fort Leavenworth, July 30, 1877; National Archives.

CHAPTER FOURTEEN   The Schools

1. General Orders NO. 42, Headquarters of the Army, Washington, D.C., May 7, 1881; National Archives.

2. Hunt, *Supra,* Page 161.

3. General Orders NO. 8, Headquarters of the Army, Washington, D.C., January 26, 1882; National Archives.

4. General Orders NO. 17, Headquarters of the Army, Washington, D.C., March 17, 1888; National Archives.

5. Hunt, *Supra,* Page 176.

6. General Orders NO. 49, War Department, 1897; National Archives.

7. General Orders NO. 115, War Department, Washington, D.C., 1904; National Archives.

APPENDICES

COMMANDING OFFICERS AT FORT LEAVENWORTH

Name	From	To
Leavenworth, H., Col., 3d Inf.	1827	1829
Riley, B., Capt., 6th Inf.	1829	1830
Davenport, W., Maj., 6th Inf.	1830	1832
Riley, B., Capt., 6th Inf.	1832	1833
Wickliff, W. N., Capt., 6th Inf.	1833	1834
Riley, B., Capt., 6th Inf.	1834	1834
Dodge, H., Col., 1st Dragoons	1834	1836
Kearny, S. W., Col., 1st Dragoons	1836	1841
Mason, R. B., Lieut. Col., 1st Dragoons	1841	1843
Kearny, S. W., Col., 1st Dragoons	1843	1844
Wharton, C., Maj., 1st Dragoons	1844	1848
Ketchum, W. S., Capt., 6th Inf.	1848	1849
Sumner, E. V., Lieut. Col., 1st Dragoons	May, 1849	June, 1850
Lovell, C. S., Capt., 6th Inf.	June, 1850	Aug., 1850
Plymton, J., Lieut. Col., 1st Dragoons	Aug., 1850	Sept., 1850
Beale, B. L., Maj., 1st Dragoons	Sept., 1850	Oct., 1850
Sumner, E. V., Lieut. Col., 1st Dragoons	Oct., 1850	March, 1851
Beale, B. L., Maj., 1st Dragoons	March, 1851	March, 1851
Fauntleroy, T. T., Col., 1st Dragoons	March, 1851	1853
Hunt, F. E., Capt., 4th Art.	1853	1855
Cooke, P. StG., Lieut. Col., 2d Cav.	1855	1856
Sumner, E. V., Col., 1st Dragoons	1856	July, 1856
Wood, T. J., Capt., 1st Cav.	July, 1856	July, 1856
Johnston, J. E., Lieut. Col., 1st Cav.	July, 1856	Aug., 1856
Sturgis, S. D., Capt., 1st Cav.	Aug., 1856	Sept., 1856
Hendrickson, T., Capt., 6th Inf.	Sept., 1856	Oct., 1856
Sumner, E. V., Col., 1st Dragoons	Oct., 1856	Oct., 1857
Harney, W. S., Brig. Gen., U. S. Army	Oct., 1857	Oct., 1857
Belton, F. S., Col., 1st Dragoons	Oct., 1857	Jan., 1858

Name	From	To
Harney, W. S., Brig. Gen., U. S. Army	Jan., 1858	May, 1858
Sherman, T. W., Maj., 3d Art.	May, 1858	May, 1858
Monroe, J., Lieut. Col., 4th Art.	May, 1858	June, 1859
Dimmick, T., Col., 4th Art.	June, 1859	Nov., 1859
Brooks, H., Capt., 2d Art.	Nov., 1859	Dec., 1859
Magruder, J. B., Lieut. Col., 2d Art.	Dec., 1859	Sept., 1860
Barry, W. F., Capt., 2d Art.	Sept., 1860	Oct., 1860
Brooks, H., Capt., 2d Art.	Oct., 1860	Oct., 1860
Magruder, J. B., Col., 2d Art.	Oct., 1860	Oct., 1860
Brooks, H., Capt., 2d Art.	Oct., 1860	Feb., 1861
Steel, W., Capt., 2d Dragoons	Feb., 1861	April, 1861
Miles, D. S., Capt., 2d Inf.	April, 1861	May, 1861
Sully, A., Capt., 2d Inf.	May, 1861	May, 1861
Sackett, D. B., Maj., 1st Cav.	May, 1861	June, 1861
Sturgis, S. D., Maj., 1st Cav.	June, 1861	June, 1861
Prince, W. E., Maj., 3d Inf.	June, 1861	June, 1862
Burris, J. T., Lieut. Col., 10th Kans. Inf.	June, 1862	Dec., 1863
Jennison, C. R., Col., 15th Kans. Cav.	Dec., 1863	July, 1864
Goodwin, J. A., Col., 138th Ill. Vol. Inf.	July, 1864	Sept., 1864
Davis, W. R., Lieut. Col., 16th Kans. Cav.	Sept., 1864	April, 1865
Heinrichs, G., Lieut. Col., 41st Mo. Vol. Inf.	April, 1865	June, 1865
Carahar, A. P., Col., 2d U. S. Vol. Cav.	June, 1865	Sept., 1865
Fleming, R. E., Lieut. Col., 6th W. Va. Cav.	Sept., 1865	Sept., 1865
Clinton, W., Maj., 13th Inf.	Sept., 1865	Nov., 1865
Reeve, I. V. D., Col., 13th Inf.	Nov., 1865	1866
Hoffman, W., Col., 3d Inf.	1866	April, 1868
Gibbs, A., Maj., 7th Cav.	April, 1868	Sept., 1868
Huntington, H. S., Maj., 7th Cav.	Sept., 1868	Oct., 1868
Hasbrouck, H. C., Capt., 4th Art.	Oct., 1868	March, 1869
Graham, W. M., Capt., 4th Art.	March, 1869	April, 1869
Snyder, S., Capt., 5th Inf.	April, 1869	June, 1869
Lidell, W. H., Lieut. Col, 10th Inf.	June, 1869	Oct., 1869
Sturgis, S. D., Col., 7th Cav.	Oct., 1869	April, 1871
Parker, D., Capt., 3d Inf.	April, 1871	April, 1871
Miles, N. A., Col., 5th Inf.	April, 1871	July, 1876
Lyman, W., Capt., 5th Inf.	July, 1876	July, 1876
Wildrick, A. C., Capt., 2d Art.	July, 1876	Dec., 1876
Davis, J. C., Col., 23d Inf.	Dec., 1876	Feb., 1878
Dodge, R. I., Lieut. Col., 23d Inf.	Feb., 1878	May, 1878
Davis, J. C., Col., 23d Inf.	May, 1878	Jan., 1879
Randall, G. M., Capt., 23d Inf.	Jan., 1879	Feb., 1879
Smith, C. H., Col., 19th Inf.	Feb., 1879	Nov., 1881
*Otis, E. S., Col., 20th Inf.	Nov., 1881	June, 1885
*Ruger, T. H., Col., 18th Inf.	June, 1885	May, 1886

*From the time of the establishment of the Cavalry and Infantry School in 1881 to the outbreak of the Spanish-American War in 1898, the post commander was likewise commandant of the school.

Name	From	To
*McCook, A. McD., Col., 8th Inf.	May, 1886	Aug., 1890
*Townsend, E. F., Col., 12th Inf.	Aug., 1890	Oct., 1894
*Hawkins, H. S., Col., 20th Inf.	Oct., 1894	April, 1898
*Augur, J. A., Maj., 4th Cav.	April, 1898	1899
O'Connell, J. J., Maj., 1st Inf.	1899	1900
Lee, J. M., Lieut. Col., 6th Inf.	1900	1902
Miner, C. W., Col., 6th Inf.	Sept. 1902	June, 1903
**Bell, J. F., Brig. Gen., U. S. Army	July, 1903	Jan., 1904
Duncan, J. W., Col., 6th Inf.	Jan., 1904	1905
Hall, C. B., Col., 18th Inf.	1905	1906
Paulding, W., Lieut. Col., 18th Inf.	1906	1906
Loughborough, R. H. R., Col., 13th Inf.	1907	1907
Davis, T. F., Col., Inf.	1907	1909
Loughborough, R. H. R., Col., 13th Inf.	Jan., 1909	Aug., 1909
Nichols, W. A., Lieut. Col., 13th Inf.	Aug., 1909	Oct., 1909
Loughborough, R. H. R., Col., 13th Inf.	Oct., 1909	March, 1911
Lindsay, J., Capt., 15th Cav.	March, 1911	April, 1911
Lenihan, M. J., Maj., 25th Inf.	April, 1911	July, 1911
Loughborough, R. H. R., Col., 13th Inf.	July, 1911	Sept., 1911
Lenihan, M. J., Maj., 25th Inf.	Sept., 1911	Jan., 1912
Cornman, D., Col., 7th Inf.	Jan., 1912	Feb., 1913
Johnston, W. T., Capt., 15th Cav.	Feb., 1913	Oct., 1913
Martin, C. F., Capt., 15th Cav.	Oct., 1913	Nov., 1913
Mowry, P., Capt., 15th Cav.	Nov., 1913	Dec., 1913
Barnes, J. F., Capt., F. A.	Dec., 1913	Dec., 1913
Smith, C. C., Capt., 20th Inf.	Dec., 1913	April, 1914
Burnham, W. P., Lieut. Col., 20th Inf.	April, 1914	Aug., 1914
Roberts, Harris L., Col., 22d Inf.	Aug., 1914	March, 1916
Comstock, H. E., Capt., Q.M.C.	March, 1916	June, 1916
Warfield, A. B., Capt., Q.M.C.	June, 1916	March, 1917
Shunk, William A., Col.	July, 1917	July, 1919
Muir, Charles H., Maj. Gen.	July, 1919	Aug., 1920
Holbrook, Lucius H., Col.	Aug., 1920	Sept., 1920
Drum, Hugh A., Brig. Gen.	Sept., 1920	July, 1921
Ely, Hanson E., Brig. Gen.	Aug., 1921	June, 1923
Smith, Harry A., Brig. Gen.	July, 1923	June, 1925
King, Edward L., Brig. Gen.	July, 1925	July, 1929
Heintzelman, Stuart, Maj. Gen.	July, 1929	Feb., 1935
Brees, Herbert J., Maj. Gen.	Feb., 1935	June, 1936
Bundel, Charles M., Brig. Gen.	June, 1936	March, 1939
McNair, Leslie J., Brig. Gen.	April, 1939	Oct., 1940
Gruber, Edmund L., Brig. Gen.	Oct., 1940	May, 1941
Fuller, Horace H., Brig. Gen.	June, 1941	Nov., 1941
Lewis, Converse R., Col. (Acting)	Nov., 1941	March, 1942
Truesdell, Karl, Maj. Gen.	March, 1942	Nov., 1945

*See Footnote page 190.

**From January 11, 1904, to July, 1917, the post and the school had separate commanders. From the latter date on, the commandant of the school was likewise commander of the post.

Name	From	To
Gerow, Leonard T., Lieut. Gen.	Nov., 1945	Jan., 1948
Eddy, Manton S., Lieut. Gen.	Jan., 1948	July, 1950
Hartness, Harlan N., Brig. Gen. (Acting)	July, 1950	Oct., 1950
McBride, Horace L., Maj. Gen.	Oct., 1950	March, 1952
Hodes, Henry I., Maj. Gen.	March, 1952	March, 1954
Beauchamp, Charles E., Brig. Gen. (Acting)	March, 1954	July, 1954
Davidson, Garrison H., Maj. Gen.	July, 1954	July, 1956
McGarr, Lionel C., Maj. Gen.	July, 1956	Aug., 1960
Johnson, Harold K., Maj. Gen.	Aug., 1960	Feb., 1963
Lemley, Harry J., Jr., Maj. Gen.	Feb., 1963	Aug., 1966
Davison, Michael S., Maj. Gen.	Aug., 1966	Aug., 1968
Hay, John H., Maj. Gen.	Aug., 1968	Aug., 1971
Hennessey, John J., Maj. Gen.	Aug., 1971	-------

COMMANDANTS OF THE COMMAND AND GENERAL STAFF COLLEGE

Name	From	To
Otis, Elwell S., Col.	Nov., 1881	June, 1885
Ruger, Thomas H., Col.	June, 1885	May, 1886
McCook, Alexander McD., Col.	May, 1886	Aug., 1890
Townsend, Edwin F., Col.	Aug., 1890	Oct., 1894
Hawkins, Hamilton S., Col.	Oct., 1894	April, 1898
Miner, Charles W., Col.	Sept., 1902	June, 1903
Bell, J. Franklin, Brig. Gen.	July, 1903	June, 1903
Hall, Charles B., Brig. Gen.	Aug., 1906	April, 1908
Morrison, John F., Maj. (Acting)	April, 1908	Aug., 1908
Funston, Frederick, Brig. Gen.	Aug., 1908	Jan., 1911
Potts, Ramsay D., Brig. Gen.	Jan., 1911	Feb., 1913
Burnham, William P., Lieut. Col. (Acting)	Feb., 1913	Aug., 1914
Greene, Henry A., Brig. Gen.	Sept., 1914	Aug., 1916
Swift, Eben, Brig. Gen.	Aug., 1916	Nov., 1916
McAndrew, James W., Lieut. Col.	Nov., 1916	June, 1917
Miller, Charles H., Lieut. Col.	June, 1917	July, 1917

BIBLIOGRAPHY

LIBRARIES CONSULTED

Alexandria Public Library, Alexandria, Va.
United States Military Academy Library, West Point, N.Y.
Wilmington Public Library, Wilmington, N.C.
The Library of Congress, Washington, D.C.
National Archives Library, Washington, D.C.
New York City Public Library, New York
The Army Library, The Pentagon, Washington, D.C.
National War College Library, Washington, D.C.
University of North Carolina Library, Chapel Hill, N.C.
North Carolina State Library, Raleigh
Army Historical Section Library, Washington, D.C.
Fort Bragg Post Library, Fort Bragg, N.C.
Philadelphia Historical Society Library, Philadelphia
Public Library, Arlington, Va.
Public Library, Fort Leavenworth, Kansas
Command and General Staff College Library, Fort Leavenworth, Kansas
The Handley Library, Winchester, Virginia

PUBLIC RECORDS

United States Military Academy Archives
National Archives, Washington, D. C.
  Letters In and Out, Fort Leavenworth, Kansas
  Post Returns, Fort Leavenworth, Kansas
  War Department Records

NEWSPAPERS AND MAGAZINES

The Army and Navy Journal
American Historical Review
Niles Weekly Register
Kansas City Star
Missouri Republican, St. Louis
New York Tribune
The Gazette, St. Joseph, Mo.
St. Louis Daily Union
The Weekly Tribune, Liberty, Mo.
New York Weekly Tribune
Santa Fe Republican
The New York Sun
The New York American
New York Evening Post
The New York Times
Missouri Intelligence
Army and Navy Chronicle and Scientific Repository, Washington, D.C.
The Leavenworth Times
Leslie's Illustrated

BOOKS

Adams, James Truslow, editor-in-chief, *Atlas of American History* (New York, 1943).

Alexander, Charles, See Cashin.

American Battlefield Monument Commission, *92nd Division, Summary of Operation in the World War* (Washington, D.C., 1944).

Anderson, William T., See Cashin.

Arnold, Anna E., *A History of Kansas* (Topeka, Kansas, 1914).

Asbury, Herbert, *Carry Nation, the Woman with the Hatchet* (New York, 1929).

Ashburn, Percy M., *A History of the Medical Department of the United States Army* (Boston, 1929).

Athearn, Robert G., *Forts of the Upper Missouri* (Englewood Cliffs, N.J., 1967).

Aubry, Francois Xavier, See Cooke.

Audubon, John James, *Audubon in the West*, McDermott, John Francis, Ed. (Norman, Oklahoma, 1965).

Aver, Louise C., *Famous Kansas Windwagon* (The Kansas City Historical Society, Topeka, Kansas, November, 1966).

Bacon, See Bernardo.

Baldwin, Alice Blackwood, *Memories of the Late Frank D. Baldwin, Major General, U.S.A.* (Los Angeles, 1929).

Baldwin, Sara A., *Illustriana Kansas* (Topeka, Kansas, 1933).

Bandel, Eugene, and Bieber, Ralph P. (editors), *Frontier Life in the Army* (Glendale, Calif., 1932).

Barnard, Talbott, *The History of Fort Leavenworth 1952–1963* (Fort Leavenworth, Kansas, 1964).

Bartlett, Richard A., *Great Surveys of the American West* (Norman, Okla., 1966).

Beers, Henry Putney, *The Western Military Frontier, 1815–1846* (Philadelphia, 1935).

Bender, Averam B., See Cooke.

Bernardo, C. Joseph, and Bacon, Eugene H., *American Military Policy, Its Development Since 1775* (Harrisburg, Pa., 1955).

Bieber, Ralph P., See Cooke.

Bill, Alfred Hoyt, *Rehearsal for Conflict, the War with Mexico 1846–1848* (New York, 1947).

Billington, Ray Allen, *Soldier and Brave*, (New York, 1963).

Bivens, Horace W., See Cashin.

Blackmar, Frank Wilson, PhD., *The Life of Charles Robinson* (Topeka, Kansas, 1902).

Blackwelder, Bernice, *Great Western, The Story of Kit Carson* (Caldwell, Idaho, 1962).

Blair, Walter, *Tall Tale America* (New York, 1944).

Boatner, Mark M., III, *The Civil War Dictionary* (New York, 1959).

Boyd, Mrs. Orsemus B., *Cavalry Life in Tent and Field* (New York, 1894).

Branham, Charles N., editor, *Register of Graduates and Former Cadets of the United States Military Academy* (West Point, N.Y., 1961).

Breihan, Carl W., *Quantrill and His Civil War Guerrillas* (Denver, 1959).

Brodie, Fawn M., *No Man Knows My History, The Life of Joseph Smith the Mormon Prophet* (New York, 1945).

Brown, Arthur M., See Cashin.

Brown, D. Alexander, *The Galvanized Yankees* (Urbana, Ill., 1963).

Brown, Dee, *The Gentle Tamers, Women of the Old Wild West* (New York, 1958).

Brown, Mark H., *The Flight of the Nez Perce* (New York, 1967).

Burns, Robert Ignatius, SJ, *The Jesuits and the Indian Wars of the Northwest* (New Haven, Conn., 1965).

Byrne, Bernard James, MD, *A Frontier Army Surgeon* (New York, 1935).

Caesar, Gene, *King of the Mountain Men, The Life of Jim Bridger* (New York, 1961).

Call, Lewis W., chief clerk, *Military Reservations* (Washington, D.C., 1910).

Canfield, James Hula, *History and Government of Kansas* (Philadelphia, 1894).

Carr, E. T., *Reminiscence Concerning Fort Leavenworth in 1865–'56* (Kansas State Historical Society Collections, XII).

Carson, Christopher, and Quaife, Milo M., editors, *Kit Carson's Autobiography* (Lincoln, Nebraska, 1966).

Cashin, Herschel V.; Alexander, Charles; Brown, Arthur M.; Anderson, William T.; Bivins, Horace W., *Under Fire with the Tenth U.S. Cavalry* (New York, 1889).

Castel, Albert, *William Clarke Quantrill* (New York, 1962).

Catlin, George, *Life Amongst the Indians* (London, 1867).

——————, *North American Indians* (2 Vols.) (Philadelphia, 1913).

——————, *Manners, Customs and Conditions of the North American Indian* (London, 1857).

Chandler, Lt. Col. Melbourne C., *Of Gary Owen in Glory* (Washington, D.C., 1960).

Chittenden, Hiram Martin, *History of Early Steamboat Navigation on the Missouri River* (Glendale, Calif., 1903).

Christopher, (Mrs.) O. H., *The Legend of the Wind Wagons of Westport* (Unpublished Manuscript, Kansas City Public Library, Kansas City, Mo., N.D.)

Cline, Gloria Griffin, *Exploring the Great Basin* (Norman, Okla., 1963).

Connelley, William E., See Root.

Cook, John R., Quaife, Milo M., editor, *The Border and the Buffalo* (Chicago, Ill., 1938).

Cooke, Philip St George; Whiting, William Henry Chase; Aubry, Francois Xavier (Bieber, Ralph P. and Bender, Averam B., editors), *Exploring Southwestern Trails 1846–1854* (Glendale, Calif., 1938).

—————, *Scenes and Adventures in the Army* (Philadelphia, 1859).

—————, *The Conquest of New Mexico and California in 1846–1848* (Albuquerque, N.Mex., 1964).

Coves, Elliott, editor, *History of the Expedition under the Command of Lewis and Clark* (3 Vols.) (New York, 1965).

Crittenden, Hiram Martin, *Early Steamboat Navigation on the Missouri River*, Vol. I (Glendale, Calif., 1903).

Croghan, Colonel George; Prucha, Francis Paul, editor, *Army Life on the Western Frontier* (Selections from the Official Reports Made Between 1826 and 1845, Norman, Okla., 1958).

Cullum, Bvt. Maj. Gen. George W., *Biographical Register of the Officers and Graduates of the U.S. Military Academy at West Point, N.Y.* (4 Vols.) (Boston, 1891).

Cutler, William G., *History of the State of Kansas* (Chicago, 1883).

Davison, Colonel Paul R., USA, Retired, *Old Rolling Wheels* (Fort Leavenworth, Kansas, N.D.)

De Voto, Bernard A., *Across the Wide Missouri* (Boston, 1947).

—————, *The Journals of Lewis and Clark* (Boston, 1953).

—————, *The Year of Decision, 1846* (Boston, 1961).

Dick, Everett, *The Sod House Frontier* (New York, 1943).

Dietz, James Jr., See Owen.

Dillon, Richard, *Meriwether Lewis*

Drago, Harry Sinclair, *Great American Cattle Trails* (New York, 1965).

Drake, Samuel Adams, *The Making of the Great West* (New York, 1887).

Drumm, Stella M., See Magoffin.

Drury, Robert M., *The Life of Isaac McCoy, The Trail Guide* (Kansas City, Kansas, 1965).

Duncan, Charles T., See Greeley.

Durham, Philip, and Jones, Everett L., *The Negro Cowboy* (New York, 1965).

Eldridge, William R., *Major John Dougherty, Pioneer* (Unpublished Manuscript, Kansas City, Mo., 1962).

Emory, Col. W. H., *Notes of a Military Reconnaissance from Fort Leavenworth in Missouri to San Diego, California* (Washington, D.C., 1848).

Ennis, Rees, *Windwagon Smith* (Englewood Cliffs, N.J., 1966).

Evans, Harold C., chief editor, *Kansas* (American Guide Series) (New York, 1939).

Fee, Chester Anders, *Chief Joseph* (New York, 1936).

Ferguson, Gen. Samuel W., *With Albert Sidney Johnston's Expeditions to Utah in 1857* (Kansas State Historical Society Transactions, XII).

Fisher, Anthony D., See Owen.

Flipper, Henry Ossian; Jackson, Sara D., editor, *The Colored Cadet at West Point (1878)* (New York, 1969).

——————, Harris, Theodore D., editor, *The Western Memoirs of Henry O. Flipper* (El Paso, Texas, 1963).

Fort Leavenworth from Frontier Post to Home of the United States Command and General Staff College (Fort Leavenworth, Kan., N.D.).

Fowler, Jacob, *The Journal of Jacob Fowler* (Minneapolis, 1965).

Fox, S. M., *The Story of the Seventh Kansas* (Kansas State Historical Society Transactions, VIII).

Frazer, Robert W., *Forts of the West* (Norman, Okla., 1965).

Fry, James Barnett, *The History and Legal Effect of Brevets in the Armies of Great Briton and the United States* (New York, 1877).

Gaeddert, G. Raymond, *The Birth of Kansas* (Lawrence, Kansas, 1940).

Ganoe, William Addleman, *The History of the United States Army* (New York, 1942).

Garwood, Darrell, *Crossroads of America, The Story of Kansas City* (New York, 1948).

Gerson, Noel B., *Kit Carson, Folk Hero and Man* (Garden City, N.Y., 1964).

Gihon, John H., *Geary and Kansas* (Philadelphia, 1857).

Goetzmann, William H., *Army Explorations in the American West, 1803–1863* (New Haven, Conn., 1959).

——————, *Exploration and Empire* (New York, 1966).

Goodale, Ephriam; Goodale, Roy, editor, *A Civilian at Fort Leavenworth and Fort Hays, 1878–1879 (The Kansas Historical Quarterly*, Topeka, Kan., Summer 1967).

Graham, Col. W. A., *The Custer Myth* (Harrisburg, Pa., 1953).

Greeley, Horace; Duncan, Charles T., editor, *An Overland Journey* (New York, 1964).

Green, Charles Ransley, *Pioneer Narratives, History of the Sac and Fox Indians* (Olathe, Kan., 1912).

Guide to Army Posts (Harrisburg, Pa., 1966).

Gunther, Maj. Sebastian, *Expeditions of Colonel E. V. Sumner Against the Cheyenne Indians* (Kansas State Historical Society Transactions, XVI).

Hale, William Harlan, *Horace Greeley, Voice of the People* (New York, 1950).

Halsey Jr., Milton B., *The Court Martial of Bvt. Major General George A. Custer*, The Trail Guide, Vol. XIII, Number 3 (Kansas City, Mo., September, 1958).

Hamersly, Lewis R., *Records of Living Officers of the United States Army* (Philadelphia, 1884).

Harris, Edward, *Up The Missouri with Audubon; The Journal of Edward Harris*, McDurmott, John Francis, editor (Norman, Okla., 1951).

Hawgood, John A., *America's Western Frontiers* (New York, 1967).

Heitman, Francis B., *Historical Register and Dictionary of the United States Army, 1789–1903* (Washington, D.C., 1903).

Herr, Major General John K., *The Story of the U.S. Cavalry* (Boston, 1953).

History of Clay and Platte Counties, Missouri (St. Louis, Mo., 1885).

Hoffhaus, Charles E., *De Bourgmont* (Unpublished Manuscript, Kansas City, Mo., 1969).

——————, *Fort de Cavagnial (The Kansas Historical Quarterly*, Vol. XXX, Number 4, Topeka, Kan., Winter, 1964).

————————, *The Coutum de Paris and the Jus Civile in Mid-America (Kansas City Law Review,* Vol XXXIII, Number 2, Kansas City, Mo., Summer, 1965).

Holden, Bernice B., *Origin of the State of Kansas* (New York, 1962).

Hollon, W. Eugene, *The Great American Desert* (New York, 1966).

Holloway, John N., *History of Kansas* (Lafayette, Ind., 1868).

Houck, Louis, *A History of Missouri,* Vol. I. (Chicago, 1908).

Howes, Charles C., *This Place Called Kansas* (Norman, Okla., 1952).

Hughes, Willis B., *The Heatherly Incident of 1836 (Missouri Historical Society Bulletin,* Vol. XIII, St. Louis, Mo., 1957).

Hunt, Elvid, *History of Fort Leavenworth, 1827–1927* (Fort Leavenworth, Kansas, 1926).

Indian Affairs, Report On, 1825–1837 (Dept. of War, Washington, D.C., 1838).

Information Office Fort Leavenworth, *Fort Leavenworth, Kansas* (Fort Leavenworth, Kansas, 1964).

Isley, Bliss, and Richards, W. M., *Four Centuries in Kansas* (Wichita, Kansas, 1936).

Jackson, Sara D., See Flipper.

————————, *The Colored Cadet at West Point* (Unpublished Manuscript, Washington, D.C., 1968).

Jacobs, James, *Tarnished Warrior* (New York, 1918).

Jacobs, Major James Rixley, *The Beginning of the United States Army 1783–1812* (Princeton, N.J., 1947).

Jenkins, Evan Jefferson, *Life Among the Homestead Settlers* (Topeka, Kan., 1880).

Jennison, Keith, See Tebbel.

Johnson, Samuel, *The Battle Cry of Freedom* (Lawrence, Kansas, 1954).

Jones, Everett L., See Durham.

Jordan, A.M. Ewing, M.D., *University of Pennsylvania Men Who Served in the Civil War, 1861–1865* (Philadelphia, N.D.)

Josephy, Alvin M., Jr., editor, *The American Heritage Book of Indians* (New York, 1961).

————————, *The Nez-Perce Indians and the Opening of the Northwest* (New Haven, Conn., 1965).

Kahn, Ely J., Jr., and McLemore, Henry, *Fighting Divisions* (Washington, D.C., 1946).

Kent, Ruth, *Great Day in the West; Forts, Posts, and Rendezvous Beyond the Mississippi* (Norman, Okla., 1956).

Kinsley, D.A., *Favor the Bold* (New York, 1968).

Ladd, Horatio O., *History of the War With Mexico* (New York, 1883).

Lavender, David, *Bent's Fort* (Garden City, N.Y., 1954).

————————, *Climax at Buena Vista* (Philadelphia, 1966).

————————, *The Rockies* (New York, 1968).

————————, *Westward Vision, The Oregon Trail* (New York, 1963).

Lavt, Aenes C., *The Overland Trail, the Epic Path of the Pioneers to Oregon* (New York, 1929).

Leavenworth, Elias W., *A Genealogy of the Leavenworth Family in the United States* (Syracuse, N.Y., 1873).

Leckie, William H., *The Buffalo Soldiers* (Norman, Okla., 1967).

Lee, Irvin H., *Negro Medal of Honor Men* (New York, 1967).

Lee, Dr. William, *The Journal of Dr. Lee while on a Journey Across the Plains to Utah* (Unpublished Manuscript, Manuscript Division Library of Congress, Washington, D.C., 1858).

Lewis, Captain Meriwether and Ordway, Sergeant John; Quaife, Milo M., editor, *The Journals of Captain Meriwether Lewis and Sergeant John Ordway, Kept on the Expedition of Western Exploration, 1803–1806* (Madison, Wisconsin, 1916).

Lewis, Oscar, *Sutter's Fort: Gateway to the Gold Fields* (Englewood Cliffs, N.J., 1966).

Lowe, Percival G., *Address* (Kansas State Historical Society, Topeka, Kan., 1894).

_____, *Five Years a Dragoon* (Norman, Okla., 1965).

Magoffin, Susan Shelby; Drumm, Stella M., editor, *Down the Santa Fe Trail and into Mexico, The Diary of Susan Shelby Magoffin, 1846–1847* (New Haven, Conn., 1926).

Malin, James Claude, *John Brown and the Legend of Fifty-Six* (Philadelphia, 1942).

Malone, Dumas, editor, *Dictionary of American Biography* (New York, 1933).

March, David D., Ph.D., *The History of Missouri* (New York, 1967).

Martin, Geo. W., editor, *Collections of the Kansas State Historical Society* (Topeka, Kansas, 1910).

Masland, John W. and Radway, Laurence I., *Soldiers and Scholars* (Princeton, N.J., 1957).

Mattis, Merrill J., editor, *Fort Laramie to Fort Leavenworth Via Republican River in 1849 (Kansas Historical Quarterly,* XX Topeka, Kansas, 1953).

McLemore, Henry, See Kahn.

McNeal, Thomas Allen, *When Kansas Was Young* (New York, 1922).

McPherson, James M., *The Negro's Civil War* (New York, 1967).

Merrill, James M., *Spurs to Glory, The Story of the United States Cavalry* (Chicago, 1966).

Moody, Ralph, *Stagecoach West* (New York, 1967).

Moore, Miles, *Early History of Leavenworth City and County* (Leavenworth, Kansas, 1906).

Mulder, William and Mortensen, A. Russell, editors, *Among the Mormons* (New York, 1958).

Mullen, Robert, *The Latter Day Saints* (Garden City N.Y., 1966).

Murdock, Robert, See Richmond.

Murray, Sir Charles Augustus, *Travels in North America*, Vol. I (London, 1839).

Musick, John R., *Stories Of Missouri* (New York, 1897).

Nadeau, Remi, *Fort Laramie and the Sioux Indians* (Englewood Cliffs, N.J., 1967).

Nichols, Alice, *Bleeding Kansas* (New York, 1954).

Nichols, Roger L., *General Henry Atkinson, A Western Military Career* (Norman, Okla., 1965).

Oliva, Leo E., *Soldiers of the Santa Fe Trail* (Norman, Okla., 1967).

Ordway, Sergeant John, See Lewis.

Owen, Roger C.; Dietz, James F., Jr.; Fisher, Anthony D., *The North American Indians* (New York, 1957).

Paden, Irene D., *The Wake of the Prairie Schooner* (New York, 1943).

Paris, The Comte De, *History of the Civil War in America* (Philadelphia, 1876).

Parker, Rev. Samuel, *Journal of an Exploring Tour Beyond the Rocky Mountains* (New York, 1838).

Parkman, Francis, Jr., *The California and Oregon Trail* (New York, 1847).

Paxton, William M., *Annals of Platte County* (Weston, Mo., 1897).

Phillips, William, *The Conquest of Kansas* (Boston, 1856).

Pike, Zebulon Montgomery, *Sources of the Mississippi and the Western Louisiana Territory* (Ann Arbor, Mich., 1966).

Polk, James K.; Quaife, Milo M., editor, *Diary* (Chicago, 1910).

Portrait and Biographical Album of Washington, Clay and Riley Counties (Chicago, 1890).

Portrait and Biographical Record, Clay, Ray, Carroll, Chairiton And Linn Counties, Mo. (Chicago, 1893).

Powell, Colonel W. H., *List of Officers of the United States Army from 1776 to 1900* (New York, 1900).

Prebble, John, *The Buffalo Soldiers* (New York, 1959).

Prentis, Noble L., *A History of Kansas* (Topeka, Kansas, 1909).

—————, *History of Kansas* (Winfield, Kansas, 1899).

—————, *Kansas Miscellaneous* (Topeka, Kansas, 1889).

Prucha, Francis Paul, *Army Life on the Western Frontier* (Norman, Okla., 1958).

—————, *Broadax and Bayonet* (Lansing, Mich., 1953).

—————, Editor, See Croghan.

Quaife, Milo M., *Chicago and the Old Northwest 1673–1835* (Chicago, 1913).

—————, See Lewis, Captain Meriwether.

—————, See Cook.

—————, See Carson.

—————, See Polk.

Richards, W. M., See Isley.

Richmond, Robert W. and Murdock, Robert, *A Nation Moving West* (Lincoln, Nebraska, 1966).

Risch, Erna, *Quartermaster Support of the Army: A History of the Corps 1775–1939* (Washington, D.C., 1962).

Robinson, Charles, *The Kansas Conflict* (New York, 1892).

Robinson, Sara T. L., *Kansas* (Boston, 1856).

Root, Frank A. and Connelley, William E., *The Overland Stage to California* (Topeka, Kansas, 1901).

Sabin, Edwin L., *Buffalo Bill and the Overland Trail* (Philadelphia, 1914).

—————, *Kit Carson Days 1809–1868*, Vol. I and II (New York, 1935).

Sandburg, Carl, *Abraham Lincoln* (3 Vols.) (New York, 1925–1939).

Sandoz, Mari, *The Beaver Men, Spearheads of Empire* (New York, 1964).

Schauffler, Edward R., "Westport Windwagon," *Kansas City Times* (Kansas City, Mo., April 3, 1946).

Schoenfeld, Seymour J., *The Negro in the Armed Forces* (Washington, D.C., 1945).

Schramm, Wilbur, *Windwagon Smith and Other Yarns* (New York, 1941).

—————, "Windwagon Smith," *The Atlantic Monthly*, Vol. CLXVIII (Boston, 1941).

Scott, Maj. Gen. Hugh Lenox, *Some Memories of A Soldier* (New York, 1928).

Sellers, Charles Grier, *James K. Polk, Jacksonian, 1795–1843* (Princeton, N.J., 1957).

Settle, Raymond W. and Settle, Mary Lund, *Empire on Wheels* (Stanford, Calif., 1949).

—————, *The March of the Mounted Riflemen* (Glendale, Calif., 1940).

_____, and Settle, Mary Lund, *War Drums and Wagon Wheels* (Lincoln, Nebraska, 1966).

Shankle, George Earle, *State Names and Flags* (New York, 1941).

Sherman, General W. T., *Memorial on the Death of General Swords* (Association of Graduates of the Military Academy, 1886).

Shindler, Henry, *A Guide, Fort Leavenworth, Kansas* (Leavenworth, Kansas, 1884).

_____, *Compendium of Laws* (Fort Leavenworth, Kansas, 1909).

_____, *Fort Leavenworth; Its Churches and Schools* (Fort Leavenworth, Kansas, 1912).

_____, *History of Fort Leavenworth* (Unpublished Manuscript, Command and General Staff College Library, Fort Leavenworth, Kansas, 1929).

_____, *History of the Army Service Schools* (Leavenworth, Kansas, 1908).

_____, *Last of Army's Rank and File Whose Blood Drenched Kansas Soil*, Vol. XII (Kansas Historical Society, Topeka, Kansas, 1912).

_____, *The First Capitol of Kansas*, Vol. XII of Collections of the Kansas Historical Society (Topeka, Kansas, 1912).

Smith, Elbert B., *Magnificent Missourian* (Philadelphia, 1958).

Smith, George Gardner, editor, *Spencer Kellogg Brown, His Life in Kansas and His Death as a Spy, 1842–1863* (New York, 1903).

Smithsonian Institution, *Annual Report of the Board of Regents*, July, 1885, Part II (Washington, D.C., 1886).

Speer, John, *Life of General James H. Lane, Liberator of Kansas* (Gordin City, Kansas, 1896).

Spring, Leverett Wilson, *Kansas* (Boston, 1913).

Steckmesser, Kent Ladd, *The Western Hero in History and Legend* (Norman, Okla., 1965).

Steward, George R., *The California Trail* (New York, 1962).

Stirling, Matthew, *Indians of North America* (Washington, D.C., 1955).

Streeter, Floyd B., *The Kaw* (New York, 1941).

Sullivan, Charles J., *Army Posts and Towns* (Los Angeles, 1926).

Swanberg, W. A., *Pulitzer* (New York, 1967).

Swanton, John R., *The Indian Tribes of North America* (Washington, D.C., 1952).

Tebbel, John and Jennison, Keith, *The American Indian Wars* (New York, 1960).

Terrell, John, See Walton.

Terrell, John Upton, *Zebulon Pike* (New York, 1968).

_____, *Black Robe* (Garden City, N.Y., 1964).

Thayer, Eli, *A History of the Kansas Crusade* (New York, 1889).

Thomas, Benjamin P., *Abraham Lincoln* (New York, 1952).

Tisdale, Henry, *Travel by Stage in the Early Days* (Kansas State Historical Society Transactions, VII).

Tracy, Col. Frank M., *Capture of the Iatan Flag* (Kansas Historical Collections, Vol. 1–2, Topeka, Kansas, 1881).

Tuttle, Charles R., *A New Centennial History of the State of Kansas* (Madison, Wisconsin, 1876).

Tyler, Orville Z., *The History of Fort Leavenworth, 1937–1951* (Fort Leavenworth, Kansas, 1951).

U.S. Army and General Staff College, *A Military History of 1881–1963* (Fort Leavenworth, Kansas, 1964).

U.S. Office of Education, *The United States Army Command and General Staff*

College (Information for Review Committee, Washington, D.C., 1967).

Utley, Robert M., *Frontiersman in Blue, The United States Army and the Indian, 1848–1865* (New York, 1967).

Van de Water, Frederic F., *Glory Hunter, A Life of General Custer* (Indianapolis, 1934).

Vestal, Stanley, *Kit Carson, The Happy Warrior of the Old West* (Boston, 1928).

——————, *The Missouri* (New York, 1945).

——————, *The Old Santa Fe Trail* (Boston, 1939).

Villard, Oswald Garrison, *John Brown 1800–1859* (Gloucester, Mass., 1965).

Walton, George and Terrell, John, *Faint the Trumpet Sounds* (New York, 1966).

Webb, Walter Prescott, *The Great Plains* (New York, 1931).

Weigley, Russell F., *History of the United States Army* (New York, 1967).

——————, *Toward An American Army* (New York, 1962).

Wellman, Paul I., *Death on Horseback* (Philadelphia, 1934).

Wells, Anna Mary, *Dear Preceptor, The Life and Times of Thomas Wentworth Higginson* (Cambridge, Mass., 1963).

Werner, M. R., *Brigham Young* (New York, 1925).

Wetmore, Helen Cody, *Last of the Great Scouts* (Duluth, Minn., 1899).

Whiting, William Henry Chase, See Cooke.

Whitman, S. E., *Cavalry Raid* (Boston, 1956).

Williams, Ben Ames, *Mr. Secretary* (New York, 1940).

Wilson, James Grant, editor, *Appleton's Encyclopedia of American Biography* (New York, 1888).

Wissler, Clark, *Indians of the United States* (Garden City, N.Y., 1966).

Wormser, Richard, *The Yellowlegs, The Story of the United States Cavalry* (Garden City, N.Y., 1966).

Young, Otis E., *The First Military Escort on the Santa Fe Trail* (Glendale, Calif., 1952).

——————, *The West of Philip St George Cooke, 1809–1895* (Glendale, Calif., 1955).

INDEX

Abert, Col. John J., 36
Abolitionists, in Kansas, 106
Adams, Henry J., 154
Adams, Thomas M., 96
Aglala Indians, 31
Alamo, battle at, 69
Alexander, Col. Thomas L., 81
Allen, Lt. James, 74
Allen, Col. Shubael, 58
Allis, Samuel, 44–45
American Fur Company, 66
Anderson, "Bloody Bill," 129, 131–32, 137
Anderson, Josephine, 130
Antonio, Col. José, 28
Apache Indians, conflicts with, 74, 143
Arapaho Indians, 31
Archuleta, Col. Diego, 73
Arikara Indians, conflicts with, 11–12, 30–31
Armijo, Gen. Manuel, 23
Armstrong, Capt. Francis, 122
Army and Navy Journal, quoted, 164, 172
Army School of the Line, 170
Arnold, Benedict, 10
Arter, Corp., 28
Ash Hollow, battle of, 91–92
Ashley, William H., 11–12
Assinboine (steamboat), 46
Astor, John Jacob, 60
Audubon, John J., 60

Baker, Col. Daniel, 16
Bandits, 129–32, 154–55
Barber, John, 90
Barber, Thomas, 112
Bartleson group, 63–64
Barton, Benjamin, 2
Bayard, Lt. George D., quoted, 117–18
Bayes, W.M., 100
Beecher, Henry Ward, 109
Belknap, Anne Clark, 15
Belknap, Col. William G., 8, 18, 178
Bell, Brig. Gen. Franklin, 170
Bell, John G., 60
Benét, Maj. Stephen Vincent, 158
Bent, Charles, 75
Benteen, Capt. Frederick, 153
Benton, Thomas Hart, 5, 65, 72
"Benzine Boards," 161
Berry, Capt. M.P., 125
Berryman, Jerome C., 44
Bingham, George Caleb, 130
Black Hawk War, 21
Blacks
  in Civil War, 132, 140
  in military service, 139–45
Blair, Frank P., 75
Blunt, Gen. James C., 131
Bodmer, Karl, 41
Bondi, 114
Boone, Col. Nathan, 112
Bradley, Gen. Omar, 173
Branson, Jacob, 111, 113
Bridger, Jim, 36, 63

Brown, Frederick, 114
Brown, Maj. Gen. Jacob, 5
Brown, John, 114
Brown, Oliver, 114
Brown, Reese, 112
Brown, Watson, 114
Brûlé Indians, 91
Bryant, Lt. Cullen, 158
Bryant, Thomas S., 16
Buchanan, James, 80, 86, 116
    on Mormon issue, 84
Buel, Capt. David H., 157–58
"Buffalo soldiers," 140–45
Bull Run, battle of, 125
Bunzhaf, Lt. Charles, 156

Calhoun, Lt. James, 155
Calhoun, James C., 19
California, 92
    Army conquest of, 75–77
California Gold Rush, 36
Cameron, Simon, 119, 124
Camp Lincoln, 124
Camp Martin, 9-10
Camp Union, 122–23, 126, 130
Campbell, William, 66
Carney, Thomas, 135
Carrington, Albert, 37
Carson, Kit, 63, 76
Catlin, George, 4, 43
    quoted, 17
Chambers (steamboat), 101–2, 114
Cherokee Indians, 30
    during Civil War, 127–28, 132
Cheyenne Indians, 32, 34, 39
    attacks against, 142–43, 152
Chickasaw Indians, 132
Chippewa Indians, 90
Choctaw Indians, 132
Cholera epidemics, 49–50, 90
Chorpenning, George, 92
Chouteau, Pierre, Jr., 66
Christian, James, 110
Civil War, 119–37
Clark, Malcolm, 109
Clark, Gen. Mark, 173
Clark, Lt. William, 2–3
Clark, Gen. William, 55
Clayton, Capt. Powell, 121
Cody, William, 94
Coldon, Sid, 97

Coleman, F.M., 111
Columbia River, 2, 64
Comanche Indians, 17
    conflicts with, 28, 74
Command and General Staff College,
    173–74
Conners, James, 23
Conway, Martin, 110
Cooke, Lt. Col. Philip St George, 31,
    35–36, 53–54, 67
    in Mormon War, 81–83
    quoted, 28–29
Cooke, Lt. William W., 152, 153,
    154
Covey, Trooper, 33–34
Cozzens, Capt. Edward, 122
Creek Indians, 132
Croghan, Col. George, 16, 27, 59
Cross, Col. Truman, quoted, 56
Crosman, Lt. George H., 43
Cruzatte, Pierre, 2
Cummings, Alfred, 80, 81, 84, 85
Curtis, Maj. Gen. Samuel R., 135,
    136
Custer, Lt. Col. George A., 39, 67,
    157
    defeat of, 155
    trial of, 152–54
Custer, Capt. Tom, 153, 155

Darney, Austin, 139
Davenport, Maj. William, 23
Davis, Sgt. Edward, 142
Davis, Gen. George B., 13
Davis, Jefferson, 38, 106–7, 112, 115
Davis, S.B., 133
Davison, Maj. Gen. Michael S., 177
DeBourg, Louis, 45
Delaware (Lenni-Lenape) Indians,
    20–21, 23–24, 90, 132
De Smet, Father Pierre Jean, 44, 46,
    63–64, 117
    as envoy to Indians, 100–1
    in Mormon War, 85–86
De Voto, Bernard, 42, 54
Dickens, Albert, 23
Dodge, Col. Henry, 29–30, 47, 53–
    55
Dodge trail, 31
Donelson, Israel B., 113–14

Doniphan, Col. Alexander W., 72, 74, 75
Dougherty, Maj. John, 14–15, 23, 24, 29–30, 43, 44, 58, 178
Dougherty, Mary, 53
Douglas, Stephen A., 79, 90, 103, 105
Dow, Charles M., 111
Doyle, James, 114
Drouillard, George, 2
Drum, Lt. Richard, 116
Dunbar, James, 57
Dunbar, John, 44–45
Duncan, Capt. Matthew, 58
Dunkin, Daniel, 58
Dunn, Maj. William, 155

Easton, Lt. Alton, 74
Easton, Capt. Langdon C., 32–35
Educational institutions, 161–78
Eisenhower, Dwight D., 173
Elliot, Maj. Joel, 152
Ellsworth, Henry, 24
Emancipation Proclamation, 140
Evans, Lt. Nathan George, 33
Ewell, Capt. Richard F., 38
Explorations of the Valley of the Great Salt Lake (Stansbury), 37
Exploring Tour Beyond the Rocky Mountains, An (Parker), 45

Fellowes, Benjamin F., 42, 50
Ferguson, Lt. Samuel W., 99–100
Field, Lt. Charles William, 91
Fitzpatrick, Tom, 63
Fleming, Lt. Col. Rufus E., 147–48
Flipper, Lt. Henry Ossian, 144–45
Foch, Marshal Ferdinand, 171
Forbes, J.T., 97
Fort Atkinson, 9, 11, 14, 39
Fort Bent, 39, 72, 86
Fort Boise, 64
Fort Bridger, 36, 81, 84, 85
Fort Childs, 65
Fort Clark, 9
Fort Des Moines, 53
Fort Franklin, 115, 116
Fort Gibson, 17, 53, 132, 142
Fort Hall, 36, 64

Fort Hayes, 153
Fort Kearny, 37, 38, 62, 65, 92, 99, 121, 148
    road to, 91
Fort Laramie, 31–32, 64, 66, 81, 92, 99, 119, 148
Fort Leavenworth
    army schools at, 163–78
    black soldiers at, 140–45
    bushwacking in Civil War and, 129–32
    condition of in 1836, 55–56
    daily life at, 87–103, 148–52
    discipline at, 88
    establishment of, 3, 5, 7–18
    expeditions from, 27–39
    ex-rebel recruits at, 134–35
    farm program at, 59
    foreign officers trained at, 175–77
    Indians removed to area of, 20, 22–25
    Kansas violence and, 113–17
    living quarters in 1846 at, 87–89
    Mexican War and, 71–75
    Mormon War and, 80, 81, 85, 86
    mutiny of West Virginians at, 147–48
    post-Civil War living conditions at, 148–52
    prison established at, 175
    private freight shipping from, 93–95
    role of in Civil War, 119–37
    site chosen for, 13–14
    temperance drive at, 168–70
    as territorial capital, 106–7
    violence at, 99–100
    visitors to, 41–51, 60
    World War I and, 171–72
    World War II and, 173–74
Fort Massachusetts, 84
Fort Randall, 120
Fort Ridgely, 120
Fort Riley, 37, 67, 94, 119, 142, 153
Fort St. Vrain, 38, 39
Fort Snelling, 11, 58
Fort Titus, 115, 116
Fort Towson, 33, 58
Fort Vancouver, 64
Fort Wallace, 152–53
Fox Indians, 22, 90

Franklin (Mo.), 89
Free-Soilers, 70
  convention and government of, 110–11
  in Kansas, 106–18
Fremont, Maj. John C., 76
French and Indian Wars, 21
Fugitive Slave Act, 110
Funston, Brig. Gen. Frederick, 170–71

"Galvanized Yankees," 133–35
Gantt, J.C., 30
Gibbs, George, 35
Gillsland, Dr., 47
Gilpin, Maj. William, 74
Goetzmann, William H., quoted, 2–3
Grant, Gen. Ulysses S., 133, 154
Grasshopper plague, 150–51
Greary, John W., 116
Great American Desert, myth of, 4, 63
Great Platte Road, 32
Greeley, Horace, quoted, 93–94
Grierson, Col. Benjamin, 140–42, 150–51, 153
Gunnison, John W., 36

Hagner, Capt. Peter V., 120
Halderman, John A., 107
Hamilton, Capt. Lewis, 153
Hammond, Lt. Thomas Clark, 60–61, 76
Hancock, Gen. Winfield Scott, 153
Hannah, Mary, 154
Harney, Gen. William Selby, 80, 85–86, 91, 100, 119
  Kansas violence and, 116–17
Harris, Edward, 60
Harrison, Gen. William Henry, 23
Hawkins, Alfred, 57
Hazen, William Babcock, 4
Heatherly War (1836), 57–58
Heinrichs, Lt. Col. Gustan, 149
Hennessey, Maj. Gen. John J., 177–78
Herald of Freedom, The (newspaper), 114
Hertzog, Mary, 15
Hertzog, Rachel Wilt, 53
Higginson, Col. T.W., 140

Hoffman, Col. William, 141–42, 152
Holiday, Ben, 95–96, 122
Houston, Gen. Sam, 69, 70
Hughes, M.M., 61
Hughes, Mary, 61
Huidekoper, Col. Henry S., 133
Huneau, Joseph, 33, 34, 35
Hunt, Elvid, quoted, 16
Hunt, Capt. Franklin, 106, 107, 110
Hunt, Lt. Samuel W., 17
Husbands, Bruce, 66

Ide, Gen., 77
Illinois (steamboat), 46
Indian Removal Act, 19, 23
Indian Trade and Intercourse Act, 19
Indians, 11
  broken treaties with, 105–6
  council at Ft. Leavenworth, 23
  during Civil War, 127–28, 132
  1848 council of, 90
  forced westward migration of, 19–22
  Lewis and Clark expedition and, 2
  moved to Ft. Leavenworth area, 20, 22–25
  Sumner expedition and, 37–39
  treaties with, 19–20
  See also specific tribes
Iowa Indians, 16, 17, 28, 54
Irving, John Treat, Jr., quoted, 42–43
Irving, Washington, 4, 42–43
Isacks, Andrew J., 107

Jackson, Andrew, 19, 53, 70, 141
Jackson, Congreve, 23
Jackson, Lt. Henry, 152
James, Frank, 129
James, Jesse, 129, 155
Jefferson, Thomas, 1, 2, 5
Jefferson Barracks, 13
Jesup, Maj. Gen., 60
Johnson, Maj. A.V.E., 131–32
Johnson, Andrew, 101
Johnson, Pvt. Charles, 152
Johnson, F., 127
Johnston, Capt. Andrew R., 76

Johnston, Col. Albert S., 80–81, 83–84
Jones, John S., 95
Jones, Samuel, 111, 113–14
Joseph (Nez Percé chief), 155–56

Kane, Col. Thomas L., 85
Kansa (Kaw) Indians, 4, 20, 23, 25, 90
Kansas, 105–18
    elections in, 107–9, 111
    opened to settlers, 105–6
    reign of terror in, 111–17
Kansas-Nebraska Act, 25, 105
Kansas Pacific Railroad, 147
Kaw Indians, see Kansa Indians
Kearny, Lt. Col. Stephen W., 29–32, 55–56, 71–77
Kerr, Charity, 130
Ketchum, Capt. Daniel, 14
Kickapoo Indians, 20, 21, 23, 44, 45, 90
Kimball, Heber, 82
Kimball and Young (firm), 92
Kingsbury, Lt. Gaines, 47
Knapp, Electa, 11

Lamb, Pompey, 139
Landon, Lt. William, 149
Lane, Gen., 128–29
Lane, James H., 111, 115, 124
Lavender, David, 62
Lawrence (Kansas), 106, 109, 110, 113, 114, 116
Leavenworth, Catherine Frisbie, 11
Leavenworth, Col. Henry, 5, 10–13, 18, 178
    establishment of fort by, 7, 9, 13–16
    military career of, 10–14
Leavenworth, Jesse, 10, 18
Leavenworth (Kansas), 106, 109, 159
Leavenworth, Dr. Melinas Conklin, 17
Leavenworth Times, 162
Lecomte, Lt. Henry C., 100, 175
Lee, John D., 83
Lee, Gen. Robert E., 92
Lee, William, quoted, 102

Lenni-Lenape Indians, see Delaware Indians
Lewis, Fielding, 1
Lewis, Capt. Meriwether, 1–3
Lewis and Clark Expedition, 1–3
Liberator (steamboat), 46
Lincoln, Abraham, 72, 99, 102–3, 124, 133, 140
Little Big Horn, battle of, 155
Little and Hanks (firm), 92
Long, Maj. Stephen, 4
Long Chin (Sioux), 91
Loring, Col. William W., 35, 36
Louisiana Purchase, 1
Lovejoy, Harriett, 11
Lowe, Percival G., 91
Lowe, T.S.C., 91
Lowery, G.P., 107
Lyon, Brig. Gen. Nathaniel, 128, 149

McBrayer, Sgt. William, 143
McClellan, Gen. George B., 133
McCook, Capt. Daniel, 121
McCorkle, John, 130–31
McCoy, Isaac, 22–24, 132
McCoy, John Calvin, 23
McCoy, Ross, 23
McCrea, Cole, 109
McCulloch, Hugh, 154
McDowell, James L., 120
McGraw, William F., 92
MacIntosh, Lt. Donald, 155
McIntosh, Lt. James, 113
Mackay, Lt. Col. Aeneas, 32, 33
McNaught, Maj. John S., 164
Magoffin, James Wiley, 72–73
Magruder, Maj. David L., 158
Majors, Alexander, 93
Mallet, Paul, 4
Mallet, Pierre, 4
Malone, Pvt. James M., 157–58
Manifest Destiny doctrine, 65
Marcy, Capt. Randolph, 84, 85
Marshall, George C., 171, 173
Martin, J.J., 96
Martin, Capt. Wyly, 9
Martin, Zadock, 15, 51, 90
Mary (steamboat), 90
Mason, Col. Richard, 60

Maximillian, Prince of Wied-Neu-
    wied, 41–42, 46
Meek, Joe, 63
Mella, Ferdinand, 169
Merritt, Maj. Gen. Wesley, 144
Mexican War, 37, 61, 62, 69–77,
    128
Mexico, 4, 69
    army of, 28–29, 70–71
Migg, R.S., 127
Miles, Col. Dixon S., 120
Military Review, The (journal), 178
Missouri (state), boundaries of, 54–
    55
Missouri Fur Company, 14
Missouri River
    exploration of, 2
    ferry across, 51, 90
    steamboats on, 46, 101–2, 124
Missouri–Mormon War, 51–52
Monroe, James, 12
Moore, Capt. Benjamin D., 76
Moore, F.B., 125
Mordecai, Capt. Alfred, 159
Mormons, 36, 37, 79–86, 90
    massacre by, 83
    in Mexican War, 71, 72, 77
    in Missouri–Mormon War, 50–51
    war with, 79–86
Morrill, Lot P., 155
Morrison, Elizabeth Eunice, 11
Morrison, Richard, 158
Mountain Meadows massacre, 83, 84
Mule-mounted muzzle-loader, 98
Murray, Charles Augustus, 43

Nadeau, 32
Nation, Pvt., 28
Nation, Carry, 169–70
Negroes, *see* Blacks
New Mexico, army in, 75–76
New York *Tribune*, 93–94
Newsome, Benjamin, 96
Nez Percé Indians, 155
Nichols, Capt. V., 121
Northwestern Confederation of In-
    dian Tribes, 90

O'Fallon, Maj. Benjamin, 15
Ogden, Maj. Edmund A., 91, 93
Omaha Indians, 23

Oregon Battalion, 65
Oregon and California Railroad, 95–
    96
Oregon Trail, 30–32, 59, 63–67, 110
Osage Indians, 3, 20
Otis, Capt. Elmer, 127
Otis, Col. Elwell S., 164
Oto Indians, 20, 23–24, 29
Ottawa Indians, 90

Padouca Indians, 4
Parker, J.W., 96, 97
Parker, Samuel, 41, 44–45
Parkman, Francis, Jr., quoted, 21,
    66
Parks, George B., 33
Patch, Gen. Alexander, 173
Patterson, Robert, 21, 173–74
Paul, Prince of Württemberg, 41
Pawnee–Delaware War, 24
Pawnee Indians, 3, 17, 23–24, 34–
    35, 44–45
    during Civil War, 127
Pawnee (Kansas), 109, 110
Penn, William, 20
Peoria Indians, 90
Pershing, Gen. John J., 143–44, 171
Pettis, S.N., 133
Pico, Pio, 76
Pierce, Franklin, 79, 92, 105, 110,
    112, 114–15
Pike, Zebulon, 3, 63
Pilcher, Joshua, 12
Platte Purchase, 55
Platte River, 4, 37, 38, 64, 65, 81
Pleasonton, Maj. Alfred, 136
Poinsette, Joel, 69
Poland, Maj. John S., 164
Polk, Christiana, 22
Polk, James K., 70, 73, 75
Pony express line, 98–99
Poor, Salem, 139
Pope, Gen. John, 122, 134, 156, 158
Poppard, Samuel, 97–98
Post Office Department, 92
Potawatomie Indians, 23, 35, 55,
    57–58, 90
Powell, Lt. Col. L., 65
Price, Gen. Sterling, 74–75, 128,
    135–37

Prince, Maj. William, 122–23, 126, 127, 129
Pulitzer, Albert, 155

Quantrill, William C., 129, 130, 131, 132, 137
Quarles, John C., 100
Quick, John, 23

Radford, Mary, 55
Randall, Steve, 97
Randolph, Philip G., 16
Rapp, John G., 125
Red Leaf (Sioux), 91
Reeder, Andrew H., 102, 106–7, 109–11, 113–14
Reno, Capt. Jessie Leo, 120–21, 154–55
Richardson, Lt. Asa, 50
Ridgway, Gen. Matthew, 173
Riley, Capt. Bennett, 27–28, 41–42, 53
Ringo, John W., 125
Ringo, R.A., 125
Roberts, Capt. Benjamin S., 67
Robinson, Charles, 111, 120, 127
Robinson, Mrs. Charles, 110
Rodert, August, 97
Rodman, Lt. John B., 156
Root, Elihu, 170
Root, Gen. Erastus, 10
Royall, Lt. William B., 74
Rush, Benjamin, 2
Russell, Majors, and Waddell (firm), 93–95, 99, 109
Russell, William H., 93, 94, 98
Ruxton, G. F., quoted, 72

Sac Indians, 20, 22, 54, 90
Sacramento (Cal.), 75, 77, 99
Sager, Henry, 96
Salcedo, General Don Nimesio, 4
Salem, Peter, 139
Salt Lake City, 36, 37, 85, 92, 95
San Jacinto, battle of, 69–70
Sanderson, Maj. Winslow F., 66
Santa Anna, Antonio, 69–70
Santa Fé Trail, 5, 59, 62, 67, 72
   expedition along, 27, 30
Scott, Gen. Winfield, 10, 125–26
Sedgwick, Maj. John, 38

Seminole War, 21, 33, 53, 117
Shafter, Col. William, 144–45
Shanks, Capt. John T., 134
Shannon, Wilson, 110–16
Shawnee Indians, 20, 21, 22, 23, 90
Sheridan, Gen. Philip H., quoted, 163
Sherman, Gen. William T., 92, 114, 155, 163
Sioux Indians, 12, 29, 33
   conflicts with, 31, 91–92, 142, 152
Slavery question, 70, 105–18
Sloat, Comdr. John D., 77
Smith, Lt. Algernon, 155
Smith, Joseph, 50, 79
Smith, Col. Persifor, 80, 115–16
Snively, Jacob, 31
Snyder, Capt. Simon, 158
Sou-wah-nocke (Delaware chief), 24
Spalding, Eliza, 46
Spalding, Henry, 46
Spanish army in America, 3
Spotted Tail (Sioux), 91–92
Sprague, Isaac, 60
Squires, Lewis M., 60
Staff College, 170
Stage coach transportation, 94–95
Stand Watie (Cherokee chief), 132
Stanley, Capt. David, 122
Stanley, Henry M., 134
Stansbury, Capt. Howard, 36–37
Stanton, E.M., 132–33, 161
Steamboat transportation, 46, 101–2, 124
Steel, Capt. William, 120, 121
Steen, Lt. Enoch, 52
Stephens, James, 100
Stockbridge Indians, 61–62
Stockton, Commodore Robert F., 76–77
Stolbrand, Gen. Carlos J., 148
Stone, Hiram, 149
Storm, H. S., 126
Stringfellow, Gen. Benjamin F., 108
Stuart, Lt. J.E.B., 38
Sturgis, Maj. Samuel D., 122, 128
Sublette, William, 66
Sully, Capt. Alfred, 122
Sully, Thomas, 122
Sumner, Col. Edwin Vose, 37–39, 112, 113–15

Swords, Lt. Thomas, Jr., 47–48, 52, 56, 58, 60, 71, 76, 90

Tale of the Indian Country, A (Irving), 43
Tampico, slaughter of, 69
Tappin, William H., 35
Taylor, Gen. Zachary, 71, 80
Tecumseh (Indian), 21–22
Telegraph service, 99
Terrell, John Upton, 44
Texas, revolt of, 69–70
Thames, battle of, 22
Thayer, Eli, 106
Thomas, "Windwagon," 96–97
Thompson, Henry, 114
Thompson, Col. Jeff, 121
Todd, George, 129, 137
Todd, Robert, 15, 51
Townsend, Col. Edward D., 121
Townsend, Col. Edwin F., 167
Townsley, James, 114
"Travels in North America," (Murray), 43
Truman, Harry S, 72
Twain, Mark, 101
Tyler, Lt. Charles H., 99–100
Tyler, John, 70

Upham, Maj. John J., 164
U.S. Cavalry Journal, 13
U.S. Infantry and Cavalry School, 165–66

Van Quickenborne, Charles Felix, 45
Vaughan, Jim, 129–30
Veniard, Étienne, Sieur de Bourgment, 4
Vestal, Stanley, 8–9
Vose, Lt. William P., 156

Waddell, William, 93
Wagner, Capt. Arthur, 166–68

Wakefield, John A., 107
Walker, Lt. John P., 158
Walker, Robert J., 80, 116, 117
War of 1812, 21, 22, 70, 140
Washita Massacre, 39
Wells Fargo and Company, 95
West, Capt. Robert M., 153
Western Engineer (steamboat), 46
Weston (Mo.), 88, 89–90
Westport, battle of, 136–37
Wharton, Col. Clifton, 61–62, 74, 90
Whigs, 70
White Cloud (steamboat), 126
Whitfield, Gen. John W., 107
Whitman, Marcus, 46
Whitman, Narcissa, 46
Wickliff, Capt. William, 51–52
Wiener, Theodore, 114
Wilkinson, Allen, 114
Wilkinson, James, 3, 4–5
Williams, A.W., 127
Williams, Capt. Seth, 121
Williamson, Capt. D.J.M., 148
Williston, Maj. Edward, 164
Wills, William, 97
Wilmington (steamboat), 46
Wilson's Creek, battle of, 128
Wind-driven wagons, 96–98
Wister, Casper, 2
Wood, Sam, 113
Woodson, Daniel, 92, 116
Wool, Brig. Gen. Zachary, 71
Wyandot Indians, 23, 90
Wyeth, Nathaniel J., 50

Yates, Capt. George W., 155
Yellowstone (steamboat), 46
Young, Maj. Samuel B.M., 164
Young, Brigham, 37, 79–80
  Mormon War and, 81–86
Younger, Cole, 129, 130, 154
Younger, Col. Henry, 129

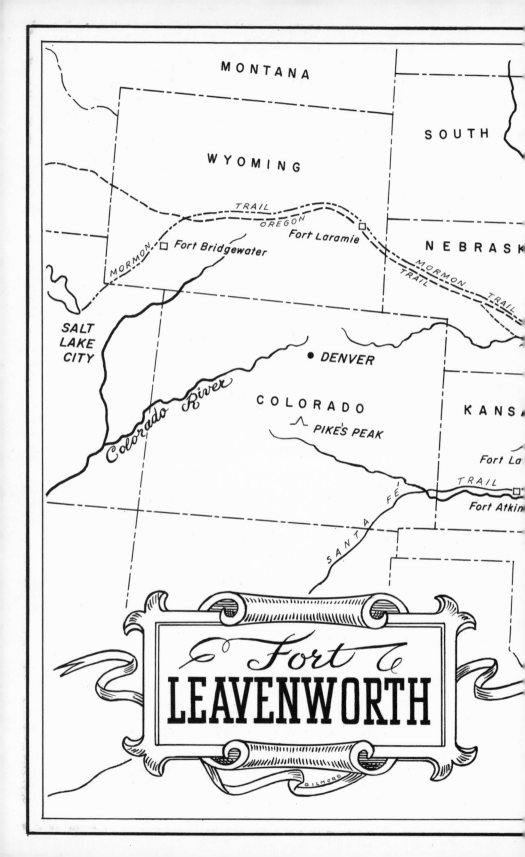